Moral Victories
in the Battle for Congress

AMERICAN GOVERNANCE: POLITICS, POLICY, AND PUBLIC LAW

Series Editors
Richard Valelly, Pamela Brandwein, Marie Gottschalk, Christopher Howard

A complete list of books in the series is available from the publisher.

Moral Victories in the Battle for Congress

Cultural Conservatism and the House GOP

Marty Cohen

PENN

UNIVERSITY OF PENNSYLVANIA PRESS

PHILADELPHIA

Published by
University of Pennsylvania Press
Philadelphia, Pennsylvania 19104-4112
www.upenn.edu/pennpress

Printed in the United States of America
on acid-free paper

10 9 8 7 6 5 4 3 2 1

Library of Congress Cataloging-in-Publication Data

Library of Congress Cataloging-in-Publication Data
Names: Cohen, Marty, author.
Title: Moral victories in the battle for Congress : cultural conservatism and the House GOP / Marty Cohen. Other titles: American governance.
Description: 1st edition. | Philadelphia : University of Pennsylvania Press, [2019] | Series: American governance : Politics, policy, and public law | Includes bibliographical references and index.
Identifiers: LCCN 2018054069| ISBN 978-0-8122-5123-4 (hardcover : alk. paper)
Subjects: LCSH: Republican Party (U.S. : 1854–)—History—21st century. | United States. Congress. House—Leadership—History—21st century. | Conservatism—United States—History—21st century. | Christianity and politics—United States—History—21st century. | United States—Politics and government—21st century.
Classification: LCC JK2356 .C63 2019 | DDC 328.73/0769—dc23
LC record available at https://lccn.loc.gov/2018054069

To Melissa, a constant source of love and strength

Contents

Preface   ix

Chapter 1. The Lay of the Land   1

Chapter 2. A Voter's Right to Choose   17

Chapter 3. Party Coalition Change and U.S. House Elections   41

Chapter 4. From the Protests to the Precincts   65

Chapter 5. Religion and Republicanism   103

Chapter 6. Overcoming the Past   138

Chapter 7. Issue Polarization and Voting Behavior
    in U.S. House Elections   178

Chapter 8. The Importance of Being Moral   199

Chapter 9. Moral Victories and a New GOP Majority   211

Notes   223

List of Interviews   235

Bibliography   237

Index   245

Preface

In the fall of 1994, my first job after graduating from Penn State University was as the College Democrats' state coordinator in charge of mobilizing students on behalf of the entire Democratic ticket in Pennsylvania. It was my first campaign job, and maybe because of the beating we took, it was my last campaign job. Two years later, I enrolled in the PhD program at the University of California, Los Angeles. Academia would be in my future and campaigns in my past. But I still could not get over the bitter defeat of 1994. It was the so-called Republican Revolution, and I became determined to learn more about how the GOP assumed control of both houses of Congress for the first time in forty years. I wanted to know that it was not entirely my fault. At the same time, I was searching for a field paper topic. I grew up in a solidly liberal Jewish home and was most interested in understanding why Jewish Americans tended to be liberal Democrats. After speaking with the great professor David Sears, I was dissuaded from studying this topic when he alerted me to the paucity of data on Jewish political attitudes at that time. I took David's advice and left his office thinking, "Why not then go to the other end of the spectrum and investigate why evangelical Christians tended to be conservative Republicans?" Thus began my long, strange trip toward the publication of this book. It began as an examination of the role evangelicals played in helping the Republican Party win the Congress in that watershed year of 1994, but it gradually morphed into a more general examination of how religiously conservative activists helped reshape the Republican U.S. House delegation.

I hope that this book contributes to the literature on parties, polarization, congressional elections, and religion in politics. My goal is to help explain the transformation of the Republican House delegation from a fiscally conservative one spread evenly throughout the country to a more morally traditional, Southern-based one that expanded to majority status and reshaped the American political landscape. To do this, I felt it was necessary to focus on the grassroots efforts of religious conservative activists and their efforts to materially transform the Republican Party from the ground up. I believed it was important to combine a statistical analysis of the voting behavior of U.S. House voters with case studies designed to flesh out the phenomena I was seeking to chronicle. I humbly hope that this methodological combination has enabled me to construct a convincing argument that not only informs but entertains the readers of this work.

Thanks to some incredibly satisfying coauthored work on presidential nominations and the inevitable intrusions of life, it took a long time getting here. Without the thoughtful guidance and enthusiastic support of Peter Agree and Rick Valelly at the University of Pennsylvania Press, this book simply would not be in print. They were a pleasure to work with throughout the process, and I would like to thank them at the outset. I am afraid I will not be able to mention everyone else who helped along the way, but you know who you are and know that I am grateful for your assistance and support. Indeed, there are many people in both my professional and personal life that are responsible for this project finally coming to fruition. At the top of the professional list is my adviser, mentor, and friend John Zaller. They say one's success in graduate school can be directly related to the quality of one's adviser. If that is the case, then I woefully underperformed. John was really the perfect adviser, providing me with countless helpful suggestions and much encouragement. During meeting after meeting while at UCLA and through many informal advising sessions after I left, I gained so much from our discussions of my project. I am grateful for our professional relationship and our friendship as well. I also owe a debt of gratitude to David Karol for his advice and encouragement. David most crucially helped guide me through the fairly intimidating process of getting my project out there in the publishing world. My other coauthors over the years—Kathleen Bawn, Marty Gilens, Seth Masket, Hans Noel, and Lynn Vavreck—all taught me a great deal about how to conduct solid, readable political science research. In addition, Larry Bartels made an important methodological contribution at a crucial point in the manuscript's development. I also would like to thank Chris Blake, who has been department chair throughout most of my tenure here at James Madison University. Chris has been and continues to be a source of support both personally and professionally that I truly appreciate. And my new colleague Mark Richardson provided some last-minute assistance with the empirical work presented in this book. Outside of academia, I have had to look no further than my immediate family for the support necessary to work so hard on a project such as this one. My mom, dad, and sister, Anita, Jay, and Rachel, have been so encouraging throughout the twenty-plus years this work has been a part of my life. And finally, my wife, Melissa, to whom this book is dedicated, and my two wonderful children, Millie and Miles: the three "Ms" are so central to my well-being and happiness that they make everything better. I thank them and love them so much for that.

Chapter 1

The Lay of the Land

A Moral Victory

Nine-term congressman Dan Glickman was on top of the legislative world in August 1994. He had represented the Fourth Congressional District of Kansas since defeating the Republican incumbent in 1976 and had just shepherded the bill of his career through the U.S. Congress. Kansas's Fourth District was home to a thriving aviation industry. Boeing and Cessna had large plants there and were the major employers in the area. However, the industry was struggling in the 1980s and early 1990s partly owing to stringent liability laws. Airplane manufacturers could be sued if someone took one of their small planes out and got injured or killed. This could happen regardless of how old the plane was or how many times ownership had changed hands. This exposure had a chilling effect on the building of airplanes, and Dan Glickman's district was feeling the brunt of this downturn. After years of failed attempts, Glickman finally got legislation passed that limited this liability. The industry was thrilled and immediately planned to hire between 1,500 and 2,000 workers to build more single-engine piston planes (Webb 1994, 1A).

This crowning legislative achievement made Glickman a hero to his constituents. He was the person most responsible for bringing jobs back to his district. It is the kind of accomplishment that can cement an incumbent in his seat for life. In fact, immediately after the bill passed, polls showed that Glickman was up by thirty points over his relatively unknown Republican challenger. Yet three months later, Dan Glickman was out of a job. He was defeated in his reelection effort by Todd Tiahrt, a one-term state senator with very little in the way of political accomplishments to his name.

How could this upset have occurred? The answer in a word was abortion. Dan Glickman was pro-choice and Todd Tiahrt was pro-life. The Fourth District of Kansas in 1994 was enflamed over the hot-button cultural issue, and Tiahrt capitalized on the burgeoning pro-life movement in the area to upset a seemingly unbeatable incumbent.[1]

Todd Tiahrt's victory was emblematic of a broader trend in American politics during this time. While Christian conservatives had been active in national politics for decades and had achieved a "seat at the table" by working with the Republican Party, the 1980s and 1990s saw them make significant strides by injecting issues of moral traditionalism into U.S. House races across the country. Christian conservative activists worked diligently to nominate friendly candidates and get them elected. These "moral victories" transformed the Republican House delegation into one that was much more culturally conservative and created a new Republican majority that with the exception of the period from 2007 to 2010 has lasted until very recently.[2]

In this book, I seek to chronicle this important political phenomenon and place it into both a historical and a theoretical context. This is a story of the growing importance of moral issues, but it is also a story of how party coalitions change and what the broader implications of these changes are. Scholars have addressed the increasing role of the Christian right at length, but nobody has focused on how this has played out in U.S. House elections over the past several decades. This book takes up that task. It shows that change began with religiously motivated activists determined to ban abortion, thwart gay rights, and restore traditional morality to the United States. Starting in the early 1980s and steadily building from that point, these activists backed like-minded candidates. Traditional Republican activists, more concerned about taxes and small government, resisted the newcomers but were often defeated. As a result, increasing numbers of House Republican nominees were against abortion and gay rights. Voters responded by putting more weight on their feelings of moral traditionalism, which led to the election of more socially conservative U.S. representatives. In this way, the House Republican caucus was transformed from a body that cared mainly about low taxes and small government to one that also cared about issues of moral traditionalism, especially abortion and gay rights. The new moralistic Republican candidates were able to win in districts where more traditional business Republicans could not, thereby creating the foundation for a relatively durable Republican majority in the House.

Christian Right Gains at the Presidential Level

The Christian right and its emergence within the Republican Party has been intensely researched by political scientists, historians, and scholars of religion. The story has been well documented especially at the national level. The Republican Party, starting to some extent with President Richard Nixon and even more so with President Ronald Reagan and followed by President George H. W. Bush, began to benefit electorally from appealing to white Southern Protestants on issues of traditional morality, such as abortion, gay rights, and school prayer. There has been a great deal of focus in this literature on the importance of such nationally known televangelists as Jerry Falwell and Pat Robertson along with the organizations they led, the Moral Majority and the Christian Coalition. This "marriage of convenience" between religious conservatives and the Republican Party seemed to benefit both sides, giving access and attention to the issues of the former while providing votes and other resources to the latter. The burgeoning relationship seemed to culminate in the presidential election and reelection of a born-again Christian, George W. Bush, in 2000 and 2004 (Diamond 1995, Diamond 1998, Williams 2010), and in 2008, a presidential candidate was made very aware of how much sway Christian conservatives had within the Republican Party.

History will always remember the selection of Sarah Palin as John McCain's vice-presidential nominee in August 2008. Palin's lack of readiness for the upper echelons of national politics combined with her quirky personality and subsequent entrance into the national zeitgeist ensured her place in the annals of infamous running-mate selections. According to the McCain campaign, Palin held the potential to be a "game changer," promising an appeal to disaffected women who voted for Hillary Clinton during the Democratic primaries, independents who would appreciate her maverick tendencies, and social conservatives who would respect her moral traditionalism, especially when it came to the issue of abortion. While the McCain team may have misjudged the first two target groups, the third segment of the electorate was "beyond ecstatic" according to Ralph Reed. The former head of the Christian Coalition continued, "This is a home run. She is a reformer governor who is solidly pro-life and a person of deep Christian faith." Palin was known in conservative circles for refusing to have an abortion when faced with the knowledge that her youngest son would be born with Down syndrome. "It is almost impossible to exaggerate how important that is to the conservative faith community," Reed concluded (Cooper and Blumenthal 2008, 1).

"Ecstatic" is certainly an appropriate way to describe the evangelical community's reaction to McCain's vice-presidential selection. Another apropos description involved quite a different emotion: relief. Evangelicals were relieved that John McCain had resisted the strong urge to really shake up the presidential contest that fall with the selection of a Democrat: Senator Joseph Lieberman of Connecticut. The vice-presidential nominee in 2000 had grown very close to McCain since crossing party lines to endorse his fellow U.S. senator in December of the previous year. Lieberman and McCain shared many political beliefs and personal traits. They were both rather hawkish when it came to foreign policy and the fight against terrorism. They also relished their role as thorns in the sides of their respective parties. Lieberman was the real "game changer" McCain wanted to spring on the American people—a bipartisan, unity ticket chock full of experience and pragmatism. There were many potential advantages to this unorthodox pick, and once McCain made up his mind, it was difficult to persuade him to change course. But he did change course, going 180 degrees in the other direction. Instead of experience, he chose inexperience. Instead of a Democrat, he chose a staunch Republican. Instead of a Jewish man, he chose an evangelical Christian woman. Instead of a longtime senator from Connecticut, he chose a first-term governor from Alaska. So what prompted the change of heart and the drastic shift?

The move away from Lieberman and toward Palin began when Senator Lindsey Graham, a strong McCain backer and longtime friend and confidant, floated the possibility of a pro-choice vice-presidential nominee to a group of social conservatives in Birmingham, Michigan. The reaction was far from positive. When Graham asked them if they would rather have a pro-life candidate and lose or a pro-choice candidate and win, quite a few said they would rather lose. This chilly response from a grassroots group of social conservatives gave the McCain campaign pause. And when Rush Limbaugh warned on his nationally syndicated radio show that picking Lieberman would "not be pretty," the dream of a so-called unity ticket died (Bumiller 2008, 18).

It is telling that a local, grassroots gathering of social conservatives played a pivotal role in determining the vice-presidential choice of the Republican nominee for president of the United States. This is just one of many instances over the past several decades that highlight the increased influence of moral traditionalists on the GOP. But it was not always this way. Twenty-eight years earlier, a Republican presidential candidate faced a similar decision about who his vice-presidential choice would be, but the process and the outcome were quite different. Ronald Reagan originally wanted former president Gerald Ford to be his running mate in 1980. It would be a "dream ticket" according to the Reagan camp, but after days of wrangling and machinations, Ford declined Reagan's offer. Reagan's next choice was his fiercest rival for the nomination, former Central Intelligence Agency director George H. W. Bush. Reagan had his reservations about Bush personally and politically. The former governor of California felt Bush had wilted under pressure during a contentious debate in Nashua, New Hampshire. Reagan also was worried that Bush was not sufficiently pro-life and would therefore violate a pledge Reagan made to the anti-abortion movement to pick a like-minded vice president. Reagan supported a constitutional amendment to ban abortion, and the best Bush could summon on this subject was opposition to federal funding of abortions for the poor (Evans and Novak 1980, A19).

Grassroots conservatives and pro-life activists were at best lukewarm to Bush. Members of the Young Americans for Freedom booed Bush at the convention the day before he was announced as the pick (Frankel 1980, A2). And when Reagan met privately with right-to-life leaders in California a few days before the convention, he prepared them for a letdown, saying there was "irresistible pressure" behind Bush (Evans and Novak 1980, A19). But when the pick was made, there was no significant outcry from these skeptics. Young Americans for Freedom was the first major right-wing group to announce their support for George H. W. Bush, saying they were not happy about it but they had worked too hard for Ronald Reagan to let this get in the way of their wholehearted support of the GOP ticket (Frankel 1980, A2). In the end, Reagan officials believed that Bush could be made acceptable on the constitutional amendment issue by simply agreeing not to oppose such an amendment even if he could not support it (Schram 1980, A3). Throughout the process of finally settling on Bush, Reagan's own misgivings were front and center, and nobody in the Reagan camp was ever too worried about the reaction of Christian conservatives (Meachem 2015, chaps. 18–22). Furthermore, Reagan had other reservations about Bush apart from the abortion issue and still picked him, whereas McCain loved the idea of Joe Lieberman on the ticket but simply could not get away with it owing to the abortion issue. From 1980 to 2008, the landscape of American politics had changed dramatically, especially within the Republican Party. In 1980, Rowland Evans and Robert Novak could say the following about Reagan's concern with Bush's position on abortion: "The immediate cause for Reagan's stated opposition is one that seldom gets into the public debate" (A19). However, by 2008, no reporter would ever write that abortion and other moral issues were anything other than frequently present in the public debate.

While much of the literature on the Christian right focuses on presidential politics and the role of national figures and organizations, the role played by local activists in House elections has largely been ignored. Several studies have drilled down to the state level, including a nearly biennial series of edited volumes (Green et al. 1996; Rozell and Wilcox 1997; Green and Rozell 2000; Green, Rozell, and Wilcox 2003; Green, Rozell, and Wilcox 2006; Dochuk 2011). So far, however, no one has examined this religious realignment as it has affected the House of Representatives. I intend to address it in the pages that follow.

Christian Right Gains at the Congressional Level

The widely heralded Southern strategy put into place by Richard Nixon in 1968 sought to exploit racial resentment among white Democrats who lived south of the Mason-Dixon Line. They looked at the national Democratic Party and saw it increasingly aligned with antiwar protestors, feminists, and most troubling for these Southerners, civil rights activists. Nixon clearly had the right idea, winning several Southern states, including Florida, Virginia, and North Carolina. He did have to settle for splitting the region with George Wallace, who won five states in the Deep South, including his home state of Alabama. Most important, though, Hubert Humphrey won only Texas. But thanks to Watergate and the presence of Georgian Jimmy Carter at the top of the ticket in 1976, the Democrats maintained their hold on the South for a bit longer. It was not until Reagan's landslide win in 1980 that the Republicans truly made headway in the South. The Reagan Revolution saw conservatives of all stripes rally around the Gipper, but it was really the first time a Republican presidential candidate had made an overt appeal to evangelical Christians. Sixty-one percent of white Southern Protestants voted for Reagan in 1980, and 70 percent did the same four years later.

But despite this success at the presidential level, Ronald Reagan's coattails were not strong when it came to U.S. House elections. In the four House elections during which Reagan was on the ballot or in the White

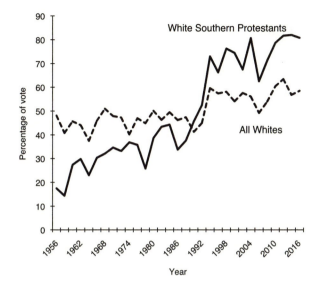

Figure 1.1. Republican U.S. House vote among whites

House, the average Republican vote from white Southern Protestants was only 41.1 percent. The racial realignment evident at the presidential level had not filtered down to the congressional level. As I will argue later on in this book, racial issues simply were rarely stressed by U.S. House candidates, and relatively conservative Democrats representing Southern districts were able to use the perks of incumbency to hold onto their seats during the Reagan-Bush era. These races were mostly fought on economics, and the absence of moral and racial issues, in my view, kept the Republicans from achieving more success in House elections. The first year Republicans gained a majority of white Southern Protestants was 1992. After that, the group was firmly in the GOP camp. When the Republicans took control of the House of Representatives for the first time in forty years, white Southern Protestants led the way. Figure 1.1 compares the voting behavior of white Southern Protestants to all whites nationally from 1956 to 2016. The early 1990s saw a rapid increase in support from the formerly strong Democratic subgroup. And when voting for GOP House candidates leveled off overall, white Southern Protestant support continued to rise.

This book is not solely about 1994, but it does have a great deal to say about that watershed election and the ramifications it had for American electoral politics and legislative governance. I will be arguing that the increased salience of moral issues to voters and the proliferation of polarization on those issues aided the Republicans in their efforts to take back the House during President Bill Clinton's first midterm election. New candidates were being nominated by morally conservative activists, and they ran successfully in districts that were friendly toward their morally traditionalist message. These "new" Republicans changed the nature of the Republican House delegation, making it more Southern, more conservative, and less willing to cooperate with moderate Republicans, let alone Democrats. Congressman Newt Gingrich's Republican Revolution changed the nature of House politics almost immediately and likely for the foreseeable future. The bomb throwers were now in charge, and they made their presence felt by helping to forge two government shutdowns, the second of which lasted twenty-one days. This new Republican majority lasted twelve years until George W. Bush's disastrous second midterm election in 2006. But the GOP was only out of power for four years when they administered a shellacking to President Barack Obama and the Democrats in 2010. This wave election was powered by a new movement that many have compared to the efforts of the Christian right sixteen years earlier.

How Comparable Are the Tea Party and the Christian Right?

On the surface, there seem to be some important similarities between the Christian right's infiltration of the Republican Party during the 1980s and 1990s and the Tea Party's political activism in the late 2000s and early 2010s. Both styled themselves as grassroots movements designed to push a specific issue agenda and make the GOP more responsive to their concerns by unleashing movement passion in the form of demonstrations, protests, challenges to Republican incumbents, and prominent endorsements. In addition, there were national leaders and local activists from the Christian right who played a significant role in the development of the Tea Party, as well as considerable overlap in mass support for each of these movements, as self-described Tea Partiers were disproportionately from the ranks of the religiously conservative (Montgomery 2012, chap. 10; Abramowitz 2012, chap. 8). And, of course, both groups led the Republican Party to major gains in midterm elections, seizing control of the House from the Democrats in 1994 and 2010, respectively.

However, as I have argued elsewhere (Cohen 2012), looks may be deceiving when it comes to comparing these two movements. In the process of assessing the probability that the Tea Party would become an entrenched faction within the Republican Party, as the second wave of Christian right activism had, I note several differences between the movements that might work against the Tea Party following the same trajectory as the Christian right.[3] I identify three criteria on which the two waves of Christian right activism and the Tea Party could be compared.

The first criterion is issue extremism. I argue that the Tea Party must try to emulate the Christian right's second wave by being very careful not to push extreme positions on the issues they most care about. These positions would alienate independents and moderate Democrats, preventing the Tea Party from achieving their policy goals within the Republican Party. The second criterion used to predict how the Tea Party would fare in the near future, both within the Republican Party specifically and American politics more generally, has to do with electoral gain. In other words, how much could the Tea Party help the GOP win elections, and how does its electoral potential compare with the potential of the earlier Christian right movement? In both waves of the Christian right, religious conservatives, who were of course the target population of the movement, were more likely to be Democrats and less likely to vote than the population at large. This created ample opportunity for the Republicans to gain by addressing the moral issues prioritized by these citizens. They were essentially an untapped reservoir of electoral support. The Tea Partiers, on the other hand, were already conservative Republicans who had been very involved in politics. It was unclear how much support could be added to the GOP's electoral base by catering to Tea Party wants and desires. They were already a part of it. Finally, the third criterion is whether the Tea Party could "play nicely." This metric deals with the tone of Tea Party rhetoric and its tactics. Throughout 2009 and 2010, the Tea Party, much like the first wave of Christian right organizing, was plagued by intemperate rhetoric that led to charges of intolerance and even racism. Calling President Obama a Muslim, accusing him of not being born in the United States, and suggesting armed rebellion against a "tyrannical Democratic regime" rivals anything ever said by Christian conservatives in terms of combative rhetoric. This kind of language worked against early leaders of the Christian right as it appeared to do to the Tea Party. The second wave, led in large part by Ralph Reed, avoided this kind of rhetoric and moderated its language to at least appear more inclusive and less insulting to others who might not be as passionate as the activists fueling the movement.

Indeed, the Tea Party seems to have receded from the spotlight or at least rebranded itself. Many argue that by early 2017, the Freedom Caucus became the best representation of the Tea Party. If so, they are not acquitting themselves well with the Republican leadership and hierarchy. They have taken extreme and uncompromising positions on virtually every issue that has come down the legislative pike over the past several years. It was one thing when they were bucking the Obama administration. But now they have proved to be a major thorn in the side of President Donald Trump and Speaker of the House Paul Ryan in their ability to achieve such legislation as an overhaul of Obamacare, tax reform, and an infrastructure bill. Their harsh and strident rhetoric does not help the situation as they only seem to be seeking the support of strong partisans within their heavily gerrymandered districts. While all of the Freedom Caucus members identify as Republicans, they do not seem very welcome in the GOP, which does not echo the experience of the Christian right, especially the second wave, which was much better integrated with the Republican Party than the first wave. That is not to say the remnants of the Tea Party (in the form of the Freedom Caucus) are not a powerful group of legislators. They have proven to be able to exact concessions in exchange for support. But often they will still withhold that support, making them unreliable coalition partners for more moderate, establishment Republicans. Furthermore, the grassroots base of the Tea Party does not appear to have remained a separate entity from the broader Republican Party, if it ever was.

The Roles of Moral Traditionalism and Racial Prejudice in Creating a GOP Congressional Majority

I will argue throughout this book that the combination of increased moral issue salience, a more intense and thorough partisan polarization on moral issues, and a Republican Party better in tune with the voting public on these types of issues have created the conditions necessary for the Republican Party to compete and win House elections all across the country but especially in the South. The notable realignment of white Southerners at the presidential level clearly began in the 1960s with the Democratic embrace of the civil rights movement. Racial matters have been pointed to by scholars and pundits alike to explain the drastic shift in party dominance from

Democrat to Republican south of the Mason-Dixon Line. However, this shift in voting behavior was limited to the presidential level for approximately twenty-five years. In Figures 1.2 to 1.4, I highlight a lag when it comes to voting for the House of Representatives. This lag shows up visually in the gap between the two lines present in these graphs. The corresponding realignment of these subgroups at the congressional level does not emerge until the late 1980s and early 1990s. This was a time of increased salience and polarization on such moral and cultural issues as abortion, gay rights, and the general role of religion in public life. More and more Republican candidates began stressing these issues in their campaigns for the House of Representatives, and in turn they began winning nomination fights and going on in many cases to defeat Democratic incumbents throughout the nation during this general time frame. I do not discount the importance of race in driving the presidential realignment and concede that racial issues still divide the parties. Indeed, the birth of the modern Christian right was not without its racial overtones. In fact, one of the major issues that activated the Christian right in the late 1970s was the Internal Revenue Service threat to revoke the tax-exempt status of churches that operated what were commonly referred to as "segregation academies" in the aftermath of *Brown v. Board of Education of Topeka* (1954). Along with abortion, school prayer, and gay rights, the defense of these Christian schools was pivotal in motivating evangelicals to return to politics after decades of inaction. And more recent events, namely, the nomination and election of Donald Trump with his somewhat surprising appeal to evangelicals, does raise the question of how race continues to linger below the surface and may indeed interact with moralistic appeals to white Southern Protestants. Certainly, Trump was going to get the vote of a big majority of evangelicals in a general election where the only other reasonable alternative was Hillary Clinton. This was especially the case after candidate Trump put out a list of pro-life judges that he would choose from if he got the chance to replace Antonin Scalia on the Supreme Court. But gaining a plurality of evangelicals in key primary and caucus states as President Trump did was downright shocking considering they had other seemingly more logical Republican candidates to choose from, such as Ted Cruz, Marco Rubio, Jeb Bush, and Rick Santorum. Trump's raw racist and ethnocentric appeals may have made up for his lack of personal piety in an intraparty battle with other more obviously religious candidates who were just as morally traditional if not more so. Despite all of this, my research into

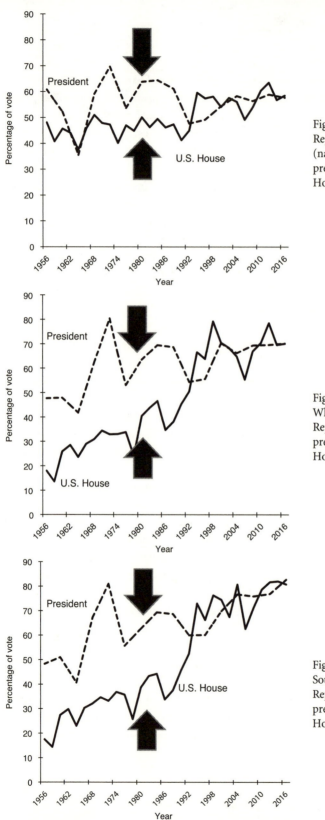

Figure 1.2. White Republican vote (nationally) for president and U.S. House

Figure 1.3 White Southern Republican vote for president and U.S. House

Figure 1.4. White Southern Protestant Republican vote for president and U.S. House

candidate messages does not show much of an overt reliance on racial issues to win elections. My congressional voting model does show that when voters are given a choice on these issues, they ascribe great importance to them. This level of importance rivals that of moral issues. But during the period of study, fewer voters were actually given a choice on race than on moral traditionalism. This, along with the evidence presented in my case studies, leads me to believe that race played much less of a role in Republican House success in the late 1980s and early 1990s than it did at the presidential level decades earlier.[4]

The Way Forward

Chapter 2 describes how the Republican delegation changed during my period of study. From 1978 to 2012, it became larger, more Southern, and more culturally conservative. Republican candidates for the U.S. House became much more likely to espouse morally traditional campaign messages. They railed against abortion and gay rights and for school prayer, as well as in favor of a more durable confluence of evangelical Christianity and politics. Moreover, now that these types of issues were on the table in House elections, Democrats followed suit and moved left. Thus, the moral issue polarization that is so evident today was birthed. These new Republican candidates did not emerge out of thin air, nor were they the product of a party establishment that realized the electoral potential of espousing a morally traditional message. These Republican candidates came to power thanks to the grassroots, locally based efforts of Christian conservative activists. These activists were largely outsiders and had to fight their way into the party in order to get their voices heard. Moreover, preliminary data analysis shows that these "new" Republican candidates and the issues they were prioritizing led voters to give more consideration to those issues when deciding whom to elect to the House of Representatives.

In Chapter 3, I examine more closely the general process, squaring the phenomenon introduced in Chapter 2 with an emerging literature that advances a novel idea regarding the way groups and parties interact. Unlike previous research that places politicians at the center of the party and conceives of parties as the creation of ambitious politicians, I emphasize the role of activists or intense policy demanders in driving a party's actions.[5] In this study of the Christian right, I will lean heavily on this new conception of what a political party is and how it operates. The relationship between groups and political parties is one that has been studied extensively in our discipline. My focus is on the replacement of House Republican candidates through the nominating process. At the local level, it was activists who came into the party and forced their issue positions and candidates onto existing politicians and party structures, often facing intense resistance from the old guard in the process. I identify many cases across the country where morally conservative candidates got nominated and elected, shifting the position of the Republican delegation on moral issues. Chapters 4 through 6 focus on particular cases—districts where Christian right activists got "their" candidates nominated and elected, taking what were previously Democratic districts and transforming them into safe Republican seats.

Chapter 4 takes the reader to Kansas's Fourth District where Todd Tiahrt, a relative newcomer, pulled off a stunning upset of nine-term Democratic incumbent Dan Glickman. Tiahrt was outspent five to one but took advantage of the increased salience of the abortion issue stemming from the Summer of Mercy protests that took place in Wichita in 1991. Tiahrt partnered with the newly pro-life Sedgwick County Republican Party and Kansans for Life to defeat Glickman, who had just realized his greatest legislative achievement: passing a bill that would bring thousands of jobs and millions of dollars to the Fourth District of Kansas. Constituency service of this magnitude would normally be enough to fend off any challenge, let alone an underfunded one that began thirty points down in the polls. However, the intensity of these new Republican activists, along with a political sophistication heretofore unseen from the Christian right, combined to upend the Democratic incumbent.

Sophisticated intensity was also the story in South Carolina's Fourth District, and Chapter 5 tells the story of Bob Inglis's 1992 victory over three-term Democratic incumbent Liz Patterson. Patterson was also skilled in constituency service and seemed to have created a relatively safe seat by establishing a fiscally responsible record in a conservative district. But the local Republican Party apparatus had been strengthened by an influx of religious conservatives in the wake of Pat Robertson's presidential campaign, and Inglis, a lawyer who had never run for public office before, mined the copious number of fundamentalist and evangelical churches for volunteers and votes leading directly to his historic upset. In many ways, Inglis's victory presaged the Republican Revolution of 1994 by exposing Democratic vulnerabilities in districts that had been voting Republican for president for years.

And finally, the Third District of Tennessee was another one of those districts that continued to elect a Democratic representative to the House despite giving Republican presidential candidates solid majorities. Chapter 6 follows the sudden and dramatic rise of Zach Wamp from personal troubles and political oblivion to the halls of Congress. Wamp, a former drug addict and convicted felon, was able to unite Christian conservatives and old-guard fiscal conservatives behind his candidacy against Randy Button. Before Wamp's victory in 1994, Democratic incumbent Marilyn Lloyd had benefited from bitter intraparty squabbles that kept the Republicans from presenting a united front in the general election. This failure to unite ensured Lloyd's long tenure in office and kept the Republicans from picking up a seat they really should have taken long before they did.

An important aspect of these three case studies is the increased salience voters ascribed to moral issues when casting their votes for the House of Representatives. The qualitative evidence presented in Chapters 3 through 6 is complemented by my empirical analysis in Chapters 7 and 8. Chapter 7 presents a congressional voting model that posits a central role for issues in determining candidate selection for the U.S. House. I outline the interaction of voter ideology, voter knowledge, and district issue polarization to see what impact these issues have on voters when they go to the polls to elect their member of Congress. This model will be used to determine the impact of issues on congressional vote choice and the electoral benefit accrued to these new kinds of Republican candidates who stress morally conservative messages.

Chapter 8 presents the substantive results from my congressional voting model. Moral issues play a major role in congressional voting behavior over the period of study. This is essentially true regardless of a voter's knowledge level and district polarization. Complementing this analysis is a discussion of the relative importance of economic and racial issues. Finally, I attempt to show the practical impact of the Republican Party's increased emphasis on moral traditionalism. Issue salience, that is, the ability of issue positions to predict congressional vote, is one part of the practical impact. Polarization, that is, the prevalence of difference on moral issues between the major-party candidates that allows voters to make a choice based on the particular issue or issue dimension, is another part of the practical impact. And partisan congruence, that is, how well a political party's candidates jibe with the voting public on a set of issues, is a third aspect of the practical impact. The results of my congressional voting model show robust effects for moral and racial issues with less potent effects for economic issues. The results of my candidate message coding reveal significant polarization on moral and economic issues with much less choice for the voters on racial issues. The potential for racial issues to influence voters is large, but it is mostly unrealized owing to the reluctance of Republican candidates in particular to openly advocate racially conservative positions. Republicans and Democrats are extremely polarized on economic and moral issues, but only moral issues exhibit significant predictive value when determining a citizen's vote choice. And finally, partisan congruence is greatest for the Republicans on issues of moral traditionalism.

Chapter 9 summarizes the book's thesis and the evidence presented in service of my main argument. I believe the Christian right's increased influence on the kinds of candidates fielded by the Republican Party in the 1980s and 1990s set the stage for the obstinacy and polarization that we see today in our politics. Through both original quantitative and qualitative analyses, this book tells that story and provides crucial background and understanding about the situation we find ourselves in today. It also highlights the contribution of religious conservatives to the Republican takeover of the House in 1994 and their role in keeping it under GOP control for most of the ensuing two decades. My book will combine a systematic empirical examination of House voting behavior with several in-depth case studies designed to shed light on exactly how and why moral issues became influential in U.S. House elections and how and why the Republicans were able to benefit electorally from this new primacy.

Chapter 2

A Voter's Right to Choose

Running on Economic Issues, Governing on Moral Issues

The 2010 midterm elections were a rousing success for the Republican Party. The president's party is commonly expected to lose some seats in Congress during its first midterm election, and with a relatively unpopular president, it should lose even more. Barack Obama's approval rating on the eve of the 2010 midterms was hovering around 45 percent, with a dismal 9 percent among registered Republicans. And so it was that on November 2, the Democratic Party was administered a shellacking by the nation's voters, flipping sixty-four seats to the GOP. This turned a healthy Democratic majority into an almost equally comfortable Republican majority.

The year 2010 brought back memories of the 1994 Republican Revolution, which actually was smaller in magnitude, with the Republican Party gaining fifty-four seats. The 1994 elections were more historic, though, considering how long it had been since the Republicans had controlled the House of Representatives. The 2010 results simply erased gains made by Democrats four years earlier during George W. Bush's second midterm election as president. The electoral landslide of 2010 was largely driven by unhappiness with Obama's first two years in office and in particular his economic stimulus bill and the Affordable Care Act, pejoratively referred to as Obamacare. The new vehicle for dissent was the nascent Tea Party, which emerged on the scene during the summer of 2009 and came into its own during the run up to the 2010 midterm elections. Tea Party–backed candidates sprang up across the nation and targeted not just Democrats but so-called establishment Republicans. The Tea Party focused mostly on fiscal issues and the size of government, with some groups taking the acronym

TEA to mean "taxed enough already." Unlike 1994 when many House candidates stressed such moral issues as abortion and gay rights, successful Republican candidates in 2010 were sidestepping those issues in favor of what they saw, and maybe what the electorate saw, as more pressing concerns, such as government spending and government-subsidized health care. All elections are assigned a narrative, and the story of 2010 had little to do with moral traditionalism. However, the incoming class of freshmen in January 2011 would turn out to be plenty conservative on social issues, and many of them took the lead in advancing morally traditional causes in the lower house of Congress. Of the eighty-six new Republicans, eighty-one of them voted to defund Planned Parenthood in February 2011, and their average Family Research Council rating was eighty-eight (Barone and McCutcheon 2013). In fact, eighty-seven votes were taken to defund Planned Parenthood during the 112th Congress (Center for Reproductive Rights 2013, 5).

This aspect of the 2010 midterms shows that narratives assigned to particular election seasons do not necessarily foreshadow what the following congressional session will be about. But a candidate's campaign message usually is a good harbinger of how he or she will legislate once elected to office. Aggregating the messages of a particular party's crop of House candidates says a great deal about what the party stands for. According to my analysis, the Republican Party became much more conservative on moral issues during the past three-plus decades. More and more candidates began taking morally traditional positions on such issues as abortion, gay rights, and school prayer, and these candidates became more successful in winning office, which radically changed the GOP House delegation. This chapter presents the results of an ambitious project to code the issue positions of every major-party House candidate from 1978 to 2012 on three dimensions: moral, economic, and racial.[1] It is clear from this data and the subsequent analysis that party polarization on moral issues increased dramatically during the period of study, giving more citizens a choice on these issues and allowing them to have an impact on who would be selected at the polls.

Before presenting and analyzing the original data on candidate messages, I will briefly review the recent literature on polarization in American politics. This will of course be done with an eye toward how my study can add to what has already been written on this timely subject. After this literature review, I will return to the results of my original data collection. In that section of the chapter, I will first document and justify the methodology used for the analysis of candidate messages. Second, I will present the raw data on moral messages along with measures of party polarization. Then, I will briefly present data on the other two dimensions for comparison's sake. And finally, I will present the results of a preliminary empirical test showing the potential effects of moral issues on the vote. At the end of this chapter, the reader will have a firm grasp of how and why I chose to quantify candidate messages the way I did. The coding of candidate messages is an essential building block in the construction of my congressional voting model, which will be presented in Chapter 7.

How Polarized Are We?

In their 2016 book on political polarization, Steven Schier and Todd Eberly (2016, 6) identify two characteristics of this phenomenon. First, those who are politically active must be divided strongly on the many major issues of the day. Second, party activists must hold relatively uniform and consistent issue positions. They conclude, and I would agree, that we have met these standards in current American politics. More specifically, I would argue that while the parties have been divided on economic, racial, and foreign-policy issues for some time, intense party polarization on moral and cultural issues has been a more recent phenomenon.

When Pat Buchanan addressed his rabid supporters at the 1992 Republican National Convention in Houston, he famously, or infamously depending on your point of view, identified what he believed was a culture war being waged for the soul of America. "There is a religious war going on in this country. It is a cultural war, as critical to the kind of nation we shall be as the Cold War itself. For this war is for the soul of America" (American Rhetoric 1992). Buchanan went on to identify the issues over which this war would be waged. Abortion, gay rights, discrimination against religious schools, and women in combat would be the battle-grounds, and Buchanan clearly situated the Republicans on the side of moral traditionalism in opposition to the Democrats.

Despite a decade and a half of bitter disputes over all of these issues and an influential scholarly tome on the subject (Hunter 1991), Morris Fiorina and his colleagues famously, or infamously depending on your point of view, argued that in fact the existence of a cultural war among the people is a myth. According to Fiorina and colleagues, the electorate only appears to be deeply divided because candidates and other party elites are polarized, and therefore the voters can only choose between extreme liberals and extreme conservatives (Fiorina, Abrams, and Pope 2006).

Alan Abramowitz (2013) takes issue with Fiorina's characterization of the public as evenly but not deeply divided. He presents compelling data that clearly shows a huge gap in party identification and voting behavior between religious and secular voters. Abramowitz goes on to say that the reason for this growing cultural divide is the emergence of a new set of issues, mainly abortion and gay marriage, which divide Democrats and Republicans and tap into voters' moral values and religious beliefs (chap. 4).

In this book, I side with Abramowitz and Buchanan over Fiorina and believe I can provide at least a partial explanation of how and why this culture war has intensified over the past forty or so years. My focus is on House elections, and I argue that a major component of the culture war was jump-started by culturally conservative activists who began backing a new breed of Republican candidate—those who began to stress moral traditionalism in their campaigns. These candidates experienced varying degrees of success, but ultimately, they conquered the Republican Party and remade its congressional delegation in their image. The result has been a GOP taken over to a large extent by Christian conservatives and a Democratic Party that has chosen to fight back with a secular, liberal agenda, creating fertile ground on which a culture war has developed.

Coding Candidate Messages

For this project, I needed to find a source that discussed the issue positions of challengers and incumbents over a period of several decades. These requirements disqualified common source material, such as Nominate scores, Project Vote Smart surveys, and interest-group ratings. The source that I settled on was *The Almanac of American Politics*. It is published every two years, and one of the useful attributes of the *Almanac* is that the authors focus their attention on the most recent electoral cycle. Therefore, if a challenger is at all viable, they will talk about him or her. This allowed me to code both incumbents and challengers in the same fashion, which is critical to my analysis since, especially during the early years of my sample, there is no other source for challenger information.

My primary interest was the moral tone of the messages candidates conveyed to the voters in a given election cycle. If the *Almanac* mentions

Table 2.1. Moral issue coding scheme

Label	Description
Very liberal	Avowed liberal on more than one moral issue and/or a leading liberal fighter for one moral issue OR Openly affiliated with a well-known morally liberal group
Liberal	Avowed liberal on one moral issue
Moderate/Neutral	Conflicting mentions (at least one liberal mention and one conservative mention) OR No mention on the moral dimension
Conservative	Avowed conservative on one moral issue
Very conservative	Avowed conservative on more than one moral issue and/or a leading conservative fighter for one moral issue OR Openly affiliated with a well-known morally conservative group

Note: The predominant moral issues were abortion, school prayer, censorship of obscene art, gay rights, religion's role in public life, and women's issues with a moral tinge.

that Congressperson "X" is pro-life, then I accept that as his or her stance on that issue. In addition, I accept that this is a belief publicly held by Congressperson "X" and that a subset of his or her constituents will know this. I devised a five-point scale that arrays the candidates on a left-to-right moral issue continuum. Coding guidelines are presented in Table 2.1. Randy Tate is a good example of a congressional challenger who is very conservative on moral issues. Tate defeated incumbent Mike Kreidler in 1994 and went on to represent the Ninth District of Washington State. According to the *Almanac*, Tate is strongly motivated by his religious faith and was a supporter of Pat Robertson's presidential campaign (Barone and Ujifusa 1995 1424). Patricia Schroeder anchors the opposite end of the moral spectrum. The longtime congresswoman from Colorado was "a symbol of feminism and liberalism. . . . She was an early supporter of legalized abortion, the sponsor of the law to make a federal crime of obstructing

Table 2.2. Distribution of Republican candidates on moral issues, 1978–2012

Total number of districts	7,830
Districts uncontested by Republicans	637
Number of Republican candidates	7,193
Very liberal	47 (0.65%)
Liberal	235 (3.27%)
Neutral	5,547 (77.12%)
Conservative	724 (10.07%)
Very conservative	640 (8.90%)

access to abortion clinics, a crusader for abortions at military hospitals, one of the leaders of the bloc who pledged to oppose any healthcare finance reform that didn't cover abortion" (Barone and Ujifusa 1995 238–239). Congressional candidates who took clear, albeit less extreme stands on a moral issue were classified as conservative or liberal. There were a few candidates who had conflicting viewpoints on these subjects and a significant number for whom their beliefs on these issues did not warrant a mention by the *Almanac*. These individuals were considered "moderate/neutral" and placed in the center of the scale.

Increasing Polarization on the Issues

Table 2.2 displays the distribution of Republican congressional candidates that were coded into each moral message category. While this table suggests a relative dearth of candidates invoking a conservative stance on cultural issues, Figure 2.1 shows a sharp upward trend in those types of candidates. During the late 1970s and 1980s, only a handful of candidates espoused morally conservative messages. There was a significant increase in 1990, which was the year the Christian Coalition was founded and first got involved in grassroots politics mostly on behalf of the Republican Party. In 1992, the percentage of conservative candidates exceeded 20 percent, and the rest of the 1990s and early 2000s saw consistent increases. By 2004, more than 30 percent of Republican candidates were broadcasting a conservative moral message. That year turns out to be the peak, as we have observed a slight downward trend since then, possibly related to the financial crash in 2008 and the subsequent Great Recession.[2]

Generally, polarization is a two-way street. As one party begins to stress new issues and move away from the center, the other party is compelled to take opposing stands on the new issues. And so it was with moral issues and the Democratic Party. Figure 2.2 shows a similar pattern as Figure 2.1, albeit with fewer Democrats left of center than Republicans right of center. Another way to chart the polarization that developed on moral issues is to assign each category a numerical value and calculate the mean ideology in each year. Referring back to Table 2.1, we can assign a -2 to very liberal, a -1 to liberal, a 0 to neutral, a 1 to conservative, and a 2 to very conservative. Figure 2.3 plots the divergence of the two parties' House candidates on moral issues over the period of study. Both parties start very close to the center, with the Republicans moving first but ever so slightly in the mid-1980s. Democrats remain close to parity thanks to the existence of some moral conservatives within their ranks. In the early 1990s, Republicans move more to the extreme as do Democrats, although not as drastically. During the 2000s and beyond, the Republicans stay further from the center than the Democrats, but both sides remain increasingly ideologically distinct from one another. In fact, 2012 gives us the largest difference between the two parties.

Another way to measure polarization is to look at the percentage of contests in which the Republican was more conservative than the Democrat on moral issues. In other words, in how many districts did voters actually have a choice to make on these issues? In Figure 2.4, we see several distinct eras within the period of study. During the late 1970s, there is virtually no polarization on these issues. During the 1980s, there is consistent albeit small growth in the percentage of districts where the Republican is more conservative than the Democrat. Then, a huge jump begins in 1992, with continued growth through the 1990s and early 2000s. The peak is 2004, with a slight downtick in 2006 and 2008 followed by recovery in 2010 and 2012.

By means of comparison, Figures 2.5 and 2.6 display both parties' candidates on all three coded issue dimensions. On the Republican side, all three dimensions show an increase in conservative messages espoused by House candidates over time, however economic issues outpace the other two dimensions, especially at the beginning and the end of the period of study. Each dimension shows times where that set of issues seems to gain in salience. For moral issues, the 1990s is a time when the Christian Coalition was at peak influence and the Republican Party took over control of the U.S. Congress. The increasing importance of moral issues tapers off

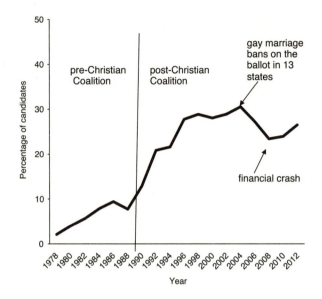

Figure 2.1. Percentage of Republican U.S. House candidates stressing conservative moral messages

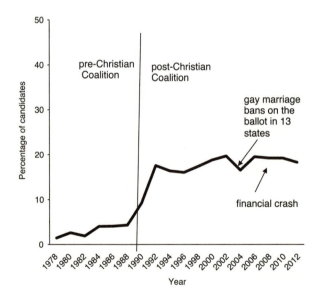

Figure 2.2. Percentage of Democratic U.S. House candidates stressing ~~conservative~~ moral messages

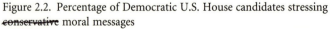
LIBERAL

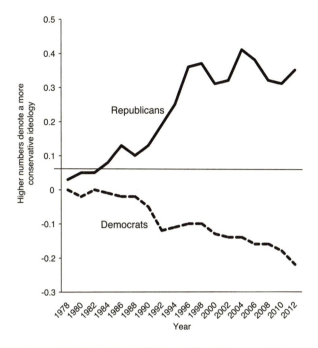

Figure 2.3. Mean ideology on moral issues of Republicans and Democrats nationally

slightly after the millennium. For economic issues, we also see big increases in the percentage of Republicans espousing a conservative message in 1992 and 1994 in particular. But contrary to attitudes toward moral issues, we see a second dramatic rise in 2008 and 2010. The latter period clearly coincides with a Tea Party movement that at least at the outset and in public was fiercely focused on fiscal matters. Finally, racial conservatism does not appear to be that great a factor until illegal immigration bursts onto the national scene in the mid-2000s.

Among Democratic candidates, economic issues clearly are more salient throughout the period from 1978 to 2012. Additionally, the salience of these issues as measured by the percentage of Democratic U.S. House candidates espousing a liberal message rises steadily over time. Liberal moral messages are largely absent until the early 1990s, coinciding with the Republicans moving to the right on the same issues. Finally, racial issues start out in between moral and economic issues, increasing slowly but

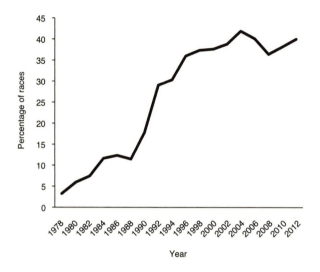

Figure 2.4. Percentage of races where the Republican U.S. House candidate was more conservative than the Democratic candidate on moral issues

surely throughout the period of study and ending up very close to where moral issues are in 2012. Figure 2.7 adds economic and racial issues to the rendering of moral issue polarization in Figure 2.4. On moral issues, we get the most polarization in 2004, with roughly 40 percent of races giving voters a clear choice. On economic issues, the most polarization comes in the most recent year of study, which is 2012. A whopping 70 percent of contests featured a Republican who was more conservative than the Democrat. And finally, on race, 2010 showed the most polarization, with about 25 percent of districts giving voters a clear choice on such issues as immigration and affirmative action.[3]

Further leveraging my candidate message data, I have created a new variable called "district issue polarization" that separates districts based on differences between the Democratic and Republican candidates on the issues. With my original campaign message coding scheme ranging from −2 (very liberal) to 2 (very conservative), I can compute district issue polarization as the Republican score subtracted by the Democratic score. This variable would then range from −4 to 4. A score of 4 for district issue polarization would mean that the Republican was very conservative (2) and the Democrat was very liberal (−2). A score of 3 could come from the

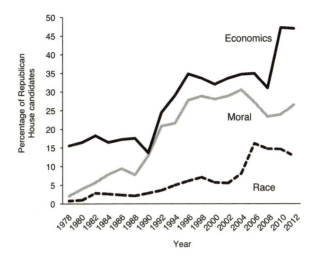

Figure 2.5. Percentage of Republican U.S. House candidates espousing a conservative message on moral, economic, and racial issues

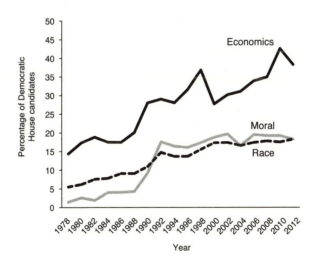

Figure 2.6. Percentage of Democratic U.S. House candidates espousing a conservative message on moral economic, and racial issues

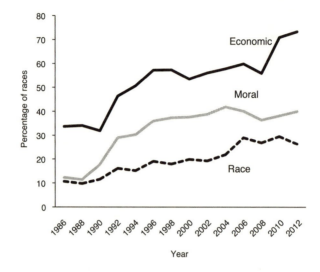

Figure 2.7. Percentage of races where the Republican U.S. House candidate was more conservative than the Democrat

Republican being very conservative (2) and the Democrat being liberal (–1) or from the Republican being conservative (1) and the Democrat being very liberal (–2). Scores of 2 and 1 could each result from several different combinations of the two candidates' positions. A score of 0 would mean there was no difference between the candidates. Negative values of district issue polarization figure to be rare since they would mean the Democrat was more conservative than the Republican. Figure 2.8 computes mean district issue polarization for each of the three issue dimensions over time, while the underlying, raw data used to create Figure 2.8 are presented in Tables 2.3 to 2.5. The first thing to notice when looking at the distribution on moral issues is how little polarization there was before 1990. In none of the first six electoral cycles did more than 18 percent of the districts give voters a choice on moral issues. Not only that, some differences between the candidates in those districts resulted from the Republican actually being more liberal on those issues than the Democrat (see the columns left of center). Beginning in 1990, there are significantly more districts exhibiting the expected pattern on moral issues (the columns right of center). For most of the period since 1990, roughly 40 percent of contested districts show the Republican to the right of the Democrat on moral issues. When

Table 2.3. District polarization on moral issues

Year	No challenger	-4	-3	-2	-1	0	1	2	3	4	Total Contests
1978	66	0.0	0.0	0.5	0.8	95.4	1.4	1.9	0.0	0.0	369
1980	49	0.0	0.0	1.0	0.8	92.2	2.6	3.4	0.0	0.0	386
1982	58	0.0	0.0	2.1	2.7	87.8	3.2	4.2	0.0	0.0	377
1984	65	0.0	0.0	1.9	3.8	82.7	5.4	5.9	0.3	0.0	370
1986	70	0.0	0.0	1.1	3.8	82.7	4.7	7.1	0.3	0.3	365
1988	77	0.0	0.0	0.8	4.2	83.5	6.1	4.7	0.3	0.3	358
1990	81	0.0	0.0	0.6	7.9	73.7	7.9	8.8	1.1	0.0	354
1992	32	0.0	0.0	2.0	8.9	60.0	14.6	12.4	2.0	0.0	403
1994	43	0.0	0.0	1.3	8.5	59.9	17.2	11.6	1.3	0.3	389
1996	21	0.0	0.0	0.5	8.7	54.8	18.8	14.5	1.9	0.7	414
1998	95	0.0	0.0	1.5	8.8	52.4	18.5	17.6	0.9	0.3	340
2000	63	0.0	0.0	1.3	9.1	51.9	22.6	14.0	1.1	0.0	372
2002	82	0.0	0.0	1.1	6.2	53.8	24.6	13.3	0.6	0.3	353
2004	65	0.0	0.0	1.1	6.2	50.8	23.2	16.2	1.6	0.8	370
2006	56	0.0	0.3	2.4	5.3	52.0	19.5	19.0	1.1	0.5	379
2008	56	0.0	0.0	2.9	5.0	55.7	19.5	15.6	1.1	0.3	379
2010	29	0.0	0.0	1.7	6.4	53.7	22.4	15.0	0.0	0.7	406
2012	45	0.0	0.0	1.3	3.3	55.4	22.3	16.9	0.3	0.5	390

Note: Cell entries in the bold bordered section are percentages.

examining economic issue polarization, we see that throughout the period of study there is more public polarization than on the other two issue dimensions. There is a large jump in the first half of the 1990s and an even bigger one in 2010. It appears as if Democratic presidents and their economic visions spark a conflict among House candidates that is reflected in this district polarization variable. Bill Clinton's tax increase in 1993 and Barack Obama's stimulus package in 2009 along with the Affordable Care Act forced many candidates for the House of Representatives to take a public stand. In 2010 and 2012, almost 75 percent of contested districts gave voters a real choice between the two major party candidates on economic issues. And finally, looking at race shows that little by little such issues as illegal immigration, affirmative action, and making English the official language of the United States became more polarizing. After 1988, when moral issues and racial issues are almost identical in their mean district polarization scores, racial issues lag behind the other two dimensions, although the gap between issues of race and moral issues closes considerably in the age of Obama.

Table 2.4. District polarization on economic issues

Year	No challenger	−4	−3	−2	−1	0	1	2	3	4	Total Contests
1978	66	0.0	0.0	0.3	0.5	71.5	20.6	7.1	0.0	0.0	369
1980	49	0.0	0.0	0.3	1.0	67.1	23.8	7.8	0.0	0.0	386
1982	58	0.0	0.0	0.0	2.7	63.7	23.9	9.8	0.0	0.0	377
1984	65	0.0	0.0	0.0	1.6	65.4	23.2	9.7	0.0	0.0	370
1986	70	0.0	0.0	0.0	1.6	64.7	23.8	9.9	0.0	0.0	365
1988	77	0.0	0.0	0.3	1.7	64.0	22.4	11.5	0.3	0.0	358
1990	81	0.0	0.0	0.0	2.3	65.8	24.9	7.1	0.0	0.0	354
1992	32	0.0	0.0	0.0	1.7	51.9	31.5	13.2	1.5	0.3	403
1994	43	0.0	0.0	0.0	1.3	48.1	38.6	11.3	0.8	0.0	389
1996	21	0.0	0.0	0.0	1.9	40.8	36.0	17.9	3.4	0.0	414
1998	95	0.0	0.0	0.3	1.5	40.9	33.2	21.2	2.9	0.0	340
2000	63	0.0	0.0	0.5	2.2	43.8	38.4	14.5	0.3	0.3	372
2002	82	0.0	0.0	0.3	2.0	41.6	37.7	17.6	0.6	0.3	353
2004	65	0.0	0.0	0.0	0.8	41.4	37.6	19.2	1.1	0.0	370
2006	56	0.0	0.0	0.0	1.6	38.5	34.0	23.2	2.6	0.0	379
2008	56	0.0	0.0	0.0	3.2	40.9	31.1	21.9	2.6	0.3	379
2010	29	0.0	0.0	0.3	2.7	26.1	28.8	33.0	7.1	2.0	406
2012	45	0.0	0.0	0.0	1.0	25.6	33.3	35.6	2.8	1.5	390

Note: Cell entries in the bold bordered section are percentages.

Discussing and Defending the Almanac *as a Measure of Candidate Ideology*

The Almanac of American Politics is far from a perfect source of information when it comes to measuring candidate ideology. Relying exclusively on the *Almanac*, of course, leaves me vulnerable to the whims of the authors and what they choose to cover for each district. It is a blunt measure of candidate positions and one that forces the researcher to translate a general narrative into quantitative ideological measures. Despite these flaws, I simply cannot think of a better way to get at candidate positions for incumbents and challengers alike in every congressional district over the span of several decades. Voting records and interest-group scores are limited to incumbents. Project Vote Smart's Political Courage Test goes back only so far and suffers from low response rates, and the Cooperative Congressional Election Study only came into existence in 2006 and does not provide candidate positions on the three dimensions I am interested in. So I am left with the

Table 2.5. District polarization on racial issues

Year	No challenger	-4	-3	-2	-1	0	1	2	3	4	Total Contests
1978	66	0.0	0.0	0.3	1.4	92.4	3.3	2.7	0.0	0.0	369
1980	49	0.0	0.0	0.3	0.0	93.3	2.3	4.2	0.0	0.0	386
1982	58	0.0	0.0	0.0	0.0	90.7	4.2	5.0	0.0	0.0	377
1984	65	0.0	0.0	0.0	0.8	88.9	4.9	5.4	0.0	0.0	370
1986	70	0.0	0.0	0.0	0.3	89.0	5.5	5.2	0.0	0.0	365
1988	77	0.0	0.0	0.0	2.2	88.0	5.6	4.2	0.0	0.0	358
1990	81	0.0	0.0	0.0	2.0	86.4	7.3	4.2	0.0	0.0	354
1992	32	0.0	0.0	0.0	1.5	82.4	10.9	5.2	0.0	0.0	403
1994	43	0.0	0.0	0.0	1.0	83.8	7.2	8.0	0.0	0.0	389
1996	21	0.0	0.0	0.2	0.7	80.0	9.7	9.4	0.0	0.0	414
1998	95	0.0	0.0	0.3	1.8	80.0	9.7	8.2	0.0	0.0	340
2000	63	0.0	0.0	0.0	2.2	78.0	10.0	10.0	0.0	0.0	372
2002	82	0.0	0.0	0.0	2.0	78.8	8.8	10.5	0.0	0.0	353
2004	65	0.0	0.0	0.0	1.4	76.8	11.4	10.3	0.3	0.0	370
2006	56	0.0	0.0	0.3	1.6	69.1	17.7	10.8	0.5	0.0	379
2008	56	0.0	0.0	0.3	2.9	69.9	14.5	12.4	0.0	0.0	379
2010	29	0.0	0.0	0.3	2.7	67.5	12.3	17.0	0.3	0.0	406
2012	45	0.0	0.0	0.3	1.3	72.1	11.0	15.1	0.0	0.3	390

Note: Cell entries in the bold bordered section are percentages.

Almanac. But that does not mean I cannot leverage some of these other possibilities to test the validity of the *Almanac.*

The way I see it there are two potential worries a thoughtful reader might have regarding the *Almanac.* The first is that my coding of the *Almanac*'s narratives are not actually describing the true positions of the candidates. For incumbents, I can test this by looking at interest-group ratings, which are, in essence, measures of the actual voting records of members of the U.S. House. For the 2012 cycle, I have compared my incumbent measures to corresponding group ratings, and the results are quite favorable. Table 2.6 shows the average rating for each category of incumbent. In that table, I have chosen the Family Research Council to compare to my moral coding, the Club for Growth to compare to my economic coding, and the American Civil Liberties Union to compare to my racial coding. There is a strong, linear relationship between my coding and average interest-group ratings for all three issue dimensions. The correlations are 0.567, 0.834, and −0.560 for moral, economic, and racial issues, respectively. Another test of

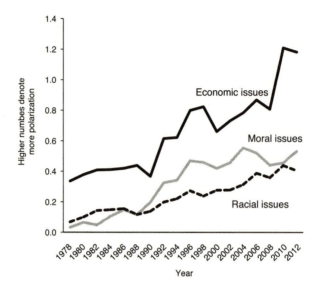

Figure 2.8. Mean district issue polarization on moral, economic, and racial issues for all districts nationally

Table 2.6. Accuracy of candidate placements using interest group ratings

Political Ideology	Average FRC Rating (%) (moral issues)	Average CFG Rating (%) (economic issues)	Average ACLU Rating (%) (racial issues)
Very liberal	4.7%	13.0%	91.0%
Liberal	16.4%	15.0%	78.4%
Moderate/neutral	51.2%	44.8%	33.4%
Conservative	80.8%	67.1%	10.3%
Very conservative	88.2%	79.7%	7.6%

ACLU = American Civil Liberties Union; CFG = Club for Growth; FRC = Family Research Council.

the veracity of my *Almanac* coding comes from a look at Project Vote Smart's Political Courage Test. Project Vote Smart sends an issue questionnaire to all candidates running for the U.S. House. Candidates are said to have passed the test if they answer a certain percentage of the questions and send back the form to Project Vote Smart's offices. Project Vote Smart then

Table 2.7. Accuracy of candidate placements on the moral dimension

Party Affiliation	Percentage Coded Conservative	Percentage Pro-Life
Republican candidates	85.8	92.6
Democratic candidates	24.0	24.0

Table 2.8. Accuracy of candidate placements on the economic dimension

Party Affiliation	Percentage Coded Conservative	Percentage Against Public Option
Republican candidates	96.7	94.7
Democratic candidates	8.9	12.6

Table 2.9. Accuracy of candidate placements on the racial dimension

Party Affiliation	Percentage Coded Conservative	Percentage Wanting to End Affirmative Action
Republican candidates	91.3	88.8
Democratic candidates	14.3	13.0

publishes the results for their members and other interested parties. I have obtained the raw data from these questionnaires for 2010 and found questions that were emblematic of the moral, economic, and racial dimensions present in my candidate data. For moral issues, I use a simple question about whether the candidate is pro-life or pro-choice. For economic issues, I use a question asking whether the candidate supports a public option for health insurance. For racial issues, I use a question asking whether affirmative action programs should be ended. In Tables 2.7 to 2.9, I compare my coding to the results of Project Vote Smart's 2010 Political Courage Test. In these tables, I am comparing the percentage of candidates I gave a conservative rating to with the percentage who answered the various issue questions in a conservative fashion. My coding closely mirrors the self-placement of the candidates for both parties' candidates on all three issue dimensions.

From the results presented in Tables 2.6 to 2.9, the reader should be reassured that my coding was an accurate portrayal of candidate ideology for those positions discussed by the *Almanac*. Now that last phrase is one that should not be glossed over. In fact, it is this phrase that gets at the second potential drawback of using *The Almanac of American Politics*. As argued above, we can be pretty sure that what the *Almanac* picks up is legitimate and accurate. However, the potentially greater concern is what the *Almanac* does not pick up. Does the *Almanac* miss or undercount issue positions taken by congressional candidates? Remember that if the *Almanac* does not discuss a candidate's views on an issue dimension, then that candidate is assigned to the neutral category and given a 0 on the dimension in question. Also recall that a significant proportion of candidates fall into that middle category. This could be a problem, especially if the undercounting is more or less likely on certain issue dimensions. For example, we know that appeals to racial conservatism are often dog whistles and might be less likely to be noticed by those chronicling particular campaigns. It might be that political polarization is in reality higher on race than the *Almanac* would have us believe. At first blush, this appears to be a thornier question and one that does not seem to be as easily checked as the first concern. However, I believe I can once again use the Project Vote Smart data to alleviate some of the angst associated with this aspect of the *Almanac*'s efficacy.

Despite sending out surveys to all candidates running for the U.S. House of Representatives, nowhere close to a majority come back completed. There could be a variety of reasons for this empirical fact. Candidates might not want to have their issue positions placed on the record in such a complete and binding fashion. Risk-averse politicians who do not necessarily need the publicity and attention from a public airing of their views on often controversial issues would be least likely to return these surveys. Sure enough, incumbents are poorly represented in the set of survey results published by Project Vote Smart. Challengers were much more likely in 2010 to provide answers to the questions being asked of them. Ideally, for my project as well as for the voters who are hungry for information about the candidates' policy preferences, everyone would make their positions known on every issue. This, of course, is a fantasy. The relevant question in this section of the book is how good is the *Almanac*? One way to assess that is to compare it to another source, in this case, the Project Vote Smart surveys. It might be helpful to compare the response rates for

Table 2.10. Coverage of moral issues in the *Almanac*

Political Ideology (18.28% picked up)	Pro-Choice Candidates	Pro-Life Candidates
Very liberal	10	0
Liberal	8	0
Moderate/neutral	59	93
Conservative	0	8
Very conservative	0	8

Table 2.11. Coverage of economic issues in the *Almanac*

Political Ideology (28.04% picked up)	Candidates Wanting Public Option	Candidates Wanting No Public Option
Very liberal	20	0
Liberal	10	1*
Moderate/neutral	58	77
Conservative	0	17
Very conservative	0	6

* Shelley Moore Capito (R-WV) was coded "liberal" on economics, yet she was against the public option in the Project Vote Smart candidate surveys. This is the only case in any issue dimension where a candidate was on a different side of zero depending on the source.

Project Vote Smart to the percentage of candidates who warranted a nonzero rating from the *Almanac*. Candidate response to the abortion question on the Political Courage Test was 22.1 percent, while 26.6 percent of candidates got a nonzero rating from the *Almanac*. On economic issues, the corresponding figures were 22.5 percent and 47.8 percent. On racial issues, they were 21.5 percent and 18.2 percent. These numbers suggest that on moral and racial issues, the *Almanac* seems to cover roughly the same amount of ground Project Vote Smart does. There appears to be much more attention given to economic issues by the *Almanac* than what voters can glean from the Political Courage Test. The results of a slightly more refined analysis are presented in Tables 2.10 to 2.12. By cross-referencing my coding with the data from Project Vote Smart, I can calculate what the *Almanac* "picked up" from the positions publicized by the candidates in the Political Courage Test. Each candidate who returned an issue survey is

Table 2.12. Coverage of racial issues in the *Almanac*

Political Ideology (12.15% picked up)	Candidates Wanting To Keep Affirmative Action	Candidates Wanting To End Affirmative Action
Very liberal	11	0
Liberal	3	0
Moderate/neutral	76	83
Conservative	0	6
Very conservative	0	2

represented in these three tables. They are assigned to a category based on their *Almanac*-based ratings. In the tables, the percentages in the upper-left corner of the tables are the proportion of candidates whose positions were "picked up" or registered by the *Almanac*. Once again, we see that racial issues lag behind the other two dimensions, but at least compared with moral issues, it does not seem to be a huge difference. If anything, there is not so much an undercounting of moral and racial issues as there is an overcounting of economic issues. I will come back to this point in Chapter 8 when assessing the overall importance of the three issue dimensions.

Preliminary Quantitative Evidence for the Importance of Moral Issues

Chronicling the increased issue polarization in American politics and discussing the reasons for it are only parts of the story I want to tell in this book. Ultimately, I aim to show that the Republican Party took advantage of the new polarization on moral issues and leveraged it toward flipping congressional seats, ultimately taking and then keeping control of the House of Representatives. This was done by increasing the effect of moral issues on the congressional vote choice of American citizens. To that end, I have developed a communications-based model that seeks to measure the absolute and relative impact of moral issues. This model is presented to the reader in detail in Chapter 7, and the substantive results are discussed in Chapter 8. However, to give the reader a sense of the empirical plausibility of my main argument, in this section I want to provide some preliminary evidence for the effect of moral issues on the congressional vote. Applying the district polarization variable to American National Election Studies (ANES) data allows me to develop a voting model that tries to get at issue importance. Polarization should lead to a greater reliance on issue positions when individuals cast their vote. To that end, I have created a congressional voting model that includes an interaction between voter morality and district polarization. The expectation is that the interaction will be positive and significant meaning that voter morality will matter more when the Republican is more conservative than the Democrat. Greater polarization should lead to a greater importance for moral issues when voters choose between U.S. House candidates. Relying on ANES data limits me to certain years and districts. I will be running this model on 1986–2004, 2008, and 2012 since these are the years for which there are data and the chosen independent variable of moral traditionalism is present in the survey. More precisely, the following four questions were asked every year the ANES was conducted between 1986 and 2012 with the exception of 2002:

1. "The newer lifestyles are contributing to the breakdown of our society." (VCF0851)
2. "The world is always changing and we should adjust our view of moral behavior to those changes." (VCF0852)
3. "This country would have many fewer problems if there were more emphasis on traditional family ties." (VCF0853)
4. "We should be more tolerant of people who choose to live according to their own moral standards, even if they are very different from our own." (VCF0854)

Respondents were asked the aforementioned four questions and instructed to either (1) agree strongly, (2) agree somewhat, (3) neither agree nor disagree, (4) disagree somewhat, or (5) disagree strongly. To create the moral traditionalism scale, I recoded the variables so higher numbers indicated a morally traditional viewpoint and then averaged the respondents' score. The resulting scale ranged from a minimum of 1 to a maximum of 5. These values were then transformed so the minimums and maximums matched the candidate scales presented earlier in this chapter (i.e., a minimum of –2 and a maximum of 2). But first, for comparison's sake, Table 2.13 replicates Table 2.3 for ANES districts. The figures in Tables 2.3 and 2.13 are correlated at 0.95. Candidate messages and the resulting polarization witnessed in ANES districts seem quite representative of U.S. House elections as a whole.

Table 2.13. District polarization on moral issues for American National Election Studies districts

Year	No Challenger	−4	−3	−2	−1	0	1	2	3	4	Total Contests
1978	20	0.0	0.0	0.0	0.0	97.7	0.0	2.3	0.0	0.0	88
1980	17	0.0	0.0	0.0	0.0	90.1	3.3	6.6	0.0	0.0	91
1982	24	0.0	0.0	2.8	4.2	84.	72.1	6.3	0.0	0.0	144
1984	17	0.0	0.0	2.6	5.1	77.8	4.3	10.3	0.0	0.0	117
1986	35	0.0	0.0	2.1	4.8	76.6	4.8	11.7	0.0	0.0	145
1988	30	0.0	0.0	1.9	5.7	76.2	6.7	9.5	0.0	0.0	105
1990	23	0.0	0.0	2.0	7.1	68.4	11.2	10.2	1.0	0.0	98
1992	10	0.0	0.0	3.5	9.9	54.7	15.7	13.4	2.9	0.0	172
1994	24	0.0	0.0	2.4	9.0	53.0	19.9	13.9	1.8	0.0	166
1996	14	0.0	0.0	0.9	8.2	51.9	21.5	15.9	1.3	0.4	233
1998	32	0.0	0.0	2.1	3.1	52.1	25.0	16.7	1.0	0.0	96
2000	55	0.0	0.0	1.3	9.4	50.9	23.3	13.8	1.3	0.0	318
2002	74	0.0	0.0	1.6	6.2	52.0	24.8	14.4	0.7	0.3	306
2004	20	0.0	0.0	0.8	6.7	47.9	22.7	18.5	1.7	1.7	119
2006	N/A	N/A	N/A	N/A	N/A	N/A	N/A	N/A	N/A	N/A	N/A
2008	9	0.0	0.0	4.3	5.3	61.7	16.0	11.7	1.1	0.0	94
2010	N/A	N/A	N/A	N/A	N/A	N/A	N/A	N/A	N/A	N/A	N/A
2012	13	0.0	0.0	0.8	3.3	60.7	18.0	16.4	0.8	0.0	122

Note: Cell entries in the bold bordered section are percentages.

Table 2.14. Results of voting model highlighting the role of district polarization on moral issues

Independent Variables (Dependent Variable: Republican House vote)	Beta Coefficients	Standard Errors
Party identification	2.141	0.066
Incumbency	1.055	0.045
Education	0.075	0.047
South	0.231	0.091
Male	0.012	0.080
White	0.656	0.122
Age	−0.070	0.025
Guaranteed job	0.160	0.046
Aid to blacks	0.174	0.047
Moral traditionalism	0.292	0.052
Moral issue polarization	−0.084	0.047
Moral issue interaction	0.174	0.046
Constant	−0.791	0.221
N	6.483	
Adjusted R-square	0.447	

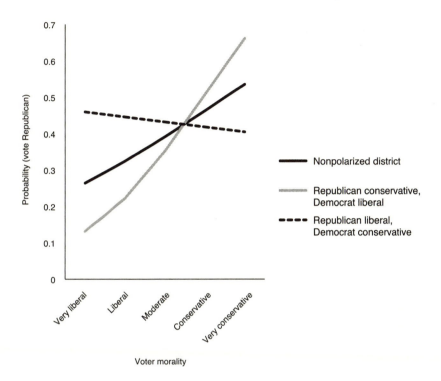

Figure 2.9. Effect of moral issues on the probability of voting Republican for U.S. House candidates

Table 2.14 shows the results of this model. The direct effect of moral traditionalism is positive and significant, meaning that even when there is no difference between the candidates on moral issues, more morally conservative voters are attracted to the Republican candidate. This type of district is represented by the solid line in Figure 2.9. This could be because Republicans during the period of study are just assumed to be more traditional when it comes to issues of morality. But where there is a clear difference between the candidates, voter morality matters even more. In the districts where the Republican is conservative on moral issues and the Democrat is liberal (district polarization equals 2), conservative voters are much more likely to vote Republican. This is represented by the lightly shaded line in Figure 2.9. In fact, the difference in a nonpolarized district (solid line) between a strong liberal and a strong conservative is roughly 27 points. In a polarized district (lightly shaded line), that difference is approximately 53 points. And in the rare cases where the Republican is liberal on moral issues and the Democrat is conservative (district polarization equals −2), more conservative voters are slightly less likely to vote Republican, all other things being equal. This is represented by the dashed line in Figure 2.9 and further buttresses the claim that moral issues matter in congressional elections. Despite the promising nature of these results, the reader should remain skeptical, considering there is no measure of whether or not the voters are actually receiving the various messages being put forth by the candidates. This concern will be addressed in the more complex communications-based model introduced and discussed thoroughly in Chapter 7. In the meantime, the next chapter reviews the theory on party coalition change and sets the reader up for the three case studies that provide the qualitative evidence for my thesis.

Chapter 3

Party Coalition Change and U.S. House Elections

A Changing of the Guard

Sedgwick County, Kansas, was officially established in 1867 and named after Major General John Sedgwick, who was killed fighting for the Union Army during the battle of Spotsylvania Courthouse in Virginia. Three years later, the first county officials were elected and Wichita was named the county seat (Sedgwick County). Wichita began as a farm market town and grew with local discoveries of oil and gas in the 1920s. During World War II and the years that followed, Wichita became the nation's major producer of small airplanes when several factories sprouted up on the Kansas plains. The big four—Cessna, Raytheon, Boeing, and Bombardier— were all located here at one time. However, by the early 1990s, the local aviation industry was harmed by the recession and by lawsuits that held manufacturers liable for planes they had produced years, and even decades, before (Barone, Cohen, and Ujifusa 2007, 670–671). The early 1990s also brought significant political change to Sedgwick County as the issue of abortion was thrust into the spotlight. The so-called Summer of Mercy generated national headlines as Operation Rescue brought its band of roving protesters to Dr. George Tiller's abortion clinic in Wichita. Thousands were arrested, and Tiller's practice was temporarily shut down owing to the demonstrations.

At the time, the Sedgwick County GOP was helmed by Republicans who were either pro-choice or did not place much emphasis on their pro-life leanings. The Summer of Mercy sparked a revolt within the county Republican Party, leading to the ouster of the existing leadership and the installation of a new chairman who was as pro-life as they come. Mark Gietzen had been active in the pro-life movement for over a decade. He fought hard to get a pro-life radio show broadcast on a station with a stronger signal. But despite being a die-hard Republican and a Reagan delegate in 1980, he and other pro-lifers were denied access and power within the local party apparatus. They did not have the numbers nor the funds to compete with the old-guard Republicans who historically controlled the levers of partisan power. Gietzen knew that to gain control of the local party and make it a pro-life institution, they had to install pro-lifers as precinct committeemen and committeewomen, giving the movement the internal strength necessary to vote the pro-choice leadership out. And it was the Summer of Mercy that provided the foot soldiers for this movement. Gietzen attended the rallies and signed up protesters to run for precinct committee positions. "I would run around to all these gatherings, a lot of them at the hotels where a lot of those people were staying, at any of these pro-life functions. And I would run around with my maps, and I'm saying, 'Here's a precinct. Do we have anybody in here? I have no pro-lifers running. I need somebody.' Somebody would raise their hand and say, 'Yeah, but I've never voted before in my life.' 'Are you a citizen? Are you of age? Can we sign you up to vote and get you written in as a precinct person?' 'Well, yeah if you tell me what to do.' And, you know, we would have another one" (Gietzen, KS04, interview with author).

Gietzen recruited 281 abortion foes to run for the 472 precinct committeemen and committeewomen positions in Sedgwick County, and many were successful. In August 1992, 83 percent of the central committee members were against abortion. A year earlier, only 49 percent were pro-life (Thomas 1992b, 1A). Now that Gietzen had the numbers in his favor, he insisted that the county party commit itself to a strong pro-life stance. After a contentious organizational meeting, the pro-choice chairwoman resigned and was replaced as county chairman by none other than Mark Gietzen. Needless to say, the official party stance on abortion shifted 180 degrees with the change in leadership.

Of course, gaining control of the formal party apparatus was only a means to an end—the end being the nomination and election of pro-life candidates to local, state, and federal government. My focus is on the House of Representatives, and as the reader will see in Chapter 4, it was too late for Gietzen's plan to have an impact on the 1992 congressional race. However, two years later. Gietzen and his backers were instrumental in helping

Todd Tiahrt upset Dan Glickman and become the U.S. representative from the Fourth District of Kansas. Tiahrt was one of many "new" Republican candidates that emerged during the 1980s and 1990s. They were fiercely conservative on social issues and boasted precious few ties to the Republican establishment. The prevalence of these types of candidates was quantified in Chapter 2, and in this chapter, I seek to explain how they came to prominence in American politics more generally and within House elections more specifically.

Winning the Conference Championship

As the onetime leader of the Christian Coalition, Ralph Reed pioneered many of the campaign strategies that have now become commonplace in American elections. Currently the head of the Faith and Freedom Coalition, Reed knows a great deal about how to effect political change. He is also a pretty big football fan. In a recent interview, he used a gridiron analogy to show how important nominations are in American politics. "If you don't win the conference championship, you're not going to win the Super Bowl" (Reed, interview with author). The logic is clear. You cannot win the general election and get to Washington without first winning the primary. But the importance of nominations goes well beyond the logical necessity of succeeding in them. Nominations are central to the workings of political parties and undergird a new theory of politics that has been put forth recently.

Kathleen Bawn and colleagues (2012) challenge the conventional wisdom on political parties. Instead of elected officials being at the center of political parties and acting as the driving force behind party formation and party change, they argue that parties are best understood as coalitions of interest groups and activists that seek to capture the government for their particular goals. "The coalition of policy-demanding groups develops an agenda of mutually acceptable policies, insists on the nomination of candidates with a demonstrated commitment to its program, and works to elect these candidates to office" (Bawn et al. 2012, 571). These scholars elaborate on the importance of nominations by focusing in on the ultimate goals of what they call intense policy demanders. They want certain policies from elected officials, and there are a number of ways they can try to secure these friendly policies. They can lobby existing officeholders. But this strategy will only be effective if the policy is broadly acceptable or if it already lines up with what the officeholder wants or believes. Intense policy demanders can attempt to win over officeholders with campaign contributions. But here a principal-agent problem looms. The money comes in, but how does the group know whether the politician is actively fighting for the group's agenda? Officeholders always have an informational advantage over policy demanders. The most reliable way to get a politician to do what you want is to put someone in there who is already in favor of your goals. Nominate a genuine friend and try to get them elected. Fortunately for interest groups, the nomination process is very conducive to influence.

In seeking to control a nomination as opposed to lobbying entrenched officeholders, interest groups and activists are in a stronger position. There are multiple office seekers who need support in the form of money and other campaign resources. Promises to support a group's policy demands can be made in return for these resources. Additionally, in the small world of local politics, leading politicians are well known to one another, and therefore policy-demanding groups can be fairly certain they are getting the kind of candidate they want. And finally, nominations are relatively low-information and low-cost contests. For House races, a little bit of money and organization can make a big difference when the cue of party identification is inoperable, media coverage is sparse, and voter interest is very low (Bawn et al. 2012, 575).

The relative lack of knowledge that House primary voters have also allows intense policy demanders to nominate candidates closer to their ideal points and further from the median voter. Bawn and colleagues (2012, 577) posit the existence of an electoral blind spot within which voters cannot tell the differences between their own views and that of the major party candidates on the issues. If the voters cannot perceive policy differences, then the parties do not have to cede very much to them. They can try to stretch the limits of what will be allowed in the nominating process while still achieving victory in the general election. The blind spot is quite relevant to my analysis since in many districts the median voter was not as fervently pro-life as the candidates put forth by the Republican Party. Thus, we see examples of Ralph Reed's notorious stealth campaigns, which are essentially efforts to expand the blind spot and sneak candidates into office without tipping off moderate voters to their extreme stances on moral issues such as abortion. However, there were also instances where the median voter was quite traditional on moral issues, and here the theoretical concept of the blind spot is not quite as relevant. In these cases, voter preferences simply needed to be expressed, and the "new" kinds of Republican candidates discussed throughout the book—candidates with strongly moralistic positions on cultural issues—finally provided them with an outlet for their viewpoints. As the reader has already observed and will continue to see, there were multiple examples of each case during the period of study.

Republican Versus Republican

Nominations are a natural focal point for intense policy demanders, and the Christian right was no exception. Beginning in the 1980s, contested Republican primaries for the House of Representatives often pitted pro-life, pro-family candidates against more moderate, more establishment politicians who were less concerned with the moral issues that animated their opponents. These campaigns were often bitter, and the internecine warfare in some cases handed congressional seats to the Democrats in November. The year 1986 saw several high-profile primary battles of this nature. In Indiana's Fifth District, an evangelical Christian and former state senator named James Butcher opposed the state treasurer, Julian Ridlen, who was a longtime party loyalist and had the support of the district party chairman and most of the county chairmen. Therefore, Butcher had to rely on the evangelical community for building his organization. Butcher was very unhappy that the party organization effectively chose sides: "Until now, I've never had a primary fight. I'm in a swing state Senate district, and they've been perfectly happy that I've been able to hold onto it. . . . But now I'm running against one of the good ol' boys, and when the going gets tough, the good ol' boy—who is a moderate and whom they can pretty much control—gets their support" (CQ Press 1986, 20). For its part, the establishment was very worried about the general election where the Democrats were fielding a solid candidate. Butcher was seen as too one sided thanks to his evangelical background and his extreme views on social issues. The party chairman thought that Ridlen was a broader candidate with a better chance of winning in November. Butcher upset Ridlen in the primary thanks to an endorsement from Pat Robertson and good turnout among evangelicals. However, the fears of the GOP establishment were realized when Butcher was defeated in the general election 52 percent to 48 percent.

In North Carolina's Fifth District, Stuart Epperson was a religious broadcaster who managed to defeat Lyons Gray, a member of one of Winston-Salem's richest families. This was a classic battle between Republican factions. Like Butcher, Epperson could not broaden his base of support in the general election and lost to Democratic incumbent Stephen Neal. South Carolina's Fourth and Tennessee's Third also were home to similar factional battles. In the Palmetto State, the Christian right candidate was defeated in the primary, and the party never united around the winning establishment candidate. He lost the open seat race that November. In Tennessee, the evangelical faction was victorious but was actively opposed by establishment Republicans in the general election, and the Democratic incumbent returned to Washington.[1] The year 1986 was indeed a watershed for these factional battles, but in the four districts discussed above, the GOP compiled a batting average of .000. Democrats kept or took the House seat in all four instances. It was not until the early 1990s that Republicans began to benefit electorally from the prevalence of these new kinds of candidates. It was this success that transformed the House delegation and created a relatively stable majority for the Republican Party.

Party Coalition Change

How party coalitions change is an important subject and one that touches on the role groups can play in party politics. If one conceives of parties as coalitions of intense policy demanders as Bawn and colleagues (2012) do, the overall direction a party will take on issues comes as a result of the mix of activists within the party coalition. It follows that changes in the makeup of the coalition will lead to changes in the party's agenda and the issue positions that their elected officials espouse. As discussed in the previous chapter, the Republican delegation of recent years looks a lot different on moral issues than it used to. Many more Republican members of Congress are espousing morally traditional views, and while the result has not always been legislative success in these areas, what it means to be a national Republican on these issues has clearly changed over the past forty years or so. The ideology of elected officials can change in the aggregate in one of two ways. Politicians can simply change their views on these subjects or they can be replaced by candidates who hold different opinions. In his book on party position change, David Karol (2009) looks at several cases in which the parties repositioned themselves on salient issues and finds that elite conversion occurs much more often than has originally been thought. Even on controversial, high-profile issues, such as gun control and abortion, politicians have been able to flip-flop and live to tell about it. Karol presents many instances of sitting members of Congress simply switching their positions either to help maintain a coalition, incorporate a new group into an existing party coalition, or expand a coalition. This is a convincing argument that challenges the existing realignment and issue evolution literature. Undoubtedly, more than a few high-profile Congress members did indeed switch positions on an issue such as abortion. The anecdotal evidence on this is clear. However, as I show in Chapter 2 and will delve into more deeply in the upcoming case studies, new kinds of candidates bear significant responsibility for the rightward shift among Republicans on such issues as abortion and gay rights. In Karol's defense, he does state that conversion accounts for less of the change on abortion than on all of the other issues he includes in the book (Karol 2009, 81).

In addition, as an example of Karol's coalition group incorporation, party politicians are seen as the instigators of change on abortion in particular (Karol 2009, 19). Katherine Krimmel (forthcoming) also argues that the Reagan administration in particular sought out Christian right groups to help the Republican Party build itself into a majority coalition to rival and replace the vaunted New Deal Coalition that had broken apart a decade earlier. She argues further that the GOP's decision to ally with these evangelical Christian groups was not driven by ideological change but was a party-building exercise. Reagan and his administration were chiefly concerned with passing their economic program and needed to enlist social conservatives to help the cause (Krimmel, forthcoming).

Krimmel uses archival evidence to make a serious case. However, she is focused on the presidential level and also concludes her analysis in the 1980s with the departure of the Reagan administration. Beginning in the late 1970s but extending to the early 1990s, I find little evidence at the congressional level that federal officeholders or party officials began actively pursuing pro-life voters of their own volition. In fact, in many cases, entrenched party leaders resisted the advances of pro-life activists and saw them as a threat to their own hegemony within the Republican Party apparatus, both formal and informal. I believe local activists were most often the initiators of change within the GOP on issues of moral traditionalism such as abortion.

In the opening chapter of *The Great Divide*, Geoffrey Layman (2001) seeks to explain religious change in the party system. In Figure 1.1 of his book, Layman sketches out an eight-step process starting with the traditionalism-modernist religious cleavage that has always existed in America and has taken on a particular political salience since the 1960s (Layman 2001, 24). He ends with a change in the religious composition of the party coalitions. Each of his steps along the way makes intuitive sense and fits the pattern I find in my case studies with one exception. After culturally based political issues emerge (as they did dramatically after the tumult of the 1960s), he believes strategic politicians champion noncentrist stands on cultural issues and this inspires culturally liberal and culturally conservative activists to respond, leading the parties to take distinct stands on these cultural issues. I would argue from my qualitative research into House elections and from the extensive work I and my colleagues (Cohen et al. 2008) and Bawn and colleagues (2012) have done on this that these two steps should probably be transposed. I believe activists took the lead on these issues, and ambitious politicians, seeing the writing on the wall, followed by taking more extreme positions on these issues, creating the elite polarization we see today and that I documented in the previous chapter. In my research, elected officials and nonelected party leaders were often forced to acknowledge the moral traditionalism championed by activists who foisted themselves and their issues onto the Republican Party. Karol's work on the flip-flopping of elected officials also fits my story.

Daniel Schlozman (2015) also has something to say about this, arguing that coalitions are built neither from the top down nor the bottom up but from the inside out and the outside in. In Schlozman's words, parties stitch together different blocs of supporters and find policies and candidates with appeal across them (Schlozman 2015, 5). Schlozman's work is directly relevant to my research considering he surveys the history of electoral alignments and argues that certain movements have served as anchors for parties. One of the groups that achieved incorporation was the Christian right within the Republican Party beginning in the 1970s (Schlozman 2015, 19). Schlozman's main argument is as follows:

Political parties have achieved durable alliance with social movements when two conditions intersect. First, winning coalitions inside parties perceive that the party can achieve durable electoral majority with the movement incorporated. Not all these partisan actors, and certainly not the pivotal ones, agree with the movement in all its particulars. Rather, they favor alliance over alternative paths to build the coalitions that will win them elections. Second, for parties to pay movements' price of admission, they must believe that movements control resources—votes, money, and networks— unavailable to parties themselves. That judgment in turn requires serious organization building on movements' part, tying together grassroots supporters with elite brokers whom parties trust to deliver on their electoral bargains. (Schlozman 2015, 14)

I have no quarrels with Schlozman's main contention, and I think he does an excellent job of chronicling the Christian right's incorporation into the Republican Party at the national level. However, within his story lurks another dynamic that occurred in local politics throughout the nation and consisted of many different parochial fights about the direction of the party in the form of congressional nomination contests. As I have alluded to in this chapter and will elaborate on considerably in the next three chapters, Christian Republicans stressing moral traditionalism had to fight their way to relevance within the party. These fights produced mixed results. The process began after the GOP and the Christian right had already consummated a relationship at the presidential level. But as has been well documented, the realignment of white Southern Protestants did not trickle down to the congressional level for at least two decades after they started voting Republican for president. There was a need for candidates to provide a voice for these Americans in House elections, and it took a while for them to emerge and then to win nominations to challenge Democratic incumbents, holding onto what Gary Jacobson referred to as "at-risk" districts. At-risk districts, according to Jacobson, were seats in the 1980s and 1990s held by Democrats but where Republican presidential candidates were getting majorities (Jacobson 2001). There was a significant number of split-ticket voters—Republican for president but Democratic for Congress —during this period. By 1992 and 1994, a great many of these at-risk districts flipped to the GOP, giving the Republican Party their long-awaited majority in the House of Representatives.

Moral Versus Economic Issues

Part of the purpose of this book is to account for why the Republican Party finally broke through in the House of Representatives in 1994 after being

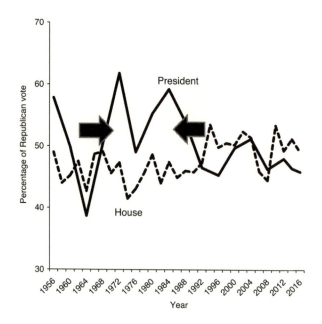

Figure 3.1. Percentage of Republican votes for president and U.S. House

stuck in the minority for decades while their presidential candidates were largely successful. A majority of voters seemed to favor Republican policies, but that preference was clearly not in evidence in congressional elections. During the 1980s, when Reagan and Bush were handily winning a majority of electoral votes, Democrats continued to hold comfortable majorities in the House.

The failure of the Republican Party to make more headway in congressional elections during this period caught the attention of notable scholars in the field. Incumbency advantage obviously favored the Democrats. The Democrats also possessed more resources and ran stronger candidates—even for open seats (Mayhew 1974; Jacobson 2001, chaps. 3–5). In addition, Democrats enjoyed an edge among the electorate when it came to the social welfare issues that seemed to dominate congressional politics. Jacobson explains the gap between presidential and congressional voting observed in Figure 3.1 by arguing that voters use different criteria to judge presidential and congressional candidates. Presidential candidates are evaluated according to their views on national issues and their ability to deal with national problems, while congressional candidates are evaluated on their personal character, experience, and ability to provide services for the district and its constituents (Jacobson 1990, 115). The issue ownership literature is also relevant here (Petrocik 1996). And consider this quote from Byron Shafer: "Ever since 1968 and the coming of the era of divided government, Democrats had been trying to push economic/welfare issues up from Congress to the presidency, just as Republicans had been trying to push cultural/national issues down from the presidency into Congress" (Shafer 1998, 23). However, neither party was successful. And on the local level, Republicans actually resisted the advances of religious conservatives and their focus on issues of moral traditionalism. In the qualitative section of this book, I make the case that the congressional realignment driven predominantly by moral issues was more of a bottom-up story than anything else. In grassroots battles across the country, religiously motivated conservatives had been fighting for a place within the party beginning in the 1980s. A decade later, those efforts bore fruit when candidates espousing morally conservative messages began winning Republican primaries, running energetic and sophisticated general election campaigns and eventually taking over numerous Democratic seats in the early 1990s.

Even after the Republican takeover of Congress and the closing of the gap in Figure 3.1, such scholars as Alan Abramowitz did not include cultural issues in their theories for why the realignment had finally trickled down to the congressional level. Abramowitz (1995) believed that ideology mattered in 1994, yet his main focus is on the Contract with America, which did not include any controversial moral issues. He does not mention moral issues or the role of the Christian right when analyzing the Republican takeover in 1994. More recently, despite the now-famous exit poll after the 2004 presidential election that ascribed moral issues top priority among the electorate, several scholars continued to downplay the role of cultural issues, such as abortion and gay marriage. Sunshine Hillygus and Todd Shields (2005) disputed these exit poll findings and argued that moral issues only serve to reinforce vote choice, not to determine it.

And then the debate over the relative salience of issues took a rather public turn with the somewhat acrimonious back and forth between Thomas Frank and Larry Bartels. Frank (2004) argued that white working-class voters were being sidetracked by moral conservatism, and it was moving them to vote for the Republican Party against their material self-interest. Bartels (2006) argued that Frank had gotten it wrong. He showed that white working-class voters were not primarily concerned with cultural issues but instead were moved to vote on the basis of economic issues. Bartels goes on to say that economic issues have lost none of their potency in the past several decades and continue to structure presidential vote choice more than social issues.

Several scholars have attempted to mediate the Frank-Bartels debate. Peter Francia and Nathan Bigelow (2010) argue that working-class voters can be pressured by unions to vote on economic issues but that churches, at the same time, are also pressuring voters to decide on moral issues. They have the answer to "what's wrong with Kansas." It is low union member-ship and high church attendance that leads Kansans away from voting their economic self-interest. Mark Brewer and Jeffrey Stonecash (2007) take the view that both Frank and Bartels can indeed be correct. In their book, *Split*, they present evidence that indicates both cultural and economic issues are extremely salient and are both in play simultaneously. In particular, they are critical of Fiorina's take on the culture wars. Fiorina and colleagues (2006) believe the existence of a cultural war among the people is a myth, and the electorate only appears to be deeply divided because candidates and other party elites are polarized and therefore the voters can only choose between extreme liberals and extreme conservatives. Alan Abramowitz and Kyle Saunders (2008) also dispute Fiorina's findings and provide credence for the notion that polarization has drastically increased since the 1970s, especially among the most informed and most active citizens. They high-light the ascendant role of moral issues and argue that political issue posi-tions are increasingly dependent on religious beliefs and practices. They argue that the religious divide is now much deeper than the class divide.[2]

A Watershed Election: 1994

The 1994 midterm elections were notable for the wave of Republicans swept into Congress, giving the GOP control of the House of Representatives for the first time in forty years. The conventional wisdom on this event in 1994 was that the Republican Party nationalized the midterm elections and ran successfully against a president and his party. President Clinton infuriated many voters with the policies he pursued during his first two years in office. Bill and Hillary's health care plan, gays in the military, the North American Free Trade Agreement (NAFTA), and the crime bill were deplored by a large swath of the electorate. Even more important than being against Democratic policies was the fact that the Republicans made an effort to be "for" something. Led by House Minority Whip Newt Gingrich, the Republicans drafted the Contract with America. The contract was signed by more than three hundred Republican incumbents and challengers on a sunny day in late September on the Capitol steps. The media ate it up, and Gingrich promised a vote on all ten items in the contract during the first one hundred days of a Republican-led House (Gimpel, 1996, chaps. 1–2). Very few imagined they would actually get the opportunity to make good on that promise since it would take a forty-seat swing to put the GOP in control the following January. Nonetheless, the spectacle of the signing and the focus on popular legislation, such as term limits, a balanced budget, and the line-item veto, enabled the Republicans to present themselves as united behind proposals the voters liked.

In the weeks leading up to the election, pundits sensed the influence the contract and its nationalization of the election was having in local races. A *Washington Post* article from late October profiled the congressional race in Virginia's Eleventh District. The reporter cites anger against President Clinton and incumbency as the main reasons the GOP challenger was able to raise more money than the Democratic incumbent. Both candidates embraced similar themes, but the Democratic label was just too unpopular in the fall of 1994. "Leslie Byrne is vulnerable to the anti-Clinton, anti-Congress, time-for-a-change attack from a moderate Republican in what is basically a swing suburban district," said Stuart Rothenberg, author of the *Rothenberg Political Report*. "He (the Republican challenger) can raise plenty of money, and the wave that is crashing across the country is probably going to drown Byrne" (Lipton 1994, B5). In another part of the country, "the anti-Clinton, anti-Washington mood among voters has put Democratic congressional candidates on the defensive all across Georgia." Democratic incumbents had to explain votes on President Clinton's tax increase and ward off charges that they were "career politicians" (Cooper 1994, A23).

Gingrich, as the face of the contract and of the Republican Party as a whole, was also having a considerable personal effect on the political environment. In Tennessee's Sixth District, Steve Gill was one of many self-described "Sons of Newt" running credible races against Democratic incumbents. These Republican challengers shared Gingrich's zeal and political philosophy on government and politics (Shribman 1994, 3). GOPAC, a political action committee linked closely with Gingrich, claimed to have trained thousands of candidates and activists since its establishment (Gaines 1994, A22).

In the days and weeks following the Republican takeover, the plaudits poured in for Gingrich, the Contract with America, and the strategy of nationalizing the election. Voters repudiated Clinton, the Democrats, incumbents, and liberals on crime, taxes, spending, morality, and ethics. Gingrich, as the driving force behind it all, assumed his rightful role as leader of the revolution and star of the show (Dowd 1994, A1; Hasson 1994, 3A; Manegold 1994, A11; Nyhan 1994, A4).

The Christian Coalition also emerged from the 1994 midterm elections with its reputation burnished. Ralph Reed's organization claimed a good deal of credit for the tidal wave that drowned the Democrats, despite the fact social issues were left out of the Contract with America.[3] The Christian Coalition was designed to influence politics at the local level and create a pro-family organization in every precinct in America (Reed 1994). In 1992, the group was heavily involved in certain congressional elections, including the distribution of 200,000 voter guides in the churches of South Carolina's Fourth District on the Sunday before the election. They were hoping to aid Republican Bob Inglis's attempt to upset the Democratic incumbent. Inglis succeeded, and the participation of the Christian Coalition was widely regarded as a major factor in that race.[4] Two years later, white evangelicals made up 20 percent of the midterm electorate, and the Christian Coalition could boast 1.5 million members. Reed's organization endorsed sixty of the seventy-three House Republican freshmen, and according to J. Christopher Soper (1996), the Christian Coalition supplied the Republican Party with grassroots support, financing, and well-trained and devoted activists. In a boast reminiscent of but not as outrageous as when Jerry Falwell claimed credit for Ronald Reagan's 1980 victory, Ralph Reed contended that the Christian right was responsible for half of the fifty-two-seat gain in the House (Soper 1996, 115).

Much of the conventional wisdom dealing with national-level influences on 1994 came from New York; Boston; Washington, D.C.; and Chesapeake, Virginia, home of the Christian Coalition. Most of it also focused on the final six weeks of the campaign. To get a fuller story of what happened in some of these districts where Republicans took seats from the Democrats, I believe it is necessary to get the local perspective and take a longer, broader view of the political landscape in these areas. There is no doubt that Newt Gingrich was the single most important person in the Republican takeover of the House. Furthermore, the Contract with America provided much-needed legitimacy and media coverage, aiding the GOP's efforts to paint themselves as more than obstructionists taking partisan shots at Bill Clinton and the Democratic Congress. And the Christian Coalition was indeed a powerful force in American politics, making a national network available for morally conservative Republican candidates across the country to access in support of their candidacies. However, after visiting three of Jacobson's "at-risk" districts, I gained some perspective that challenges the conventional wisdom of how the Republicans took over the House in 1994.

While Gingrich may have been the personality and driving ideological force behind the Republican revolution, he was nowhere to be found in the three districts I studied. He did promise to visit Wichita, Kansas, to host a fundraiser for Todd Tiahrt when Tiahrt made the announcement that he would be challenging Democratic incumbent Dan Glickman. However, Newt backed out when he saw that Glickman led by thirty points in the polls. Tiahrt had to settle for Dick Armey, the second most visible Republican member of Congress in 1994. Unfortunately for the Tiahrt campaign, Armey was a very distant second (Dave Hanna, KS04, interview with author). The only candidate in the three districts I visited who was affiliated in any way with GOPAC was Ken Meyer, a candidate for the Republican congressional nomination in Tennessee's Third District, and Meyer was defeated soundly in that primary by the eventual winner of the seat, Zach Wamp (Ken Meyer, TN03, interview with author). Steve Gill, one of the so-called Sons of Newt I mentioned earlier, actually ended up losing a close race to incumbent Bart Gordon in Tennessee's Sixth District. Further, the Contract with America did not play a prominent role in either Kansas's Fourth or Tennessee's Third. While both Tiahrt and Wamp went to Washington and signed the contract, local political operatives thought it was less relevant to the outcomes of their races than other themes, such as abortion, guns, and grassroots organizing (Billy Linville, TN03, interview with author; Hanna, interview with author).

Such national organizations as the Christian Coalition, and even such entities as the Republican National Committee and the Republican National Congressional Committee, also did not appear to be significant factors. When they did get involved, it was generally late in the game after the most difficult work was done. Local parties and interest groups were in the vanguard, providing money, volunteers, and such materials as voter guides and issue alerts.[5] These observations shed considerable light on what happened in 1994, but they also can be generalized and expanded upon to challenge the conventional wisdom regarding House elections more generally.

House Elections from a Different Perspective

I believe the role of religiously conservative activists and the increased importance of moral issues can shed some light on more general aspects of congressional elections. A main line of research revolves around what are referred to as candidate-centered elections. The basic idea is that in this age of decentralized parties both inside and outside the legislature, primary elections to determine nominations, independent political consultants, and expensive media strategies, the locus of power has shifted from the organized party structure to the individual candidate.[6]

Gary Jacobson is one of several scholars to have written extensively on this topic.[7] In his well-respected text on congressional elections, he defines candidate-centered politics and lays out the corollaries of candidate-centered congressional elections. In a candidate-centered world, most candidates "operate, out of choice or necessity, as individual political entrepreneurs" (Jacobson 2001, 5). "Most instigate their own candidacies, raise most of their own resources, and put together their own campaign organizations" (8). According to Jacobson, the long-term deterioration of party organizations and the weakening of partisan ties from the 1950s to the 1970s contributed to the separation of congressional elections from national political forces. The result, for Jacobson, has been the rise of candidate-centered campaigns (12).

Paul Herrnson says similar things regarding congressional elections. "Candidates, not political parties, are the major focus of congressional campaigns, and candidates, not parties, bear the ultimate responsibility for electoral outcomes" (Herrnson 2004, 6). Further, "the need to win a party nomination forces congressional candidates to assemble their own campaign organizations, formulate their own election strategies, and conduct their own campaigns" (7). This becomes a self-fulfilling prophecy, and as candidates find ways to accomplish things on their own that they previously needed the party for, the formal party structure further weakens.

The conventional wisdom holds that since candidates must be self-starters, for the most part building organizations and raising money on their own, they need to possess a great deal of political skill, experience, and ambition. The "quality" of the candidate is at a far greater premium than it was in the days when local party machines did all the work and could get even the most untalented hack elected to Congress if they so desired. Jacobson places a great deal of emphasis on candidate quality. He has developed a simple yet effective tool for discerning whether congressional candidates are of good quality. If they have been elected to office previously, they are high-quality candidates. Jacobson posits that these office seekers figure to be more successful than low-quality candidates who have not held public office before (2001, 174).

Indeed, higher-quality challengers tend to do better than lower-quality challengers. They have the experience and have demonstrated their skill in past electoral endeavors. Past success figures to predict future success partly because of an inherent degree of talent but also because campaign donors are trained to recognize a good bet when they see one. Higher-quality challengers are more successful in large part because they attract more money. For obvious reasons, individual and political action committee (PAC) donors are much more inclined to give funds to someone who has a greater probability of winning. And Jacobson provides ample evidence for the importance of challenger spending in congressional elections, showing that challengers rarely win without spending a great deal of money (2001, 38–46).

The candidate-centered story has been widely accepted by those who study American politics, especially those who focus on congressional elections. However, there has been a recent line of research that argues for a resurgence of parties at both the national and local levels. This work goes back to E. E. Schattschneider's renowned definition of a political party. In *Party Government*, the author defines a party as simply "an organized attempt to get control of the government" (Schattschneider 1942, 35). No more, no less. Schattschneider does not have much to say about what this party might look like. It could be that the supposed absence of local party activity is due to researchers failing to notice party activity conducted by people and organizations that do not conform to their ideas of what a party should look like.

Seth Masket (2009), in his research into California politics, discovered several informal party organizations wielding power in a state where parties were long thought to be weak. These informal organizations recruit candidates, bundle money, control nominations, and emphasize certain issue positions and policy goals. In short, they make an organized attempt to get control of the government. The complicating thing for most political science researchers is that these activists often do not work within the formal party structure. They often do not have public meetings, and they are not easily recognized from afar. However, they act like a party and have a major influence on the politics going on in their areas.

Most of the influence occurs in nominating campaigns. In research into the presidential nominating process, I and my colleagues (Cohen et al. 2008) argue that parties have reasserted control over presidential nominations by seeking to coordinate behind a favored candidate in an effort to shepherd him or her through an increasingly volatile and unpredictable primary election season. Since Jimmy Carter's improbable run to the 1976 nomination and Gary Hart's near upset of front-runner Walter Mondale, many pundits and scholars have posited that reforms designed to increase rank-and-file participation have seized control of the process from the parties that once dominated in the infamous smoke-filled rooms. I and my colleagues (Cohen et al. 2008) argue further that the new party does not need to meet in smoke-filled rooms to figure out who they want nominated and what help is needed to succeed in that endeavor. There are other ways they can communicate with each other and confer important resources without formally getting together to decide these things. It may not look like a party, but according to Schattschneider it is one. It is an organized attempt by a group of individuals to gain control of the government. I and my colleagues (Cohen et al. 2008) have identified a fairly stable cadre of players who are consistently involved in the relatively informal selection process.

I do not believe that Jacobson and others, when dismissing local party activity in congressional elections, are necessarily wrong. I agree with much of what they have to say. However, their accounts are misleading in that they fail to account for informal party structures that have a great degree of power over local elections owing to their ability to control nominations. Focusing primarily on the formal party structure and general elections might lead an observer to conclude that we are living in a candidate-centered world. However, drawing on previous research and my own evidence from three congressional districts, I believe congressional elections still very much operate in a party-centered world. This important theoretical difference will be addressed throughout the rest of the qualitative section of this book.

Three Case Studies

By shifting the focus to moral issues, providing campaign resources, and displaying a more conciliatory attitude to fellow Republicans, groups and individuals associated with the Christian right enabled the Republican Party to take control of the House of Representatives. This was done in many districts across the country. From Randy Tate's victory in Washington's Ninth District to Joe Scarborough's win in Florida's First, morally conservative Republicans took seats from the Democrats in 1994. The district-level dynamics most certainly differed throughout the country but in varying forms: issues, resources, and attitudes interacted in such a way as to make the Republican candidate more formidable. In an effort to better understand how the Republican Party flipped the House of Representatives in 1994 and created a fairly durable majority, I traveled to three at-risk districts that shifted from Democratic to Republican in either 1992 or 1994. These three districts have remained Republican all the way up to the present time. Through a review of secondary source material, interviews, and archival newspaper research, I have crafted three case studies I believe will help shed light on the phenomenon of interest.

The three districts included in my research are Kansas's Fourth, South Carolina's Fourth, and Tennessee's Third. The first seat had not been held by the GOP since 1976, the second not since 1986, and the third not since 1974. Yet when the votes were counted on the evening of November 8, 1994, all three were represented by Republicans. In the Fourth District of Kansas, a first-term state senator by the name of Todd Tiahrt ousted a longtime Democratic incumbent in one of the signature upsets of the 1994 elections. Tiahrt expressed his conservative religious beliefs often during the campaign and benefited from the takeover of the Sedgwick County Republican Party by Christian conservatives, most of whom were brought into politics by the antiabortion rallies that took place during the so-called Summer of Mercy in Wichita in 1991. In South Carolina's Fourth, a virtually unknown lawyer with no political experience named Bob Inglis defeated a three-term Democratic incumbent in 1992. This race marked one of the first concerted efforts by the Christian Coalition to influence the outcome of a congressional election. On the Sunday before the election, the coalition distributed roughly 200,000 voter guides in churches across the district, highlighting the issues on which the candidates differed. Inglis was able to appeal to the large number of religious conservatives in the district without alienating the ever-powerful business community. Finally, in Tennessee's Third District, Zach Wamp defeated Randy Button in a race for the open seat vacated by the retiring Democratic incumbent Marilyn Lloyd. Lloyd was pushed hard by Wamp two years earlier and must have sensed the political winds blowing against her and her party. Wamp was a born-again Christian who, with the support of the local power structure and an active religious community, overcame a drug problem and other legal mishaps to defeat his well-known Democratic challenger.

I do not imagine these three districts are representative in any way of the country at large or even the subset of districts that were vulnerable for the Democrats. I selected these districts as clear examples of the vital role played by the Christian right in the transfer of congressional power. I believe the political phenomena described in these three case studies occurred elsewhere, if not in exact style at least in substance. The goal of the case studies is to flesh out the dynamics that took place, provide some qualitative evidence for my main arguments, and give the reader some names, faces, and quotes to go with the extensive data analysis presented elsewhere in this book. Tables 3.1 to 3.3 provide thumbnail sketches for the three districts I visited.[8]

Demographically, the first point to take away from these three tables is that these districts, despite being redrawn five times during the period of study, really did not change very much. South Carolina's Fourth got a bit older, and Kansas's Fourth became a bit more rural relative to the rest of the country. Other than that, the makeup of these three districts does not seem to have changed that much between 1972 and 2012. Kansas's Fourth is right around the median on all five demographic categories presented in Table 3.1. South Carolina's Fourth is near the median on education, has below-average median income, and is slightly more rural than the rest of the nation. The percentage of African-Americans in the population is consistently near the eightieth percentile throughout the period. Finally, Tennessee's Third District population is relatively poorer, older, and less well educated. It is also a rural district with a large African American population.

In presidential voting, each district in every year gave the most recent Republican presidential candidate a majority of its votes. Only in South Carolina's Fourth in 1980 did a district not place in the upper half of the nation in Republican presidential vote. In the 2012 election between Barack Obama and Mitt Romney, each district was in the mid- to upper eightieth percentile in terms of voting Republican. At the congressional level,

Table 3.1. Case study 1: Kansas, Fourth Congressional District

Redistricting Year	Median Income ($)	Percentage Black	Percentage with College Degree	Percentage over Age 65	Percentage Urban	Republican Share of the Most Recent Two-Party Presidential Vote (%)	Republican Share of the Two-Party House Vote (%)
2012	48,100 (48th)	6.3 (46th)	26.9 (52nd)	13.3 (50th)	79.8 (41st)	63.1 (85th)	66.3 (82nd)
2002	40,917 (49th)	6.9 (54th)	23.0 (52nd)	13.0 (59th)	78.8 (43rd)	61.5 (81st)	62.2 (60th)
1992	28,308 (46th)	6.5 (57th)	19.6 (57th)	13.5 (66th)	75.8 (47th)	54.8 (77th)	44.9 (49th)
1982	17,609 (63rd)	7.1 (57th)	17.0 (65th)	10.9 (48th)	80.6 (57th)	58.7 (58th)	24.8 (21st)
1972	9,097 (42nd)	6.6 (58th)	N/A	10.1 (51st)	81.9 (57th)	68.0 (69th)	74.7 (96th)

Note: Percentiles are in parentheses.

Kansas's Fourth District was solidly Republican in 1972, solidly Democratic in 1982, marginal in 1992, and solidly Republican again in 2002 and 2012. South Carolina's Fourth District was solidly Democratic in 1972, solidly Republican in 1982, flipped barely to the Republicans in 1992, and solidly Republican in 2002 and 2012. Finally, Tennessee's Third District was solidly Republican in 1972, solidly Democratic in 1982, marginal in 1992, and solidly Republican in 2002 and 2012.

In my case studies, I will concentrate on the impact religious conservatives have had on each of the three districts, while repeatedly highlighting evidence that challenges or supports the main arguments presented in this book. Table 3.4 summarizes the arc of my case studies. I have selected three districts where by all rights the Republicans should have sent one of their own to Washington well before they finally did. Instead, these districts voted for Democrats, albeit moderate ones, during that period.

The second column of Table 3.4 outlines the reasons for GOP failure during the Reagan-Bush years. The third column explains when and how the seat went Republican. Finally, in the fourth column, the role of the Christian

Table 3.2. Case study 2: South Carolina, Fourth Congressional District

Redistricting Year	Median Income ($)	Percentage Black	Percentage with College Degree	Percentage over Age 65	Percentage Urban	Republican Share of the Most Recent Two-Party Presidential Vote (%)	Republican Share of the Two-Party House Vote (%)
2012	45,108 (35th)	19.7 (82nd)	27.5 (55th)	13.2 (49th)	84.9 (47th)	63.2 (85th)	65.8 (81st)
2002	39,417 (42nd)	19.8 (80th)	22.3 (49th)	12.2 (47th)	73.5 (37th)	66.0 (91st)	70.4 (77th)
1992	27,703 (44th)	19.7 (83rd)	17.6 (46th)	12.3 (49th)	64.4 (34th)	62.1 (94th)	51.5 (62nd)
1982	15,537 (36th)	19.4 (81st)	13.9 (46th)	10.1 (32nd)	67.3 (41st)	54.6 (38th)	63.3 (82nd)
1972	8,416 (29th)	18.4 (77th)	N/A	7.9 (18th)	56.4 (31st)	80.0 (99th)	33.9 (32nd)

Note: Percentiles are in parentheses.

Table 3.3. Case study 3: Tennessee, Third Congressional District

Redistricting Year	Median Income ($)	Percentage Black	Percentage with College Degree	Percentage over Age 65	Percentage Urban	Republican Share of the Most Recent Two-Party Presidential Vote (%)	Republican Share of the Two-Party House Vote (%)
2012	38,020 (12th)	10.9 (65th)	19.9 (21st)	16.1 (88th)	62.8 (20th)	64.3 (88th)	63.4 (76th)
2002	35,434 (23rd)	11.1 (68th)	18.9 (33rd)	13.6 (69th)	64.2 (24th)	58.2 (73rd)	65.7 (66th)
1992	24,687 (22nd)	11.6 (71st)	16.0 (36th)	13.7 (67th)	64.6 (35th)	50.0 (61st)	49.3 (58th)
1982	15,241 (30th)	12.4 (71st)	13.9 (46th)	10.8 (46th)	68.0 (42nd)	57.7 (54th)	37.0 (41st)
1972	7,940 (23rd)	11.3 (68th)	N/A	10.8 (62nd)	45.0 (17th)	72.0 (85th)	56.9 (67th)

Note: Percentiles are in parentheses.

Table 3.4. Arc of my case studies showing Republican failure and success
over time

Case Study	Why Failure	Winning the Seat	Role of Religious Conservatives
Kansas, Fourth Congressional District	Republican candidates did not stress moral issues and did not have the money or the volunteers.	Defeated a nine-term incumbent in 1994.	Took over the local party in 1992. Local interest groups galvanized their membership.
South Carolina, Fourth Congressional District	Bitter primary fights. Democratic incumbent was challenged primarily on economic issues.	Defeated a three-term incumbent in 1992.	Voter guides focused on moral issues. Assimilated into the party, creating a larger and better-organized GOP.
Tennessee, Third Congressional District	Conservative incumbent. Internal rifts within the local Republican Party.	Won a Democratically held open seat in 1994.	Provided the foot soldiers and energy for the victory.

right in these partisan swings is sketched out. Though I believe the role of
religious conservatives was necessary in all three of these partisan takeovers,
I do not think it was sufficient. There are numerous reasons why the Republicans struggled at the congressional level during the 1980s, and there were
certainly many things having very little to do with religion and morality that
contributed to the GOP's successes in 1992 and 1994. That said, I believe the
role of the Christian right in the Republican Revolution of the early 1990s
was tangible, has been somewhat overlooked, and deserves our attention here.
The fact that these seats remain safely in Republican hands also makes them
important markers for understanding how the GOP remained in the majority
for all but four years between 1994 and 2018. Additionally, these cases contribute to our general understanding of how congressional elections are conducted.

The Limitations and Dangers of Personal Interviews

Before turning to the first of my case studies, I do want to address the
limitations and dangers of relying too heavily on personal interviews to

draw conclusions about political events. There would seem to be several inherent problems that could affect the veracity of the accounts. First, memory fades, and I am focusing on episodes that occurred as much as thirty years before the interview dates. Second, there is a tendency for individuals to exaggerate their own role in a particular situation. Third, there is an equally enticing tendency for individuals to cast themselves in a positive light. To combat all of these difficulties, I made a concerted effort to ask objective observers, such as reporters and academics, all of the questions I posed to the politicians and activists who were intimately involved with the district's politics. When there were conflicting reports, I address this in the text or hold back that information so as to keep the reader from drawing flawed conclusions. In addition, reading local newspaper accounts of these events as they happened cleared up a lot of hazy recollections and conflicting versions of what was really going on. To give the reader a sense of the types of individuals I spoke with and to provide a who's who of sorts for the next three chapters, the list of interviews I conducted throughout the course of my research appears in the back of the book.

Chapter 4

From the Protests to the Precincts

An Incumbent Realizes His Greatest Legislative Achievement

As a nine-term incumbent Democratic congressman from the Fourth District of Kansas, Dan Glickman was well connected in Washington. He was a high-ranking member of the Agriculture Committee and the chair of the permanent Select Committee on Intelligence. Glickman had cultivated many personal and professional friendships throughout his time on Capitol Hill. All of his experience, connections, and political savvy would soon be tested as he embarked on the most important legislative endeavor of his career. If successful, it would be his greatest political achievement. More important, it would be a big shot in the arm as he ran for his tenth term in 1994.

Aviation has historically dominated Kansas's Fourth. Boeing and Cessna had large plants there and were the major employers in the area. But during the 1980s and early 1990s, the aviation industry was struggling. Nationwide, between 1980 and 1993, more than 46 percent of the nation's airframe building jobs disappeared, and Wichita did not escape the trend (Higdon 1993, 1A). Part of the difficulty was liability. Cessna built thousands of airplanes on the east side of Wichita in the years after World War II. Fifty years later, these aircraft were antique biplanes. Yet if someone took one out and got killed, Cessna would still be liable. Regardless of how much time went by or how many owners the plane had, the manufacturers could still be held responsible for the pilot's death. This had a chilling effect on the building of smaller airplanes. Many Wichita residents felt it was only common sense that Cessna should not be liable for an indefinite period.

However, Dan Glickman, along with Kansas senators Nancy Kassebaum and Bob Dole, had labored unsuccessfully for years to limit that liability.

Glickman's latest legislative effort was gathering steam during the spring and summer of 1993. "If the bill becomes law, the benefits to Kansas would be swift and immediate," reported the *Wichita Eagle*, which covered the issue heavily (Webb 1993, 1A). The Senate passed the legislation on March 16, 1994. The battlefield then shifted to the House of Representatives, with Dan Glickman clearly the commanding general. Coverage in the *Eagle* remained heavy as the battle reached its climax. The Association of Trial Lawyers of America was the main lobbying group opposing the legislation, and Jack Brooks, the powerful judiciary chair from Texas, was the main foe in the chamber. All the while, Boeing continued to lay off workers in Wichita. Russ Meyer, the chair of Cessna, said that his company would resume piston airplane production the day after the law passed.

On August 3, the House finally signed off on Dan Glickman's liability limit, and the bill was headed to President Clinton for his signature. Years of cajoling had paid off. The General Aviation Revitalization Act of 1994 was the capstone to Dan Glickman's legislative career, and glowing reviews came from all over. It is worth quoting extensively from the August 4, 1994, front-page article in the *Wichita Eagle* titled "Light Plane Industry Hopes Soar: Clinton Ready to Sign Bill" to hammer home the significance of Glickman's accomplishment.

> Capping an eight-year congressional battle, the bill received a final thumbs-up from the U.S. House, prompting a jubilant Rep. Dan Glickman to bear-hug anyone nearby including a pair of notably un-huggable congressmen.
>
> Glickman's joy was understandable. When President Clinton signs the bill into law, and he intends to sign it, the White House confirmed Wednesday, Cessna Aircraft Co. says it will hire hundreds of Kansas workers and resume building its famous line of single-engine airplanes for the first time since 1986.
>
> "Yahoo," said Jim Beckley, director of trade for the Kansas Department of Commerce. "We have all dreamed about the day when Cessna would get back into the single-engine airplane production."
>
> The Machinists Union in Wichita put up a sign outside its office that read, "A very happy day. Let's build airplanes," minutes after

Glickman called from the House floor Wednesday afternoon to tell union representatives that the bill had passed.

The "conservative" estimate from Cessna is that the company will need to hire another 1,500 to 2,000 workers to build single-engine piston planes.

The bill would exempt from lawsuits 110,000 of the 178,000 planes that Cessna has ever built and about 65 percent of the 50,000 airplanes that Beech has built. Both companies have said they would pour money now used for defending themselves in court into the development of new products.

"Just because it passed, it's not going to be dramatic overnight," said Ed Simpson, president of the industry's trade group. "It's no panacea, but I can't think of any one factor that will re-stimulate this industry and lead to other things more than this bill." (Webb 1994, 1A)

Glickman's clout in delivering for his district had never been so clear. By wielding his legislative muscle and maximizing the advantages of incumbency, the Democratic congressman was able to save thousands of jobs and boost the economy of his home district. This is an ideal example of how incumbents have built such an impressive reelection rate. This is how the Democratic Party managed to stay in control of the House for four decades. Yet only three months later, Glickman was out of office; beaten by, of all people, a Boeing employee who believed deeply that saving the lives of the unborn was more important than restoring thousands of jobs in his hometown.

Todd Tiahrt, the new congressman from the Fourth District in Kansas, had been a one-term state senator from the town of Goddard.[1] He was able to upset the seemingly unbeatable incumbent by stressing abortion and other moral issues and, as a result, exposing Glickman's liberalism in that domain. Before 1994, Glickman's Republican challengers had usually stressed fiscal matters. Like many Democrats, Glickman had become fairly good at parrying charges of being a tax-and-spend liberal. He was able to avoid the big-spender label while taking care of the district's economic concerns. However, he was not prepared for such a spirited attack on issues of moral traditionalism. Tiahrt, backed by a county party that had recently been taken over by pro-lifers and buoyed by the intense support of Kansans for Life, overcame a thirty-point deficit in the polls and a five-to-one spending disadvantage to defeat Congressman Glickman 53 percent to 47 percent. The story of Tiahrt's victory nicely parallels those that took place elsewhere during the early 1990s. Democratic seats in moderate-to-conservative districts were going Republican owing to a new emphasis on cultural issues. Once these issues were on the table, newly empowered religiously conservative activists provided the resources and political muscle to push the Republican challenger to victory. As one of the district-level fights that has reshaped the Republican Party and led to a new and relatively stable congressional majority, it is worth studying in great detail.

Political Background

Wichita is the largest city in Kansas, and it accounts for roughly half of the Fourth District's voters. The predominant county in that district is Sedgwick. It includes Wichita as well as half of the outlying areas. The remaining quarter of the district lies in mostly rural counties. There is a large union presence mostly connected to the airplane industry that leads Wichita's economy. The rest of the district is dominated by agriculture.

In recent decades, Kansas has gone from six to five to four congressional districts. As this has occurred, the Fourth District has become more rural, making the district more conservative. Wichita has always been a blue-collar town, so when labor was strong and these workers were voting on pocketbook issues, Wichita leaned Democratic. The smaller towns and rural areas have been as reliably Republican as the state itself. Republicans have come to dominate the Fourth District at all levels of government as the GOP has once again solidified itself as the majority party in the Sunflower State.

Religion is central to the lives of most Fourth District inhabitants, and it has played a major role in Kansas politics back to the days of John Brown and his Beecher's Bibles. While Catholicism is the largest denomination in Wichita, there are scores of evangelical Protestant and nondenominational fundamentalist churches in the area. While not all church leaders and their congregations are involved in politics, the level of activity has steadily risen, and one could argue that religious conviction underlies much of what is currently relevant to Fourth District politics (Tom Schaefer, interview with author). It certainly was the driving force behind Todd Tiahrt's upset victory over nine-term Democratic incumbent Dan Glickman in 1994. The increased salience of moral issues with a religious tinge, most notably abortion, was a key factor in this race. Without the fervent support of religious conservatives throughout the district, Tiahrt would not have won, and the Democrats would have maintained their hold on this seat. With that backing, it became one of many districts to go Republican in 1994, contributing to the GOP's stunning takeover of the House and its creation of a new majority.

Abortion /moral issues w/ fervent support of rel. conserv. driving force to win of Todd Tiahrt

An Evolving Republican Party

The Republican Party has virtually dominated Kansas politics for most of the last century. Of course, Democrats have not been completely shut out of power. In fact, going back to the 1960s, Republicans and Democrats have each had their successes in gubernatorial elections. However, Kansas has not sent a Democrat to the U.S. Senate since the 1932 election, and the House delegation almost always contains more Republicans than Democrats. Kansas Democrats are currently unrepresented in Congress, and Republicans presently enjoy large majorities in both houses of the state legislature.

While Republicans have pretty consistently held power in Kansas since it gained statehood, the party looks a great deal different today than it has in the past. Before the 1980s, Kansas Republicanism had been personified by Alf Landon, former governor of Kansas and 1936 presidential nominee, and former U.S. Senator Bob Dole. This brand of moderate, even progressive Republicanism has historically been anchored by the small farmer. "As he expresses himself politically through the Farm Bureau and the Farmer's Union on the one hand, and the Republican Party on the other, this small farmer is conservative on many matters but not always subservient to business and industry; he is highly moral in his view of politics and reasonably progressive in his attitudes toward education, social welfare, and taxation" (Smith and Heil 1958, 5). Moral issues, such as prohibition, Sunday blue laws, and antigambling drives, have periodically stirred Republicans to political action. However, the moral indignation that erupted around those concerns never dominated the party and always seemed to be tempered by moderation on other issues that would appear on the political agenda.

This all changed with the backlash against *Roe v. Wade* and the rise of Ronald Reagan. The Republican Party throughout Kansas became wracked by internal conflict between two equally powerful factions. I refer to these two factions as the business, or Chamber of Commerce, Republicans and the Christian Republicans. The first faction is mostly concerned with such economic issues as taxes and regulation. They are generally conservative on such social issues as abortion and gay rights, though not always, but they certainly do not place the same emphasis on these issues as the other faction. This second bloc is most concerned with moral issues and bases many of its political stances on religious conviction.

The business Republicans had historically held sway over the Republican Party and can be seen as the heirs of the moderate, progressive Republicanism personified by Landon and Dole. In fact, the Christian Republican faction did not really exist until the mid-1980s. Chamber of Commerce Republicans were relatively moderate during this time, and Bob Dole was their standard-bearer. While Dole was seen as Mr. Republican in Kansas, he was not a fire-breathing conservative. He was not linked with the fledgling New Right, which was espousing ultraconservative views on all matters.[2] The business Republicans were friendly to agriculture and business in general. They were more on the order of Ford Republicans than Reagan Republicans, a fact borne out by Ford's selection of Dole as his vice-presidential candidate in 1976.

The Fourth District had been represented for many years by a Republican much in this mold. Garner Shriver was first elected to Congress in 1960. He routinely won comfortable victories despite being a somewhat nondescript legislator. He was moderate to conservative on the issues and rarely rocked the boat on Capitol Hill (Barone and Ujifusa 1977, 308). In the Democratic landslide of 1974, Shriver won a lackluster 49 percent against a poorly financed Democrat and a candidate from the American Independent Party who gained 9 percent of the vote. This unimpressive showing convinced several Democrats that Shriver would be ripe for the picking in 1976, and the man who dominated the Democratic primary that year was Dan Glickman.

A Democrat Takes Control of the District

Dan Glickman is the son of a Jewish scrap dealer. He grew up in a well-to-do, well-respected Wichita family. His father knew everyone, and early in his career Dan Glickman was president of the school board. He was likable, capable, personable, and smart (Hanna, interview with author). According to *Wichita Eagle* reporter Bud Norman, Glickman was astute enough to

realize what drove Fourth District politics in
before challenging Garner Shriver, Glickmai
country to talk with people who were driving
and hours doing this. Glickman realized that
had mud on his boots, he would have big p
unless he made a concerted effort to connec
Glickman made it his business to learn everytl
the macroeconomic level to the basic questioi
over there? What's the harvest season for that
(Bud Norman, interview with author).[3]

The long hours paid off. Glickman attacked Shriver for having done
nothing for the Fourth District while in office. Glickman appeared young
and energetic while Shriver appeared old and inert. The race was not about
any issues in particular. It was about a changing of the guard and voters
choosing a new, hard-charging representative for their district. Glickman
put together a coalition of blue-collar Democrats in the city and did well
enough in the country to eke out a 51 percent to 49 percent win. Once in
office, Glickman did an excellent job of solidifying his hold on the district.
He was far from a radical leftist and immersed himself in aircraft issues
that, combined with his newfound knowledge of agriculture, allowed him
to address directly the interests of a large majority of his constituents. He
won reelection easily in 1978 and, despite Ronald Reagan handily winning
the Fourth District in both 1980 and 1984, was not seriously challenged
until 1986.

That was a good year for Republicans in Kansas mostly because they
recaptured the governor's office after Democrats had held the top post for
twenty of the previous thirty years. The sitting Democratic governor, John
Carlin, was term-limited after eight years in office, and the 1986 gubernatorial election highlights the moderate tone of the Republican Party at this
point in time. Seven candidates entered the primary, including the president of Coleman, a large thermos company; the man with the most Pizza
Hut franchises in the country; the sitting secretary of state; and the reigning
speaker of the House. Speaker Mike Hayden ended up winning the primary
despite being heavily outspent. Of the seven aspirants, only one was associated with the religious right. Hayden recalls that faction as totally caught
up with the pro-life movement at the time and their candidate finishing in
the middle of the pack, well behind the leaders. After the primary, the
Republicans circled the wagons and came together to help Hayden win the

on over a Democrat whose father and grandfather had pre-
...d Kansas's top office. Hayden explains what he ran on in 1986.
...a Republican and I am a fiscal conservative. And I ran a lot on
...ditional values: small town, farm family, that kind of thing. But in those
days, traditional values were viewed considerably different than they are
today" (Hayden, interview with author). Indeed, Hayden governed as a
moderate. He raised taxes when necessary and established a pro-choice
position on abortion.

While Mike Hayden was making his play for Topeka, Dan Glickman
finally faced notable opposition in the form of a Wichita City commissioner
named Bob Knight. Knight campaigned as a fiscal conservative and tried to
paint Glickman as a big-spending liberal. Knight called Glickman "the biggest spender in the recent history of the Kansas congressional delegation."
Glickman's campaign manager responded on behalf of the candidate: "In
Dan's tenure in Congress he has had amendments adopted that have saved
the government nearly $600 million" (Polczinski 1986, 20D). The race was
mostly about economic issues, and Knight was not only vastly outspent but
did not inspire much enthusiasm among the Republican base. In the end,
Glickman won handily and returned to Washington for another term.

The important point to realize about the elections of 1986 is the low
salience of certain moral issues that would later become so important in
Kansas. There was little mention of abortion in the gubernatorial race, and
while Knight was pro-life and Glickman pro-choice, it never really became
an issue in the Fourth District either. Voters made their decisions based on
Glickman's constituency service, which was very good, and his fiscal attitudes, which were moderate to conservative. Glickman seemed a good fit
for the district.

Moral issues did not gain traction in 1986 mostly because the Republican Party was dominated by Chamber of Commerce Republicans. Abortion, gay rights, and school prayer were not high priorities for this faction,
and sometimes they took liberal positions on these issues. Ultraconserva-
tives of all stripes were lonely voices in the wilderness during this time, but
a few got elected to the state legislature in the mid-1980s. Mike Hayden
and Marvin Barkis were two prominent politicians who remembered quite
well these conservative firebrands, despite their small numbers.[4] Hayden
was governor at the time and Barkis was minority leader in the state house.

Hayden recalls these legislators as voting against everything. They were
anti-abortion, anti-tax, and anti–government spending. He did not have

fond memories of these intense ideologues who emerged from the conservative wing of the Republican Party. Ironically, Barkis, a Democrat, had some very positive dealings with these legislators. Barkis and his Democratic minority would often align with the radical conservatives to embarrass the moderate wing of the Republican Party. This unnatural bipartisan alliance had some success in thwarting the agenda of Governor Hayden and the moderate Republicans; however, these conservative troublemakers were only an irritant to the moderate wing of the GOP since they were too small a group to actually enact any of their preferred policies (Barkis, interview with author). Their criticism of the governor and his counterparts in the legislature focused on the unwillingness of the dominant faction of the Republican Party to pursue socially conservative policies. Foremost among the moral issues concerning these Republican rebels was abortion.

A Nascent Pro-Life Movement

During the mid-1980s, the pro-life movement in the Fourth District was active in education but not politics. Kansans for Life (KFL) was started in 1979 solely as an educational organization. In 1980, David Gittrich began working for KFL, and he recalls traveling to churches throughout the area to educate congregants on the evils of abortion. In the days before videotapes, Gittrich would haul around a projector and several sixteen-millimeter films. Gittrich remembers showing them so often that the reels became worn out. KFL did no legislative or electoral work during its first few years of existence. By 1982, the organization was doing some lobbying, and in 1986, it began to endorse some candidates in local elections. However, during this time, KFL was almost entirely devoted to education (Gittrich, interview with author).

Mark Gietzen was also active in the pro-life movement as well as in the local Republican Party. Gietzen was working for Boeing in the late 1970s when he decided to get involved in politics. He was a Reagan delegate and recalls being in the minority as a pro-life Sedgwick County Republican. Around this time, Gietzen achieved some local notoriety by conducting an intensive grassroots effort to ensure that a radio program called Pro-Life Perspective, broadcast by a former president of the National Right to Life Committee and one of the founders of the pro-life movement, got on a powerful station. Gietzen set up an organization to try to get him on a frequency where lots of people could listen. They were successful, and Pro-Life Perspective began airing on a powerhouse station, reaching listeners not only in Kansas but in neighboring states as well (Gietzen, interview with author). Through the educational efforts of KFL and the Pro-Life Perspective radio program, thousands of individuals were exposed to the controversy surrounding abortion, raising awareness and the salience of this issue. Both Gittrich and Gietzen played influential roles in this process.

While the seeds of a pro-life political movement may have been planted during the early and mid-1980s, they did not bear fruit quickly or on their own. As a result, abortion did not assume a significant place in Kansas politics, and the social conservative wing of the Republican Party could not gain much traction in their battles with the dominant moderate faction. Despite this fact, the clashes continued throughout Governor Hayden's term. In 1990, after a turbulent legislative session in which the group of socially conservative legislators had made life difficult for the governor, Hayden and the GOP legislative leadership decided to cut off Republican PAC money to a number of emerging Christian Republican leaders (Cigler, Joslyn, and Loomis 2003, 149). As Hayden began campaigning for reelection, his party was becoming more and more fractured. He faced a strong primary challenge from an anti-tax, anti-abortion candidate who was convinced to run by one of Hayden's enemies in the state house. Hayden narrowly won the primary but was defeated in the general election by a pro-life candidate named Joan Finney. Many pro-life Republicans deserted Hayden because of his pro-choice stance, which may have tipped the election to Finney. It was clear that abortion was becoming a bigger issue in Kansas, even trumping party identification for many voters in the 1990 gubernatorial race. However, nobody could imagine how much of an impact abortion would soon have on Kansas politics, particularly in the Fourth District.

The Summer of Mercy

The political landscape of Kansas's Fourth District was forever changed during the summer of 1991 when Operation Rescue decided to bring their roving band of abortion protesters to the Wichita area. Their main target was Dr. George Tiller, a Wichita abortion practitioner. Tiller ran an abortion clinic on Kellogg Avenue, the main drag connecting I-35 with downtown Wichita. Tiller was an appealing target for Operation Rescue because of his willingness to perform late-term abortions and his unabashed defense of his right to do so. There were not many abortion clinics in this part of the country, so women sometimes traveled hundreds of miles to Wichita to seek Tiller's services. The leadership of Operation Rescue, after conducting large-scale protests in Los Angeles, New York, and Atlanta, thought that a small Midwestern city might be more hospitable to an influx of conservative activists. In the late spring, a group of outsiders descended on Wichita and Tiller's practice. Local pro-choice activists and law enforcement geared up for the invasion, but they made a strategic blunder when they decided to temporarily shut down all abortion clinics in the Wichita area for a week to avoid a conflict and blunt Operation Rescue's momentum. This cessation of activity was seen as a miracle by many of the protesters—their actions, as they saw it, saved the lives of hundreds of unborn babies—and as word spread of this accomplishment, it inspired thousands more men and women to drop everything and travel to Wichita to keep up the protests. Tiller had always planned to reopen his clinic, and when he did, pro-life demonstrators attempted to block the entrances. Many were forcibly removed and thrown in jail. Other protesters decided to lie down in the middle of the street in an attempt to stop traffic. They were also arrested. After months of protests, Wichita police had arrested more than 2,700 people. The Summer of Mercy culminated in a rally at Cessna Stadium on the campus of Wichita State University. The 45,000-seat stadium was filled to the rafters as the crowd reveled in their accomplishments (Risen and Thomas 1998, chap. 13). What exactly they accomplished was not immediately clear. After the Summer of Mercy ended, Dr. Tiller resumed his medical practice and continued to perform abortions in Wichita until his assassination by a militant pro-life activist in May 2009.

Although the abortion protests during the Summer of Mercy were instigated by outside forces, a great many of the participants were from Wichita and its immediate surroundings. As I mentioned earlier, the pro-life movement was far from dormant in the area, and there was some coordination between local activists and Operation Rescue. According to David Gittrich of KFL, Wichita Rescue had been doing some of the same things— protesting, getting people arrested—that were the hallmarks of the Summer of Mercy. What Operation Rescue brought was a deep desire and an uncanny ability to attract media attention. The protests were so pervasive and so publicized that nobody in the area could avoid taking a stand. Abortion as an issue dominated Wichita during the Summer of Mercy. This singular event provided an outlet for the burgeoning pro-life movement.

All of the people David Gittrich had been educating over the past ten years could now act on their beliefs. They could go down to George Tiller's office and express their opposition to his activities. Thousands of people, who had never been involved in any sort of political activity, were suddenly getting arrested because of their strong opinions regarding abortion.

The partisan political consequences of the Summer of Mercy arose out of an effort, barely noticed at the time, to further involve pro-lifers in party activity. Mark Gietzen and a fellow Republican Party activist named Paul Rosell saw an opportunity to change the makeup of the Sedgwick County Republican Party, which was dominated at the time by Chamber of Commerce Republicans who were either pro-choice or did not ascribe much importance to abortion as a political issue.[5] Both Gietzen and Rosell were ardently anti-abortion and understood that the way to change their local party's structure was to place as many pro-lifers in precinct-level positions so that when the time came to elect party officers, pro-life candidates would have widespread support. There was rarely competition for precinct leadership, and the business Republicans simply assumed these positions by default since they were the only ones who bothered to run for the positions and nobody else seemed to care. But Mark Gietzen and the Summer of Mercy were about to upset this comfortable situation.

Taking Over the Party

The abortion protests mainly took place in the daytime in front of George Tiller's abortion clinic on Kellogg Avenue. At night, there would invariably be rallies at the motels where the out-of-town protesters and organizers were staying. While much of the focus was rightly on the front of the room where the speakers were, the important political activity was occurring somewhat surreptitiously in the back of the room. Astute reporters barely noticed Gietzen and Rosell sitting behind a table signing people up. One reporter recalled thinking that they were just seeking out volunteers for the next day's protests. She remembers them as representatives of a local pro-life organization. While they were certainly pro-life, they were actually representing the Republican Party. Gietzen and Rosell were looking for registered Republicans to sign up to run for precinct committee positions the following spring. Of course, if the people coming to the table were not registered, or were registered Democrats, Gietzen and Rosell would attempt to change that, undoubtedly advertising the GOP as the national party with

a pro-life plank in the platform. Gietzen recalls l
would run around to all these gatherings, a lot of tl
a lot of those people were staying, at any of these p
would run around with my maps, and I'm saying
we have anybody in here? I have no pro-lifers run
Somebody would raise their hand and say, 'Yea
before in my life.' 'Are you a citizen? Are you of age? Can we sign you up
to vote and get you written in as a precinct person?' 'Well, yeah if you tell
me what to do.' And, you know, we would have another one" (Gietzen,
interview with author). This recruitment of precinct committee candidates
was done fairly quietly, and it was done under the auspices of the religiously
conservative wing of the Republican Party. Nobody really detected what
was going on, and most of the new sign-ups were individuals who had
never been involved in politics before. The one thing they had in common
was a passion for the pro-life movement. Gietzen reasoned that if they were
sufficiently moved to go to jail for the cause, then he could certainly convince them to get involved in party politics and put their energies toward
more productive activities. The goal was the takeover of the Sedgwick
County Republican Party, and the means was to stack the precinct leadership positions with enough committed pro-life activists to sufficiently alter
the balance of power in the party and produce a new regime that was significantly more pro-life than the previous one.

When the Summer of Mercy ended and Operation Rescue left town—
taking the national media with them—quiet returned to Wichita. But Gietzen and his new recruits continued to prepare for the upcoming precinct
committee elections. Gietzen and his colleagues went about organizing
campaigns for the hundreds of pro-life candidates brought into the party
during the Summer of Mercy. Often they were running against people who
were fairly well known. However, these new candidates were dedicated and
energetic. And since many precincts consist of only a few blocks, they were
able to go door-to-door and personally ask for the votes of their neighbors.
They did not necessarily say they signed up at an Operation Rescue rally.
However, they made it clear they were pro-life and otherwise quite conservative. This kind of door-to-door campaigning occurred in virtually every
precinct in Sedgwick County. Many of the sitting party representatives had
never gone door-to-door and in the past had often been unopposed in the
precinct-level races (Gietzen, interview with author). The days of a free ride
for the Chamber of Commerce Republicans was now over owing to the

of Mark Gietzen and his new cadre of dedicated pro-life activists. Irvin Barkis, who was defeated by a social conservative in 1992, could plainly see the differences in campaign styles between the two Republican factions. He remarked that grassroots, door-to-door campaigning worked against so-called business Republicans because they felt as if they were "above it." Barkis characterized the Christian Republicans as mostly blue collar, so "they didn't mind going amongst the people" and "doing the dirty work of politics" (Barkis, interview with author).

The "dirty work" paid off. Gietzen recruited 281 abortion foes to run for the 472 precinct committee member positions in Sedgwick County, and many were successful. After the primary election on August 4, 1992, 83 percent of the central committee members were against abortion. A year earlier, only 49 percent were pro-life (Thomas 1992b, 1A). One newly elected committee member was forthcoming about his reasons for getting involved in the political process. "I'm not here because I love politics. I hate politics. I'm here because I love unborn babies. I've been to jail for the unborn" (Thomas 1992a, 1D). In fact, 19 percent of the newly elected precinct committee members had been arrested for blocking clinic access during the Summer of Mercy (Thomas, 1992b, 1A).

With the numbers in their favor, Gietzen and his anti-abortion forces insisted that the Republican Party commit itself to a pro-life stance. Following a contentious organizational meeting that took place days after the primary election, the pro-choice chair resigned and was replaced as the top official in the Sedgwick County Republican Party by none other than Mark Gietzen.

Both factions worried about how the split would affect the Republicans in the upcoming general election. Many felt that the pro-choice members of the party would either stay home in November or vote with the Democrats. Gietzen recalled that after the shake-up the moderates abandoned the party and took all the money with them. According to Gietzen, the former chair and the newly resigned treasurer took the checkbook and began writing checks to the campaign funds of officeholders who were friends of theirs. As a result, Gietzen and his county party organization were left with a negative account balance. The newly crowned ruling faction did not even have a key to the office.

Religious conservatives were not just taking over the Republican Party in Sedgwick County. Across the country, Chamber of Commerce Republicans were losing their hold on the local party apparatus. As the Reverend

Jerry Sloan put it, "Republicans all over the country are saying, 'What's happening to my party?' "The thing that's happened is while they were busy going to the Lincoln Day dinners, the fundamentalists were going to the caucus meetings. And that's where the power lies" (Thomas 1992c, 1A). Sloan went on, "They [the fundamentalists] count on a low voter turnout. They realize you don't have to be a majority to accomplish what you want. All you have to be is an organized minority" (Thomas 1992c, 1A). Sloan's first quote highlights the value of local, retail politics. His second statement closely echoes Schattschneider in *Party Government* (1942), which the reverend probably has never read.

Christian conservatives in Kansas discovered the importance of precinct-level politics and pounced. Before the Chamber of Commerce types realized it, they had been displaced. In the following years, they made an aggressive, statewide attempt to regain their power. Adapting to the new political reality, they sought to do this by retaking the local positions. Before 1992, elections for precinct committee members were rarely even contested. By 1998, then-Governor Bill Graves and then-Senator Nancy Kassebaum were endorsing moderate candidates in these contests. This dramatic change arose directly out of the efforts of Christian Republicans in the late 1980s and early 1990s and is quite a testament to the new significance of local organizing.[6]

The Importance of Local Parties

Thanks to a concerted effort to elect abortion foes to these precinct offices, the county party was now in the hands of Mark Gietzen and his supporters. A great deal of effort went into taking over the formal party machinery, so at this juncture it makes sense to ask why it was so important for them to do so. I corresponded at length with Gietzen about the role that can be played by local parties. He told me the party is in a position to confer some important advantages to candidates hoping to gain elective office. Without the support of the party, a candidate would have to allot time, money, and volunteers to tasks that might be more efficiently accomplished by the party. For example, the county party can purchase one list of current registered voters and share it with all the candidates, paying for the list only once. That is a $50 to $150 expense for each campaign that has to buy the list itself. In addition to the money being saved, a nontrivial amount of work needs to be done to get those lists into a usable form. Again, the party can do this for every candidate in the county (Gietzen, interview with author). One can imagine many other examples where the party can save resources for a campaign and allow it to put those resources to better use. Of course, the party leadership can decide which candidates get help and which do not. This is where control of the party becomes vital. A pro-choice leadership will naturally choose to help pro-choice candidates and maybe withhold money, information, or volunteers from a pro-life candidate. Deciding which types of candidates benefit from the party's economies of scale is an important reason to seek control of the formal structure.[7] Despite this potential for power and influence, Gietzen pointed out that many county parties are nearly nonexistent and totally nonfunctioning, with figureheads that do nothing more than show up at the Chairman's Breakfast on Kansas Day. As we will see later, Gietzen's Republican Party was very active in promoting the kinds of candidates it wanted to see win office. According to Gietzen, after the 1992 takeover, it was impossible for someone to get through the primary and win in a general election without the full support of the county party.[8]

After the party was taken over, the next step was a massive voter registration drive to build a larger base of Republican voters. Most of this was done in the churches. The newly elected precinct committee members went into their home churches to get people signed up to vote. These people now had a title and were even more motivated to do whatever was necessary to make the GOP stronger. They provided the local Republican Party with access to thousands of socially conservative congregants who were not registered. From attending church services together, these political nonparticipants often personally knew the precinct committee member encouraging them to register and vote Republican. Of course, the effort was not limited to registering new voters. Part of the strategy was to convert Democrats and Independents by emphasizing the GOP's conservative stands on moral issues. If the precinct committee member was socially conservative, then it followed that most of his or her fellow parishioners would be as well. As a result, the churches were very fertile grounds for the Republican Party, and their voter registration numbers swelled accordingly.[9]

Shifting Focus

Of course, taking over the party must be seen as a means to an end for the Christian Republicans. Their main goal after gaining power was to elect

Republicans who shared their views on issues they held dear—and foremost was abortion. In 1992, George Bush was heavily favored in Kansas and figured to have no problem defeating Bill Clinton and gaining the state's six electoral votes. The GOP had lost control of the state house but was poised to gain it back. Dan Glickman was still going strong as the Fourth District's congressman, but the local Republican Party hoped to unseat him.

Glickman had cruised to victory in 1988 and 1990 in races in which his Republican challengers were poorly funded and the GOP put forth little effort on their part. The issues raised by these candidates were not winning issues either. They focused on fiscal matters where Glickman was seen as moderate and in tune with the district. In 1990, anti-tax activist Roger Grund won the Republican nomination. His campaign was focused solely on reducing the federal deficit by cutting spending. As in his race with Bob Knight in 1986, Glickman positioned himself comfortably in the middle of the spectrum on this economic issue. Like Grund, he also attacked federal spending and pledged to work on income tax reform to ease the burden on the middle class.[10] Grund only spent $2,000, and the outcome of the race was never in doubt. The liberalism of Glickman on moral issues was rarely discussed before 1992. Even in 1990, when the governor's race was as much about abortion as taxes, Glickman was permitted to be, in Bud Norman's words, "quietly and inconspicuously pro-choice" (Norman, interview with author). As a result, Dan Glickman was in a strong position heading into his eighth reelection campaign. However, local Republicans had several reasons to be optimistic. First, redistricting had made the Fourth less Democratic. Second, it was a presidential year, ostensibly making it more difficult for Glickman to distance himself from a national Democratic Party that was far more liberal than the district median. Third, the Republicans finally attracted a strong candidate to the race. As it turned out, they ended up attracting several strong candidates, setting up the potential for a divisive primary. That potential was realized, and the intraparty conflict was centered on one issue. The 1992 Republican congressional primary was the first major Fourth District election since the Summer of Mercy, and as one might expect, the contest was all about abortion.

A Factional Battle for the Republican Congressional Nomination

Eric Yost was the first candidate to enter the Republican primary. He possessed an impressive resume, having served two terms in the state house and then rising to vice president of the state senate. In the months leading up to the primary election in August, he was joined by a redistricted incumbent from the former Fifth District named Bill Nichols and the Wichita police chief, Richard LaMunyon. LaMunyon was not much of a threat to Yost, but Nichols had some name recognition as an incumbent, albeit from a different district. Nichols also gained the support of the National Republican Congressional Committee, which was first and foremost committed to reelecting Republican incumbents. There was also a calculation that Nichols was more electable, not only because of his incumbency status but owing to his more moderate tone on the issues, most notably abortion. There were credible rumors that national Republican Party officers had asked Yost to drop out so the party could avoid a divisive primary that might hurt its chances in November. Local activists worried about a divisive primary as well. The conservative wing of the party was solidly behind Yost, while the business Republicans who still ran the county party favored Nichols mostly because of his pro-choice leanings.

During the primary campaign, abortion dominated the debate. The Republicans were divided on it, and because they were talking about it so forcefully, Dan Glickman finally saw his views on abortion documented on the front pages. In fact, a July 5, 1992, *Wichita Eagle* article was devoted entirely to abortion and its potential impact on the campaign. It meticulously laid out all four candidates' positions on the subject. Glickman's numerous pro-choice roll-call votes were presented, and he was quoted as saying that there are limits to what government can do. "It is really a moral and religious matter for a woman and her family to deal with" (Cross 1992b, 1B). On the Republican side, it appeared that Eric Yost had cornered the pro-life market. "Yost's opposition to abortion is part of his larger campaign theme that the country should return to the basic 'Christian values' and 'family values' on which it was founded" (Cross 1992b, 1B). Both Dick Nichols and Richard LaMunyon described themselves as pro-choice and lamented the emphasis on the issue (Cross 1992b, 1B). However, there was no avoiding it. As Peggy Jarmin of the Pro-Choice Action League put it, "The days are gone when politicians could avoid this issue. [They] . . . know the public is concerned about this, and they need to make it clear where they stand" (Cross 1992b, 1D).[11] It was now clear that Glickman could no longer be "quietly and inconspicuously pro-choice."

It is important to recognize that abortion did not appear on the agenda in 1992 because the mainstream party saw its potential for gaining votes.

Abortion was thrust into the spotlight by Eric Yost's campaign and the pro-life activists gaining strength within the local Republican Party. These insurgents forced the issue onto the agenda and fundamentally changed the dynamics of congressional elections in the district.

Both Glickman and Yost used the abortion issue to raise money from activists who supported their positions. Glickman sent a letter suggesting contributions between $25 and $250, "to help me continue to ensure that family values which respect the role of women in society are not lost." Yost's letter was directed at those who oppose abortion and "see our nation moving away from the Christian values our founding fathers held dear. [It says that] now is the time to take a stand for pre-born children" (Cross 1992a, 1D). For their part, interest groups on both sides of the issue were prepared to have an impact on the primary and general election campaigns. Groups that supported the two candidates' respective positions on abortion provided money, campaign volunteers, and endorsements (Cross 1992a, 1D). This was especially helpful to Yost in his primary campaign since Nichols raised significantly more money and had the support of the national Republican Party (Cross 1992c, 1D). Of course, Glickman was unopposed and simply filling his coffers for the general election.

In August, Eric Yost overcame his fundraising deficit and the national Republican Party's support of his opponent to gain a spot in the November election opposite eight-term incumbent Dan Glickman. The two candidates differed sharply on many issues, most dramatically and significantly on abortion. However, Yost did not focus solely on abortion. He sounded an anti-incumbent theme in what figured to be an anti-incumbent year. He also campaigned on a philosophy of just-say-no fiscal conservatism and the general rhetoric of traditional family values. For his part, Glickman attempted to paint Yost as an extremist on abortion. He also attacked the Republican for backing the use of tax dollars to support private education (Cross 1992d, 1A). The race would hinge on the issues, but Yost also needed a united Republican Party to have any hope of defeating such a strong incumbent. Of course, this became much more difficult to envision after the takeover of the county party by Mark Gietzen and his pro-life forces. While Yost would appear to benefit from having like-minded local party leaders backing his campaign, if a large number of moderates bolted from the party, taking with them their money, volunteers, and votes, Yost would have little chance for victory in November. In fact, this is what happened, and even though Mark Gietzen had gotten the county party into the black shortly after the takeover, they were not ready to be of much help to Yost (Gietzen, interview with author) In addition, KFL used every resource they had available, but the organization was still honing its political skills (Gittrich, interview with author).

An Incumbent Is Threatened

The general election campaign focused mostly on issues of moral traditionalism with some discussion of health-care and government spending sprinkled in. Yost raised and spent considerably less money than Glickman, despite Senator Dole's help.[12] The Republican candidate collected most of his money from pro-life groups, while Glickman's came from a wider variety of groups and individuals—as one would expect from an incumbent. While Yost did not overtly associate himself with the so-called religious right, he welcomed their support. On the major issues of the day, the choice was clear, and in the end, Eric Yost fell short. He was defeated 52 percent to 42 percent, with 6 percent going to the libertarian candidate. Glickman spent over $1 million to Yost's $350,000.

It seemed as if the upheaval in the local Republican Party hurt Yost, but it was hard to tell how much. Yost had the support of local pro-life groups, but Glickman had some success painting the Republican as an extremist on the issue. Undoubtedly, Glickman received the votes of many pro-choice Republicans in the Fourth District. It was by far Dan Glickman's most difficult reelection campaign, and Eric Yost may have exposed some vulnerability in the Democratic incumbent.[13]

Enter Todd Tiahrt

Despite their loss in the Fourth District, Kansas Republicans had a good year in 1992. Bush carried the state, Dole was reelected easily, and Republican incumbents in the First and Third Districts were barely challenged. Republicans also retook the state house and gained five seats in the state senate. A worker at Boeing named Todd Tiahrt was one of the newly elected Republican state senators. Because of redistricting, he had to defeat two incumbents to make it to Topeka. Tiahrt, a solid social conservative, defeated a moderate Republican in the August primary and a Democrat in the fall.[14] Despite the effort that it took to get to the state senate, Tiahrt made up his mind rather quickly that he did not want to be there for long.

After some discussions with local Republicans and pro-life leaders, Tiahrt decided to enter the race against Dan Glickman for the Fourth District's congressional seat.

How and why Todd Tiahrt decided to run for Congress sheds light on some of the dynamics that influence congressional elections.[15] Both Mark Gietzen and David Gittrich knew Tiahrt and helped convince him to run. They made it clear that he would have the full support of pro-life forces in the area. The Sedgwick County Republican Party was now firmly under Gietzen's control, and Tiahrt would certainly be acceptable to the anti-abortion activists. So there was a built-in base for a campaign. In addition, many Republicans thought Glickman was vulnerable after Eric Yost forced him to spend $1 million in 1992. Another factor favoring a challenge in 1994 was that Tiahrt was in the middle of his term. If he failed in his bid for Congress, he would at least keep hold of his state senate seat (Hanna, interview with author).

There was another impressive candidate who was thinking of challenging Glickman in 1994. He was Frank Ojile, a former city council member from Wichita. Ojile and Tiahrt were from the same state senate district and possessed very similar positions on the issues. They were both conservative Republicans known for their opposition to abortion.[16] A primary between Ojile and Tiahrt would have been disastrous for the local Republican Party. First, Ojile and Tiahrt might have split the social conservative vote, allowing a more moderate candidate to win. Even if one of them was victorious, chances are the primary would have been bruising, and the likelihood of GOP unity in November would have been slim. Finally, a contested primary would have forced the eventual winner to spend valuable resources that would be needed to defeat a strong incumbent such as Dan Glickman. For these reasons, nobody wanted an Ojile-Tiahrt primary contest, and David Gittrich set about making sure that it did not happen. Gittrich got together with the two potential candidates, and in Gittrich's words, "they just prayed about it." Gittrich says that Ojile wanted to run but did not think he should. Tiahrt wanted to run and felt that he should. So the decision was made for Tiahrt to run and Ojile to sit this one out. There would be only one legitimate pro-life, conservative candidate running in the August primary, and he would have the full backing of the local power structure (Gittrich, interview with author). Dave Hanna, a high-ranking member of the Tiahrt campaign, adds some more detail and substance to the story of how the two conservatives coordinated on who

would run. According to Hanna, Tiahrt and Ojile had roughly the following conversation during their sit-down.

> Tiahrt: "Well, Frank, how much do you think it's going to take to
> win?"
> Ojile: "At least $150,000."
> Tiahrt: "Ok. $150,000. Well there's sixty-seven or so days. That
> means you gotta raise roughly $3,500 a day. How much you raise
> today?"
> Ojile: "None."
> Tiahrt: "Ok. How much you gonna raise tomorrow?"
> Ojile: "Well, uh, not much."
> Tiahrt: "Ok. You're already seven thousand in the hole."
> Ojile: "Well, yeah. That's a good way to look at it. You really want
> to do this?"
> Tiahrt: "Yeah."
> Ojile: "Ok." (Hanna, interview with author)[17]

A combination of prayer and common sense revealed a great deal of
intelligence and sophistication on the part of all involved. Everybody realized the dangers of a brutal primary, and a conscious effort was made to
coordinate early enough to send the chosen candidate into the general
election in as strong a position as possible. The 1992 primary—and the
related schism within the county party—hurt the GOP's chances of
defeating Dan Glickman in the general election. There would be a primary election in Kansas's Fourth in 1994, but it would be far from brutal
or divisive. Tiahrt's opponents were a cab driver and a former drug
addict. This lack of credible competition allowed the Tiahrt campaign to
do virtually no campaigning during the primary. Since Tiahrt was already
a state senator from western Sedgwick County, his campaign spent no
money and did nothing to publicize their candidate and his issue positions. They figured most voters would fail to recognize any of the names.
Those votes would be divided evenly between the three candidates, and
the people who knew him from his home district would pull him through
(Hanna, interview with author).

The Tiahrt campaign had good reasons for not wanting to spend money
and publicize his issue positions. First, they hardly had any money. If they
wanted to win in November, they could not afford to waste anything

getting to that election. Second, the strategy in the general election was going to resemble a stealth campaign. The brain trust behind the Tiahrt campaign did not want to go out of their way to alert moderate Republicans and Democrats to Tiahrt's views on such issues as abortion and guns. The press was aware of this unwillingness early on. Consider the following quote from an article written during the primary campaign: "Although Tiahrt supports policies typically associated with the Christian right or social conservative movements, in interviews he emphasizes his attempts as a lawmaker to work on a broader agenda. He has worked for bills to guarantee tax breaks for a bowling tournament in Wichita and to encourage money-saving innovation by state employees" ("Tiahrt Plans Run" 1994, 3B).

The brain trust's gamble paid off because Tiahrt coasted to an easy win in the primary. The victory party was held at the Knights of Columbus hall on West 13th Street in Wichita. According to Hanna, they had the party there because the hall was free. One television station showed up, and they all thought that was terrific. However, as they turned their attention to Glickman and the general election, they were under no illusions about the difficulty of their task. Despite the vulnerability that may have been exposed by Yost two years earlier, their best-case scenario was 60 percent to 40 percent for the Democrat (Hanna, interview with author).[18] The main reason for the low expectations was the powerful specter of incumbency that almost always creates such a tall mountain for challengers to climb. In addition, the strength of incumbency was particularly pronounced in Dan Glickman's case.

Eric Yost's formidable challenge in 1992 may have uncovered some weakness in the incumbent. It did push Todd Tiahrt into considering a run. Glickman spent $1 million and still only managed to gain 52 percent of the vote. For an eight-term incumbent, that is not a good showing. However, just getting back to Washington for the next session allowed the congressman from Kansas's Fourth District to realize his greatest legislative achievement. As noted in the beginning of this chapter, the airplane liability bill was a great boon to the local economy. Glickman received and deserved the lion's share of the credit. Coincidentally, the House signed off on the bill the day after Tiahrt's victory in the Republican primary. Glickman had graduated from being a popular congressman to something of a local hero. It was not surprising then that Todd Tiahrt trailed his Democratic opponent by thirty points in polls taken right after the primary and the passage of the airplane liability bill.

Gittrich and Gietzen Assist the Campaign

Despite the ominous poll results, Tiahrt's backers began working hard to try to get their man elected. One of Tiahrt's strongest supporters was David Gittrich from KFL. He had spoken extensively with Tiahrt about running and played at least some role in the decision of Frank Ojile not to seek the Republican nomination. Gittrich had been very busy since the Summer of Mercy. While Mark Gietzen was engineering a pro-life takeover of the Sedgwick County party, Gittrich was contributing in his own way to the reordering of the political landscape around the issue of abortion. After a decade of education and some unsophisticated attempts at political action, Gittrich set out to recruit pro-life candidates to run for local office.[19]

In the immediate aftermath of the Operation Rescue protests, KFL received a large number of phone calls from individuals wanting to help. Many of them ended up stuffing envelopes or carrying out other office duties. Gittrich would routinely ask these volunteers where they lived. If they lived in an area with a pro-choice incumbent or where there was an open seat, he would suggest they run for office. If they were not interested, he asked them to speak with local pro-life pastors to see who they might recommend as a good candidate. Gittrich related to me his pitch for involving local citizens in the candidate recruitment process. "If your state representative (or senator) died, and they came to you and said it was up to you to pick the next person to replace him, whoever you pick is going to be it, so it's all on your shoulders. Who you gonna pick? And whoever that is go ask him if they'd like to run. And if they say yes, then I wanna talk to 'em so we can help them learn how to do it" (Gittrich, interview with author). Gittrich admits that this did not happen a lot. However, they were able to bring some ordinary citizens into the political process by actively seeking out individuals who were upset with the widespread acceptance and practice of abortion.

To go along with the candidate recruitment effort, KFL was developing a better way to keep in touch with its membership. In the past, the organization contacted their supporters by mail. However, mailings were expensive and extremely labor intensive. David Gittrich oversaw the development of an automated dialing system that allowed KFL to reach its people more quickly and more cheaply. According to Gittrich, nobody in the area was using direct dialing for political purposes—only for telemarketing. In 1992, KFL picked two races to test their new system on. They called about four hundred names in each of the two state house districts. All of the calls went to pro-lifers. The incumbent they supported won handily while a long-shot protest candidate they made calls for only lost by twelve votes. This was not definitive proof that the dialing was working, but they were certainly motivated to use it again during the following election cycle.

Although Gittrich had not worked for Yost, he knew Tiahrt personally and began calling KFL supporters as soon as Tiahrt won the primary. This was done independently of the campaign and wholly separate from the Republican Party. It was strictly a KFL operation, and it was focused solely on abortion. Tiahrt's people knew about the calls only after the fact, as people would report having received them. In the words of Dave Hanna, "They didn't know about them as in, 'this is what we want you to say and this is when we'd like you to say it' " (interview with author). Gittrich estimates his group called 20,000 to 25,000 names in the Fourth District. These were names that had been collected during protests, meetings, film screenings, and other pro-life gatherings. The phone calls all had the same simple message: Dan Glickman is in favor of abortion; Todd Tiahrt is against it. Even though Gittrich believed Glickman was a nice guy, the bottom line was that he not only supported abortion but actually took money from Dr. Tiller. To the pro-life activists roused by the Summer of Mercy, this made him unworthy of holding public office. So they demonized Congressman Glickman on the issue of abortion. According to Gittrich, it took roughly a month to call all of the people on their lists twice. They were not calling the general public—just pro-lifers. These phone calls accomplished the vital task of connecting voters' opinions on a newly salient issue to the candidate with whom they agreed. This type of political activity is what helped make moral issues more important in congressional elections.

Meanwhile, KFL was continuing to ramp up the sophistication of its electioneering. One of the members developed enough expertise with computers to implement an interactive program within the automated dialing system that would make the call and ask the recipient to press "1" for a yard sign, "2" to volunteer, and so forth. Although many people might regard such calls as an imposition, Gittrich reports that these pro-lifers were encouraged not only to vote for Todd Tiahrt but to actively take part in his campaign. In this way, KFL recruited many volunteers for making literature drops, attending sign waves, and participating in other important grassroots campaign tasks. These volunteers proved to be valuable resources for an upstart campaign that needed all the help it could get.

Tiahrt's election was the top priority for KFL in 1994 (Gittrich, interview with author).[20]

It was also the top priority for Mark Gietzen as chair of the Sedgwick County Republican Party. Gietzen had solidified his hold on the party since the schism of 1992 and believed strongly in Tiahrt's ability as a candidate and his potential as a legislator. He was satisfied that Tiahrt was sufficiently pro-life and directed a large portion of the county party's resources toward the Republican challenger's campaign. He funneled money, volunteers, and organizers to the congressional race. Gietzen received a great deal of criticism, even from pro-life activists and candidates, for his decision to put so much emphasis on Tiahrt's race. The complaint was that Tiahrt was so far behind in the polls that the race was hopeless. Much of the criticism came from people who wanted the resources for their own local races in their own areas. But Gietzen stuck to his guns and put his newly won power and prestige on the line for Todd Tiahrt and his campaign (Gietzen, interview with author).

Volunteers were the key resource available to Sedgwick County Republicans, and there were a lot of them. Hundreds of people were contacting the local GOP to get involved—to do something for pro-life candidates. Many of these individuals had been brought into the formal partisan process during and immediately after the Summer of Mercy protests. Gietzen directed each precinct committeeperson to work for the Tiahrt campaign. The party did not have a lot of money, so volunteers were vital. According to Gietzen, they came early and stayed late because they had lots of fire in the belly. After all, many of them had been willing to get arrested for the pro-life cause. Gietzen recalls between five hundred and one thousand volunteers who were working regularly for the campaign. This figure becomes considerably larger when you include those who showed up once or twice to do some work. Mark Gietzen also shuttled the best organizers to the congressional race. In 1994, veterans of the Summer of Mercy were throwing virtually everything they had into the congressional contest (Gietzen, interview with author).

For the pro-life movement, the takeover of the Sedgwick County Republican Party was paying off. Any chair will naturally direct party resources to candidates he or she supports. But an active, aggressive, committed chair such as Mark Gietzen can provide a huge organizational boost to candidates that he favors. Certainly, Dot Meyer, the pro-choice county chair forced out by Gietzen and his followers in 1992, would not have divvied up the party's resources in the same fashion.

The 1994 General Election Campaign

The efforts of Gittrich and Gietzen in September and early October were designed to close the enormous deficit Tiahrt faced in the days immediately after the primary and Glickman's triumph with the aircraft liability bill in Congress. These activities, especially KFL's phone calls, were done independently of the campaign and as stated earlier, without its previous knowledge. Gietzen's volunteers assisted the formal campaign in conducting an extensive grassroots operation seen as the only way to make genuine progress since money was very slow to come in. What donations they did receive were generally small and the product of much effort. The Tiahrt campaign was raising most of their money from pro-lifers and a few union guys mad about the North American Free Trade Agreement (NAFTA) and Clinton's crime bill (Hanna, interview with author). There was no national money available to the campaign. Dave Hanna mentioned that when Tiahrt decided to run, Newt Gingrich promised he would come in for a fundraiser. Hanna then called Newt's office after the campaign got going and was told that the then-minority whip would not be able to make it. Presumably the poll numbers contributed to this change of heart. After being rejected by Gingrich, Hanna then called Dick Armey. Armey agreed to come in, and they raised $15,000 mostly from people who had been with Tiahrt since the beginning. At the time, the campaign thought that was all the money in the world. As a result, during September and most of October, the campaign was conducted strictly on the ground as opposed to over the airwaves. But it was working. A buzz was building. Dave Hanna recalls some of the events cooked up by the campaign to help build that buzz. The Tiahrts ran ice-cream socials in which they took ice cream to people. They conducted "friend-raisers" where the price of admission was bringing a friend. They had steak frys and distributed red T-shirts with Gittrich's T-heart symbol on them. These were all designed to build a following without spending lots of money. In fact, they did their best to scrape together money any way they could. They ran little auctions and sold the red T-shirts rather than just giving them away. Dave Hanna could sense the campaign was gaining some traction. In towns of three thousand or four thousand people, Dan Glickman would ride through a parade on the back of a convertible with a few people out front handing out literature. Tiahrt would come through the parade with anywhere from twenty to seventy volunteers—all in red T-shirts. According to Hanna, most of these people were social conservatives concerned primarily with abortion who saw Tiahrt as someone on the right side of the issue. They could not afford to write a thousand-dollar check, but they could and did walk in a parade.

Abortion was a major factor in the Tiahrt campaign as it was in Eric Yost's race two years earlier. However, there was one major difference. Tiahrt's brain trust was especially wary of drawing too much public attention to the candidate's pro-life stance for fear of losing moderate Republicans and repelling Democrats who might consider defecting from the incumbent. In public statements, they made a conscious effort to downplay his conservative views on abortion and other hot-button moral issues. In early October, the *Wichita Eagle* once again picked up on the Tiahrt campaign's aversion to loud, aggressive pronouncements on these subjects. "Tiahrt calls the 'Contract with America' a 'historical event' and says that such points as a line-item veto would allow the Republicans to adopt their agenda without increasing the deficit. He does not plan to emphasize the Republicans' stand on social issues, though, despite his longstanding support from conservative religious groups."[21] Later in the same article, Tiahrt is quoted in measured tones. "Glickman has the extremist record on abortion, but I choose not to make that an issue. I've worked with insurance and adoption laws to reduce the need for abortions, and support a bill that would have brought Kansas within the Supreme Court guidelines. Glickman, on the other hand, has voted the most extreme line he could possibly have voted, well outside what most Kansans want. I think most Kansans believe the Supreme Court guidelines are fair and reasonable, but I'm a pro-life candidate and would like to reduce the need for abortion" (Norman 1994a, 1C).

This strategy could only be undertaken if there was some other way of alerting, and firing up, the pro-life base that needed to come out in large numbers for Tiahrt to have any chance of upsetting Glickman. That other way involved the phone calls being made by KFL to anti-abortion residents all across the district. Dave Hanna recalled David Gittrich's advice to Tiahrt during the campaign. Hanna remembers Gittrich telling Tiahrt that he did not need to go out and talk about the abortion issue. Gittrich said he would take care of that. He told Tiahrt to go out and talk about taxes and regulation, and Gittrich would make sure the pro-lifers knew he was on their side. This independent broadcasting of the candidate's conservative position on abortion was an enormous help to the campaign. And to Tiahrt's credit, he took Gittrich's advice and trusted that the political director of KFL would convey the message to those who needed to hear it. Tiahrt did not have to go out and rail against abortion every day, and thus he avoided being pigeonholed as a single-issue crackpot.[22] The phone calls from KFL were getting little attention from the media, which played right into the hands of Gittrich and Tiahrt. They were able to reap the benefits of a pro-life message without suffering the consequences. It may not have been a prototypical stealth campaign, but it possessed some of the trappings.[23] Tiahrt may not have stressed abortion in his speeches and press releases, but all involved believed it was the most important issue in the campaign. When I asked Mark Gietzen if the main issue in the election was abortion, he responded by saying, "One hundred percent." He corroborated Hanna's comments by saying that Tiahrt rarely mentioned abortion in the presence of reporters. But according to Gietzen, abortion is the issue that drove it—"just like slavery drove the Civil War." Gietzen went on, "Abortion is what motivated these volunteers to work crazy hours for the Tiahrt campaign" (Gietzen, interview with author). Guns were also a big issue because Glickman had voted for the Clinton crime bill and its ban on assault weapons. And NAFTA may have hurt Glickman with blue-collar workers who had always given him a great deal of support.

NAFTA and the crime bill were both pushed hard by President Clinton and his administration. Glickman's votes with the president, who was exceedingly unpopular in the Fourth District, were potentially damaging to the incumbent.[24] That potential was officially realized when the Tiahrt campaign decided to air an advertisement that morphed Glickman's face into Clinton's and pointed out that Congressman Glickman had voted 86 percent of the time with President Clinton. The so-called "86 percent ad" was the brainchild of Dave Hanna. He explained to me the genesis of the ad, how it was produced, and the effect that it had. Hanna noticed that in a special congressional election earlier in the year, the Republican's campaign effectively used ads that morphed the Democratic candidate's face into Bill Clinton's. Hanna thought this was a great idea, and so he looked up Glickman's presidential support ratings and found that he voted with Clinton 86 percent of the time. Hanna was shocked because Glickman was always seen as moderate to conservative. This was the public perception, and it allowed Glickman to hold onto a district that was steadily becoming more conservative and consistently voting Republican at the presidential level. According to Hanna, Glickman "voted Democrat, but press released Republican" (Hanna, interview with author). He got away with this largely because the local television station really did not cover politics, and the Washington correspondent for the local newspaper was sympathetic to Glickman's views and did not go out of his way to expose the incongruity. Hanna felt that voters in the Fourth District would be shocked to hear how often Glickman was voting with the unpopular president. So the campaign poured all of its money into making this ad, which began running in early October. The original commercial was put together in a garage and looked every bit the low-budget production that it was. The ad morphing Glickman's face into Clinton's and trumpeting the congressman's high presidential support rating had a huge impact on the public. The campaign knew the message was really getting through when little kids would come up to Tiahrt and say "86 percent of the time" (Hanna, interview with author). Its success focused the Tiahrt campaign like a laser beam on "86 percent." Every piece of literature mentioned it. Tiahrt harped on it, mentioning it whenever the press asked him about anything. Every chance he had, the candidate put it in an answer (Hanna, interview with author).

Getting on television was very important for the Tiahrt campaign. Besides disseminating a resonant message across the district, it provided the underdog a legitimacy that he otherwise may have lacked. Before the 86 percent ad, the only campaign advertising consisted of volunteers going to the local Walmart in red T-shirts. Hanna remembers a guy seeing him in his red T-shirt and asking if Tiahrt really had a chance to win. Naturally, Hanna replied that he did. According to Hanna, the prospective voter smiled and countered, "Well, I hope so. If I see him run a television ad, then I'll believe he'll have a chance to win" (Hanna, interview with author). After seeing Tiahrt's new advertisement, another more prominent Kansan began to believe he had a chance to win. Senator Bob Dole began pestering the national party to do a poll for the Tiahrt-Glickman race since Kansas's Fourth was not included in early October polls conducted in competitive races across the country. Ten days before the election, they finally surveyed Fourth District voters and found that Tiahrt was down by only four points. A few days later, the *Topeka Capital-Journal* also did a poll and found the margin was seven. Nobody had done any polling since the first polls were taken immediately after the primary. Glickman's thirty-point lead was now down to single digits with one week left. It was clear to everyone involved that this was going to be a tight race and that it would go down to the wire. The KFL phone calls, the parades, and the "86 percent ad" had tightened the race dramatically. There was a week to go, and all the momentum was on the Republican side.[25]

With the publication of the favorable poll numbers, money and volunteers poured into the Tiahrt campaign. Dole gave $100,000, and he got the Republican National Committee (RNC) to give an additional $60,000.[26] With this money, the campaign stepped up the television advertising campaign. The headquarters was swamped with people wanting to help. Volunteers wearing red T-shirts and waving signs stretched for miles on Kellogg Avenue. Cars were honking their horns. The grassroots effort was intensifying, and the excitement was palpable. The Tiahrt people were enthusiastic and tireless back when the campaign was a long shot. When they were told they had a realistic chance to win, the intensity was ratcheted up even further. Someone from the campaign stopped for the night in a cheap motel in a small town in southeastern Kansas. When he came out in the morning, there was a Tiahrt flier on his windshield that had clearly been produced at someone's home. One day, Tiahrt was driving to work at Boeing when he saw a woman standing by herself in the rain holding a Tiahrt sign. This intense dedication gave Tiahrt and his campaign the confidence that they could pull off the upset (Hanna, interview with author).

Dan Glickman also could sense the incredible momentum building up for his opponent. He saw the poll numbers as well as the red-T-shirted volunteers all over the district. Glickman stepped up his advertising during the last week of the campaign, but there was only so much he could do—so much he could spend—in such a short period. Moreover, Tiahrt now had the cash to match him ad for ad. Furthermore, Glickman did not have a solid organization in place because he had never needed one before, and a candidate certainly cannot build a potent grassroots operation in seven days. Tiahrt closed the gap even further during the last week of the campaign and actually took the lead in some polls at the very end. It was beginning to look like a toss-up. Glickman decided his only hope was to schedule a debate.[27] He called in all his chits at Channel 10 and they agreed to host an eleventh-hour debate. Tiahrt had to agree to it, but his campaign was very worried. They feared Glickman would get all softball questions while Tiahrt would be asked the tough ones. The debate was scheduled for the night before the election. Outside the television station, there were hundreds of Tiahrt backers wearing those ubiquitous red T-shirts. Inside the studio, the only people not wearing red T-shirts were Glickman, his wife, and his campaign manager. KFL easily got supporters to come out on very short notice. Their people made three hundred calls like it was nothing.

The candidates debated a myriad of issues, including balanced budgets and private school vouchers. Most of the discussion, however, focused on the two most explosive issues in the campaign: abortion and guns. Predictably, Glickman attacked Tiahrt as extreme on both subjects while Tiahrt tried to defend his support of a Human Life Amendment, which would ban abortion even in cases of rape, incest, or when the life of the mother is endangered by pregnancy, as well as to defend his sponsorship of a concealed-carry law while in the state senate (Norman 1994b, 1A). Across the board, the ideological differences between the candidates were stark but no more so than on abortion and guns. Since these were the issues Fourth District voters cared about the most, it seemed they would determine the election.

Tiahrt appeared to emerge from the debate unscathed. He certainly did not defeat Glickman, but he avoided any huge mistakes and mostly looked the part standing next to the longtime incumbent. Tiahrt did display a lack of inside knowledge at one point during the debate, but it only increased his appeal among average voters and nicely displayed the differences between the candidates and their campaigns. Glickman attacked a Tiahrt tax-cut plan by citing an unfavorable report it received from the Concord Coalition, a budget watchdog group. Tiahrt responded by saying that it really did not matter to him what some left-wing organization had to say about his plan Tiahrt's inner circle winced because the Concord Coalition is far from liberal, and it would be clear to anybody in the audience who had more than a little knowledge of politics that Tiahrt must never have heard of the group—and if he had, that he knew precious little about it. Unfortunately for Glickman, hardly anyone attending the debate even noticed the gaffe because most of them did not know the Concord Coalition from a Concord grape. They cheered Tiahrt's response, and the look on Glickman's face was one of disbelief. According to Dave Hanna, it said, "I cannot believe I am losing to this guy" (Hanna, interview with author).

This particular incident from the debate highlighted the fundamental dynamic of the campaign. Glickman was a career legislator firmly rooted inside the Beltway. Tiahrt, on the other hand, was strictly local and also a bit amateurish. His advisers were professionals, and they contributed mightily to his victory; however, the candidate was simply one of the folks. He was seen as a champion of normal Kansans who abhorred abortion, gun control, and cultural elitism.[28] After the debate, Tiahrt and his inner circle traveled across the street for dinner at IHOP. In yet another display of how successful the grassroots effort had been, the waitress brought out a pancake in the shape of a heart. On the pancake was a T made out of whipped cream.

Less than twenty-four hours later, the votes were counted, and Kansas's Fourth District had a new congressman for the first time in eighteen years. Todd Tiahrt defeated Dan Glickman by 53 percent to 47 percent.[29] Tiahrt won Sedgwick County, barely carrying Wichita, and he won all but one of the rural counties. After Glickman conceded, the victory party began. The ballroom was packed with supporters who eventually broke into song. While they waited for the victorious candidate, the revelers sang "What a Mighty God We Serve." Not surprisingly, considering who made up the backbone of the campaign, this was also the theme song of the Summer of Mercy protests three years earlier. In his victory speech, Tiahrt went on to thank the 1,800 volunteers who made his victory possible. He credited his grassroots organization and a general disgust with the Democratic Party for enabling him to win (Norman 1994c, 1A).

The Postmortems

It is rare that a campaign is decided by one issue, or one incident, or one strategic decision. Certainly, the personalities of the candidates, the resources possessed by them, and national forces all play a role. I would argue that moral issues and the organizational effort by religiously conservative groups and their leaders were the biggest reasons why Todd Tiahrt was successful in upsetting an eighteen-year incumbent. A close look at the campaign and the history of Kansas's Fourth District suggests that the increased salience of moral issues and the increased intensity and sophistication of those on the conservative side of these issues pushed the Republicans over the hump in a district they probably should have captured a few election cycles earlier.

Now that I have taken the reader through the details of the campaign, I would like to step back and assess the causes that contributed to the surprising outcome. I asked several local observers of the campaign to describe what they believed to be the most important reasons for Tiahrt's victory. I also researched newspaper articles to account for immediate perceptions of what happened. In judging the relative significance of these factors, I think it is necessary to assess the extent to which each was in play two years earlier when Eric Yost could only manage a respectable ten-point loss. The differences between the 1992 and 1994 campaigns give us the most insight into how Glickman was finally defeated.[30]

The most obvious cause of Glickman's defeat lies in the partisanship of the district and the general Republican surge in 1994. Kansas's Fourth had voted for Reagan in 1980 and 1984 and Bush in 1988 and 1992. Of course, Glickman survived in those years as well as in all of the intervening mid-term elections. Looking at party registration, the Fourth District was becoming steadily more Republican throughout Glickman's tenure. As previously stated, voter registration efforts were the top priority for Mark Giet-zen once his forces took over the Sedgwick County GOP. During the early 1990s, the Republican advantage was roughly 11 percent. It is difficult for any politician, even one as skilled as Dan Glickman, to consistently overcome those foreboding numbers. Owing to the national Republican wave in 1994, Glickman's task became that much more difficult. Ten days out, Glickman's pollster told the Democratic candidate that there was a 47 percent to 27 percent party identification advantage for the Republicans. Glickman replied that this was impossible, that it was only an 11 percent disadvantage in the Fourth. The pollster responded by telling his boss that regardless of what it said on their registration cards, that year more people were thinking of themselves as Republicans. Glickman reached the obvious conclusion that he was in dire straits. Overcoming an 11 percent disadvantage is one thing; surviving a 20 percent disadvantage is quite another.[31]

The fact that Fourth District voters in Kansas were more inclined in 1994 than perhaps ever before to feel an affinity for Republicans of course begs the question of why that was. Yes, there were national forces at play in the Tiahrt-Glickman election but only because what was happening on the national level fit nicely into the local dynamic. Local observers such as Bud Norman, a *Wichita Eagle* reporter who covered the campaign closely, dis-counted the impact of national forces. Tiahrt signed the Contract with America but did not campaign on it. Tiahrt's people could not even get the national party to commission a poll for the candidate until late in the race, and Bob Dole had to pressure the RNC to give any money. National organizations, such as the Christian Coalition and National Right to Life, were largely absent. It was local activists recruiting local volunteers appealing to the voters on issues of local importance. The issue of abortion was one on which there was a deep and public polarization between the two candidates. Glickman was strongly pro-choice, while Tiahrt was firmly anti-abortion.

It would be almost impossible for anyone in the district paying any attention to the contest not to know where these two politicians stood on this issue. And in the wake of the Summer of Mercy, almost all Fourth District voters felt strongly about abortion and had picked a side. Everyone I talked to pointed to the Summer of Mercy as a seminal event in local politics. Before the 1991 protests, abortion was not a top issue in congressional politics. There were activists on both sides who felt strongly about their position, but the general awareness, polarization, and salience simply was not there until Operation Rescue brought it out into the open and into their backyard. Dan Glickman was pro-choice throughout his career, but until the Summer of Mercy, he rarely had to deal with the issue on the campaign trail. Starting in 1992, Glickman found himself defending his views against challengers who strongly disagreed with his liberal position. To reiterate, it was an insurgent group within the Republican Party that changed the terms of debate. After years of attacks on Glickman's fiscal record from Chamber of Commerce Republicans, moral issues assumed a prominent place in the campaign discussion thanks to the efforts of newly powerful Christian conservatives.

Eric Yost was solidly in the pro-life camp, and he made some efforts to attack Glickman on abortion. The protests were fresh in everyone's mind; however, Yost could not capitalize on the increased awareness of the issue. Todd Tiahrt was in a much better position to reap the benefits of an activated pro-life movement simply because the elites were in a better position in 1994 to harness that energy and direct it in a positive, efficient way. As the 1992 campaign got under way, Mark Gietzen had just taken over the Sedgwick County Republican Party. The moderates bolted and left Gietzen and his fellow conservatives with only the shell of a party structure. It took time for Gietzen to build the party back up, and he admits it did not happen in time to help Eric Yost. In addition, David Gittrich and Kansans for Life had not fully developed the automated dialing system that would serve Todd Tiahrt so well in 1994. There was not the same mechanism for alerting the public and drawing them into the campaign in 1992 as existed two years later. It was the combination of the increased issue salience of abortion *and* the improved organization and higher sophistication of the local political entities that made the difference for Todd Tiahrt. The issue alone was not enough. Intensity without sophistication could not upset a popular incumbent. Sophisticated intensity provided Tiahrt with the kind of grassroots effort necessary to be successful and to counteract the incumbency advantage that his opponent enjoyed. According to Bud Norman, the level of grassroots support was not there for Yost in 1992. "It was night and day, in fact" (Norman, interview with author).

An additional aspect of the grassroots effort aided Todd Tiahrt in a very important manner. Because David Gittrich was making phone calls alerting pro-lifers across the district of Tiahrt's commitment to the cause, the candidate did not have to dwell on the issue during his campaign speeches and interviews. He did not have to risk alienating moderates who might have been put off by his strong anti-abortion views. If Tiahrt had been forced to advertise his feelings on abortion wherever he went to make sure his base got the message, he easily could have been cast as a single-issue crank. When Gittrich told Tiahrt to leave the abortion issue to him, it freed the Republican candidate to talk about other issues and build broader coalitions in the district. When Mark Gietzen sent his precinct committee people into their churches to drum up support for Tiahrt, it eliminated the need for the candidate to stress his morally conservative appeal to the entire electorate. The effort was extremely well targeted within the district, which blunted the backlash that otherwise might have emerged to such a strong, moral message. Tiahrt and his campaign realized early on that they could not win with just pro-lifers. They could not even win with pro-lifers and those who were pro-gun. There simply were not enough of them to win district-wide. They made the decision early on, and Gittrich helped them achieve it, to speak to all of the voters and not concentrate on those who were against abortion and gun control.

The somewhat secretive nature of the 1994 campaign served another very important purpose and provides another contrast with 1992. Tiahrt's efforts to get in touch with his base went largely unnoticed by the media, the general public, and the Democratic Party. His popularity was building, but it was happening largely under the radar. Since the early poll that showed Glickman with a seemingly insurmountable lead, the relative strength of the candidates was changing dramatically. However, nobody conducted a poll in the two months or so after the original sampling. Therefore, nobody knew how competitive the race was getting. The phone calls and the mobilization in the churches were not registered by the media or the Glickman campaign. Everyone outside the Tiahrt camp simply assumed it would be a cakewalk for the incumbent. Glickman thought so too and took it easy during the campaign. He never developed a strong grassroots presence of his own. He did not spend a lot of money. In the hindsight of many observers, he simply took Tiahrt lightly. Here was this one-term state senator whose only legislative claim to fame was some wacky concealed-carry law. Glickman was up thirty points; he was a nine-term incumbent. Why worry? By contrast, in 1992, Glickman was keenly aware of the danger posed by Eric Yost. Yost was well respected as a public figure, and he had already defeated an incumbent backed by national and local Republican powers in the primary. Glickman fought hard and spent over $1 million. He worked the district and defended himself throughout the campaign. By contrast, in 1994, Glickman spent just under $700,000 and most of that was during the last ten days when the tide had already turned against him.

Another reason why Glickman was so confident in 1994 and maybe felt he could coast to victory was the General Aviation Revitalization Act. This was the legislative achievement of a lifetime and was extremely likely to boost the local economy and bring more jobs to the district. Unfortunately for Glickman, the nature of congressional elections had changed. In years past, a legislative accomplishment of this magnitude for a member's home district would have led to an easy victory in November. This especially would be the case, as it was for Glickman, if the local congressman could claim virtually all the credit for getting it done. In 1994, it simply did not matter. Taking care of the district economically was simply not as important as the hot-button issues of abortion and guns. This is a classic example of moral issues trumping economic issues and overshadowing the traditional opportunities for incumbents to benefit their home district.[32]

Even with the obvious focus on moral issues, the role of the Christian Coalition was less clear. Most of the people I talked to downplayed their role and, more generally, the role of all national organizations. This could be a case of local myopia; however, it appears that this race was really off the national radar until very late in the game. By the time these national organizations saw how competitive the race was, there was not much for them to do. Kansans for Life was putting out the voter guides in churches, and thousands of volunteers were already in place thanks to Mark Gietzen. I am inclined to believe that the Christian Coalition and other national groups played a very small role in Todd Tiahrt's upset of Dan Glickman. Dave Hanna told me a story that highlights how far out of nowhere Tiahrt came and how little was known about it by anyone outside of the Fourth District. In 1995 or 1996, Tiahrt found himself on a plane with Charlie Cook, one of the most highly respected handicappers of congressional elections. Cook recognized Tiahrt and told him that he had been handicapping races for a long time and there had been only two races that were utterly and completely off his radar. Tiahrt's was one of them.

After eighteen years representing Kansas's Fourth Congressional District, Dan Glickman's long, illustrious career was over.[33] The enhanced importance of moral issues and the increased sophistication of socially conservative groups and individuals were vital in switching the Fourth District of Kansas to the Republican column in 1994. Todd Tiahrt went on to represent the Wichita-based district until 2010, when he left the House to run for the U.S. Senate. Tiahrt failed to win the Republican Senate nomination in 2010 and was replaced in the House by Mike Pompeo. Pompeo ran as a pro-business and limited-government Republican in a year in which fiscal issues dominated the political discourse partly as a result of the Tea Party's ascendance. Pompeo did not openly run as a Tea Party candidate but was nonetheless able to get to the right of his three opponents in the Republican primary and win by double digits. He went on to win the general election 59 percent to 36 percent. Despite not running as a moral conservative in 2010, Pompeo went on to vote to defund Planned Parenthood in his first term and to receive a score of 95 percent from the Family Research Council as a freshman member of Congress (Barone and McCutcheon 2013, 681).

Todd Tiahrt attempted to win back his seat by challenging Pompeo in the GOP primary in 2014, but the incumbent held onto the seat rather easily. Early in the Trump era, Kansas's Fourth District was thrust into the national spotlight when the new president nominated Mike Pompeo to be director of the Central Intelligence Agency. This led to the first special election to the U.S. House in the Trump era, and the race proved much closer than expected. The Fourth District was safe for Mike Pompeo as he won reelection by thirty-one points in 2016 with Trump and Clinton battling at the top of the ticket. However, the first three months of Trump's presidency were rocky to say the least, and Governor Sam Brownback, also a Republican, was becoming less and less popular by the day. It all added up to a much closer race than anyone might have expected as the Republican Ron Estes held off Democrat James Thompson 53 percent to 46 percent. This, along with other close special elections in rock-solid Republican districts, showed just how unpopular President Trump had become and how his rise to power had energized the Democratic Party. Thompson ran again in 2018, but he could only manage 40 percent of the vote this time around in this now reliably Republican Fourth District of Kansas.

Chapter 5

Religion and Republicanism

An Early Example of the Electoral Potency of Moral Traditionalism

Two years before the 1994 Republican takeover of the House, a keen observer of American politics might have noticed a harbinger of Republican success in South Carolina's Fourth District race. A previously unknown lawyer with little name recognition and barely enough money to advertise on television shocked a three-term Democratic incumbent who tallied over 60 percent of the vote in her previous reelection bid. The race demonstrated the potential of moral issues to swing an at-risk district to the Republican column as the challenger was able to tap into a locally vibrant evangelical and fundamentalist community. It provided him with campaign resources that were essential to defeating a popular Democratic incumbent. In addition, the challenger benefited from a Republican Party that was extremely strong locally. In fact, the roots of his victory were planted sixteen years earlier when a group of young activists from Bob Jones University decided they were going to get involved in local Republican politics.

Evangelicals Storm the Republican Party

Mostly owing to Jimmy Carter's election to the presidency, 1976 was dubbed the "Year of the Evangelical." However, evangelical activity in the bicentennial year was not limited to presidential politics, and more important, it was not limited to the Democratic Party. The goal of Bob Jones University (BJU) activists was to take over the Greenville County Republican Party. The means would be precinct by precinct. There were two types of precincts as far as Republican Party organization was concerned. In some precincts, there was no organization whatsoever. In others, maybe ten people would attend the delegate selection meetings. The plan was simple. Students, faculty, and staff from BJU would show up for these precinct meetings and dominate the proceedings. The results were astounding. In 1974, the Greenville County Republican convention had roughly two hundred people. Two years later, it had 1,250. Religious conservatives made most of the difference. The leaders of the push were affiliated with the university, but the foot soldiers came from the churches.[1]

Bob Taylor, the head of the mathematics department at BJU at the time, was one of the original 1976 activists. He credits John Conlan, a Republican congressman from Arizona, for spurring on the grassroots effort in Greenville County. According to Taylor, some of the people in the county got the idea from Conlan's campaign literature to go into the evangelical churches—sometimes during the services—to get people involved. They made sure the congregants were registered to vote and suggested they go to precinct meetings. It was bipartisan in its appeal, but Taylor and his fellow activists knew the parishioners would end up registering Republican based on their ideological conservatism (Taylor, interview with author).

The BJU activists got a lot of people excited to vote, and many were inspired to go to precinct meetings during the early months of 1976. Even though they were political newcomers, the Bob Jones people had a sense that they would be successful in the months leading up to the county convention. A few months before the convention, the large group of religious conservatives began meeting to plan strategy. Closer to the date of the convention, Taylor was brought to a meeting of one of the two existing factions of party regulars and he realized, "They're just gonna be . . . their mouths are just going to drop open because the numbers coming in they're not gonna believe. And that's the way it turned out" (Taylor, interview with author). Precinct meetings that normally had two or three people now had fifteen. Those that had thirty in 1974 had sixty in 1976. This explosive growth happened in precinct after precinct across the county (Taylor, interview with author). There were many precincts that had not been organized; they had not elected officials, and there was no semblance of a partisan infrastructure. Students, staff, and faculty at Bob Jones lived in all parts of the county. According to Oran Smith, the president of a pro-family group in South Carolina and the author of a book on Baptist Republicanism, "They would organize the Oneal precinct, which had never been organized before, and show up at the county convention with a majority of delegates. And the old crowd was very concerned about these new people" (Smith, interview with author).

A Newly Vibrant Republican Party Emerges in the Fourth District

The "old crowd" had been young once, and they consisted of those Republicans who had built a state political organization from the ground up. The operation was bolstered by W. D. Workman's losing 1962 U.S. Senate campaign. Workman, from the city of Greenville, ran a very respectable race against Olin Johnston. His strong showing galvanized Republicans statewide. According to Workman's son Bill, before his father's campaign, the Republican Party in the South was full of elitists looking for patronage. Younger, more business-oriented Republican conservatives, who were driven by what was good for the country rather than what they could get out of government, started asserting themselves and assuming power. The elder Workman brought a voice to conservatism in the GOP, focusing on the increasing size of government (Bill Workman, interview with author). These bright, young business types rapidly displaced the previous party leaders and set out to make up for the hundred-year head start the Democratic Party enjoyed in most of the region.

As in the rest of the South, Palmetto State conservatism was slow to produce Republican gains. Between 1900 and 1944, the Republicans failed to win a gubernatorial, a congressional, or even a state legislative race. The GOP was completely shut out during this period. As late as 1960, the Republicans failed to contest a single one of the state's six seats in the U.S. House (Moreland, Steed, and Baker 1986, 123–24). However, thanks to the efforts of W. D. Workman and others in the early 1960s, South Carolina as a state and its Fourth District in particular can be said to have helped lead the South into the Republican Party. By the mid-1960s, Republican state party chair J. Drake Edens had earned a national reputation for his organizational skills at the grassroots level. The Republican Party further benefited from Strom Thurmond's famous party switch in 1964, two years after local state representative Floyd Spence had done the same. Congressman Albert Watson also switched parties when the Democrats stripped him of his seniority for supporting Barry Goldwater's presidential bid in 1964. Watson resigned and regained his seat in a special election as a Republican. Both

Thurmond and Watson were reelected as Republicans two years later, while Spence was elected to the U.S. House in 1970 as a Republican.

In the Fourth District of South Carolina, local businessmen have always been powerful in Republican politics. The Fourth has been centered on two counties for decades. Greenville and Spartanburg Counties dominate the Fourth District economically, politically, and socially.[2] The Upcountry, in the northwest corner of South Carolina, has always been more conservative than the rest of the state. This has as much to do with the influence of big business as it does with the large number of evangelical and fundamentalist churches that dot the area. As mentioned earlier, members of those churches insinuated themselves into Republican politics in 1976. The result was a changed party. Bill Workman was intimately involved in Republican politics when the first group of Christian conservatives made their presence felt. "To take control, you go to the precinct meetings. If a precinct that had been a country-club Republican-type of precinct or even an outskirt where they may have had two and three and four people show up for precinct meetings, . . . all of a sudden here's fifteen that show up. And then elect their own precinct president and executive committeemen and then there's a change in the formulation and the nature of the county party. And to the extent that this goes on across the state you have a new state party" (Workman, interview with author).

In the short run, the influx of religious conservatives created nothing but trouble. Oran Smith recalls the newcomers as shrill and aggressive with little desire to compromise. They had the votes at the county convention and proceeded to oust many party regulars. It was a full-blown rumble that produced bitterness and animosity within the GOP (Smith, interview with author). A divided Republican Party was certainly not conducive to electoral success in a region where the Democrats still dominated. Alan Ehrenhalt, who wrote about Greenville County in his book *The United States of Ambition*, describes the aftermath of the rumble of 1976. "In the short run the 1976 coup was a disaster for all concerned. With its factions bitterly opposed to each other, the Republican Party lost virtually all its state legislative seats in Greenville County, even as Gerald Ford was carrying the county against Jimmy Carter by more than three thousand votes. For the next four years there were essentially two Republican parties in Greenville" (1991, 97–98). Ronald Reagan was able to unite the two factions in 1980. He gave both the party regulars and the insurgent Christian conservatives reasons to support him. By 1980, the infighting had diminished, and both groups were working together for the greater good of the Republican Party.

In 1980, Republicans around the country, and in Greenville County, had a terrific year. However, 1978 produced a victory for Greenville Republicans that would eventually reverberate across the state and the nation. Carroll Campbell was a state representative from Greenville when he decided to run for the open Fourth District congressional seat. His opponent was the popular mayor of Greenville, Max Heller. It was a hard-fought campaign that at times verged into the realm of nastiness. Lee Atwater was Campbell's campaign manager, and some claim he was responsible for a variety of sordid tactics designed to highlight religious differences between the candidates. Heller was Jewish, and many voters were called in the weeks before the election and asked whether they would support a candidate who did not believe in Jesus Christ as his savior (Barone and Ujifusa 1979, 801).[3] Campbell ended up winning the race by six points and would eventually become governor in 1986. During his eight years in the state capitol, Carroll Campbell was the central figure who turned the Republican Party into the political force in the Palmetto State that it is today.

An Open Seat in the Fourth District

With Campbell's run for governor, the congressional seat was open once again. Ronald Reagan had received 70 percent of the Fourth District's presidential vote two years earlier, and with the popular Greenville native at the top of the statewide ticket, Republicans were confident they would maintain their hold on the seat. However, they were defeated in 1986, and the seeds for their defeat were sown during an extremely contentious primary that divided Republicans in several different ways.

Four Republicans sought their party's congressional nomination. They were all conservative, but that is where the similarity ended. The candidates were Bill Workman, mayor of Greenville and son of the defeated Republican Senate candidate in 1962; state representatives Thomas Marchant and Richard Rigdon; and fundamentalist Christian airline pilot Ted Adams. As mayor, Workman was seen as the candidate of the downtown business interests. He had overseen the continued economic development of the city and was in support of a proposed arena which would bring big-name entertainment to Greenville. Marchant and Rigdon had ties to the fundamentalist community through their representation of portions of the Bob

Jones University precincts. In addition, Rigdon was a graduate of BJU. Finally, Ted Adams was the quintessential political outsider. He had never run for public office and was counting on drumming up support from those in the district who were tired of "politics as usual" and instead wanted someone who would fight hard for their principles.

Substantively, the primary campaign was mostly focused on economic issues. In the first debate, Marchant charged that Workman was as liberal as the Democratic candidate, Liz Patterson. Workman countered that he was fiscally conservative, and all four candidates stressed their conservatism on taxation and government spending. Religion also played an enormous role in the contest. All four candidates recognized the importance of the fundamentalist and evangelical vote. In the Fourth District, the best way to attract that vote was to gain the support of Bob Jones Jr., or Dr. Bob, as Bill Workman called him. For that reason, each competitor actively sought his endorsement.

All four candidates supported the religious right agenda, but Workman was operating at a greater distance from the fundamentalist community than the other three. The contenders' views on religion and morality were clearly laid out in the second Republican debate. Workman said only that morality should start with individual voters. Marchant came across as "a very strong supporter of pro-life efforts." Rigdon was quoted as saying "every law that is passed dictates a morality. I've run all my campaigns based on the moral issues. I see my moral issues springing from the word of God." As for Ted Adams, he may have endeared himself most to the religious conservative movement by saying nothing. The debate was held on a Sunday, and the former pilot refused to attend because of his religious beliefs (Baker 1986a, 4).

Bob Jones University was deeply divided over whom to support in this election. Bob Jones Jr. shared the platform with Marchant when he opened his Greenville headquarters. Jones said he supported Marchant because he "from the very beginning has been very fair in his stands to protect the freedoms of political and religious minorities" (Paslay 1986, 1B). However, a large proportion of the student body and faculty seemed to support Ted Adams. According to Adams, his candidacy was "tearing the school apart" (Adams, interview with author). Indeed, in the last week of the campaign, Marchant sent out a letter, from Bob Jones III, to voters associated with the university. The letter stated Jones's support for Marchant, who was worried that many supported Adams (Baker and Perry 1986a, 2B). Workman and

Table 5.1. GOP U.S. House primary results in 1986

Candidate	District-wide	City of Greenville	Greenville County[a]	Spartanburg County	Bob Jones Precincts[b]
Workman	**49.4**	**54.0**	**42.8**	**60.0**	22.8
Marchant	22.5	19.6	24.1	22.4	28.8
Adams	20.6	21.5	24.1	10.6	**42.6**
Rigdon	7.5	5.0	9.0	7.0	6.8

Note: Numbers are percentages, and the data comes from the *Greenville News*.

[a] Not including the city.

[b] Residents of the Bob Jones University campus (which includes the homes and apartments for many of the faculty and staff).

Rigdon could not expect much institutional support from BJU, each for different reasons. Workman was associated with the downtown business crowd and was seen as insufficiently conservative on moral issues. Rigdon, on the other hand, was a graduate of BJU and had openly admitted the great extent to which his spirituality guided his political decision making. BJU's problem with Rigdon stemmed from his switch from fundamentalist to charismatic Christianity, which was seen as heretical by the ultraseparationists at Bob Jones (L. Perry 1986, 1C).[4]

The primary campaign was summed up in an article published in the *Greenville News* just days before the election. "The candidates . . . have campaigned as fiscal conservatives who support a strong national defense. They have also made overtures to voters, especially in large fundamentalist precincts near Bob Jones University in Greenville, on moral issues such as abortion, school prayer, and pornography" (D. Perry 1986, 4C). Workman had amassed twice as much as money as Marchant, who, in turn, had collected more than Rigdon and Adams combined. This huge financial advantage proved to be too much to overcome as Workman ran away with the primary election. Table 5.1 presents the results. The election returns highlight the particular strengths of the candidates. Mayor Workman did exceptionally well in the city and less well in the county at large. Workman dominated in Spartanburg County, and since none of the candidates had a base there, it is believed that his superior war chest allowed him to muster a strong majority in that portion of the district. In the Bob Jones precincts, the split discussed earlier was borne out. Ted Adams's popularity with the students, staff, and faculty allowed him to achieve a strong plurality despite the endorsement of Marchant by Jones Jr. and Jones III. Workman made a respectable showing, and the charismatic Christian Richard Rigdon was far behind. District-wide, Workman was the clear winner. However, he fell just short of the 50 percent needed to win the nomination outright. This meant a runoff with the second-place finisher, Thomas Marchant.

No candidate who wins the first round of a primary election wants to be in a runoff. A runoff siphons valuable time, energy, and resources away from the general election campaign. Republican leaders concerned with maintaining their hold on the Fourth District were not pleased with having to continue this contentious and potentially divisive intramural battle for one more day, let alone two weeks. So an effort was launched to convince Marchant to drop out of the runoff. At first, the state representative was unwilling to withdraw, and he hammered the front-runner in the media. Then Marchant had a sudden change of heart and decided to drop out. Bill Workman remembers those hectic days following the initial election. "Tom Marchant and I had a sit-down brokered by some of the guys in Columbia (the state capital), and Tom agreed that he would step aside and did so" (interview with author). Bob Taylor believes Marchant dropped out because he thought Workman's lead was insurmountable. Presumably Marchant, as a Republican interested in continuing his political career in South Carolina, was convinced that it was in his best interest not to divide the party further in a costly and divisive runoff. Unfortunately for Workman and "some of the guys in Columbia," Ted Adams had no such desire to placate the party elites, and by law as the third-place finisher, he assumed the mantle of runoff challenger. Marchant's withdrawal does provide another example of party leaders influencing nominating campaigns, although the second-place finisher was not completely cowed by elites as evidenced by his endorsement of the more conservative outsider Adams.[5]

The Dreaded Runoff

Despite all of the post-election wrangling, there would be a congressional runoff after all. It was a classic battle between the insider Workman and the outsider Adams, as well as a factional fight between the entrenched business wing and the fledgling Christian right wing of the Republican Party. A digression into how these two politicians came to this runoff is instructive for the general lessons it teaches about American politics. Their lives and careers make for an interesting contrast.

Bill Workman grew up in a family where political issues were discussed over breakfast, lunch, and dinner. His father, W. D. Workman, was a political reporter who ran a credible race for the U.S. Senate in 1962. After graduating from the Citadel and leaving the military, the son followed in the father's footsteps and became a political reporter. Workman moved to Greenville in 1969 and became a dean at Greenville Technical College. In his first year in the area, he was approached by several businessmen to run for school board. Through the 1970s, he worked for Daniel Construction and Piedmont Natural Gas, building important ties to the business and industrial communities. In 1981, he decided to run for city council and was victorious. This time around, Workman did not wait for an invitation. "I didn't need anybody to ask me for that [city council]. I realized it was a lot easier to give a speech than to cover one" (Workman, interview with author). After two years on the Greenville City Council, he ran for mayor in 1983 and was elected. As mayor, he was a champion of local businesses and went to great lengths to build and modernize the city's economy and improve its social status. The contacts he made as a reporter and as a businessman opened the opportunity to run for elective office.

Political success in South Carolina is largely about personal contacts and building networks. Workman was effective in doing that, and it landed him in the mayor's office. During his first term, the Fourth District seat opened up, and he decided to run for it. He hoped to clear the field by sending a letter to Richard Rigdon and Thomas Marchant in late December 1985 urging them to drop out of the race and support his candidacy against the Democratic candidate. Ultimately, Workman was unsuccessful in chasing those two competitors out of the race, but ironically it was his third competitor who ended up being the thorn in his side.[6]

Ted Adams is the prototype of a political outsider. For the former airline pilot, politicians are worth nothing if they fail to defend their principles. And Adams has more than his share of principles to defend. Adams lived in Greenville all his life and, after graduating from the Citadel, went into the Air Force and flew as a pilot in the Strategic Air Command. He then went to work for Pan Am as a pilot flying to the Far East. He finished his career with United and amassed extensive experience flying the 747, 757, and 767. According to Adams, "Squadron officer's school in the Air Force opened my eyes to what was going on in this country as far as it being taken over by 'globalists' and some Communists." He did not like it and was unhappy with the way the Vietnam War was fought. He felt "we were losing our freedom, losing our culture" (Adams, interview with author).

Adams started out by writing his congressman, and then he joined the John Birch Society. He also became state chairman of a tax reform group that monitored the tax and spending votes of congressmen. One of Adams's political heroes was a fellow Bircher, Congressman Larry McDonald. McDonald was a Democrat, but according to Adams, he had a perfect "constitutional" voting record.[7] McDonald was killed when the Soviet Union shot down Korean Air Lines flight 007 in 1983. The man who preached at McDonald's funeral, Joe Mulcraft, decided to run for Congress if Adams would. So Adams quit the John Birch Society and agreed to run in 1986 when the Fourth District seat opened. Adams was convinced that letter writing was no match for the "special interests that buy the elections" (Adams, interview with author).

When Adams announced his candidacy, there were 150 people at the motel ballroom where he made his first speech as a candidate. Most were Christians who were committed to better government. They did not want anything out of government, according to Adams. "They just wanted to keep the government off their backs and out of their pocketbooks and let them live the way they always lived, basically free" (Adams, interview with author). Adams came to fundamentalist Christianity after tragedy. His first wife died in a plane crash, and he barely survived one. "[After that I] . . . learned I was not the master of my fate and that there were other powers working in our life. That sense, plus the sudden responsibility of rearing my two daughters, one six weeks old and the other age three-and-a-half, really was the thing that brought me to a saving knowledge of the Lord." Eight years after he was widowed, he remarried, and "we joined a church, we got the Lord's word there, we were fed with the gospel, we accepted Jesus Christ as our Savior and our Lord and it's been that way ever since" (Baker 1986c, 1B).

Clearly the runoff would be a referendum on what kind of Republican voters wanted to represent them in the general election. Workman was the business candidate who trumpeted his support for the new arena. Adams was against the stadium for fear it would promote immorality through the various acts that might perform there. For Adams, his religion and politics were inexorably intertwined. In a speech to Bob Jones University students during the campaign, Adams described the nation's problems as a simple choice between God and Caesar. "The whole issue of politics is the issue of sovereignty. That is, who is going to control your life? Is it going to be God or the state? Who has the right to tell you what to do with your children, your time, your property and your money?" (Baker 1986c, 1B). During that same speech, Adams articulated what he believed was the proper role for religion in public policy. He said Congress should enact laws "based on our Christian heritage. Years ago we operated this country under God's law, but recently, our lawmakers have changed that, and with that change has come broken families, missing and abused children, troubled schools, unsafe streets and eighteen million unborn children murdered. I believe that if this nation is going to escape cultural collapse and divine judgment, we have got to have a change in laws" (Baker 1986c, 1B). "You and I, and all of our friends, have to start examining the way we think," he said at the BJU student rally. "Do we think like Americans, people with a Christian heritage? Or are we thinking like Marxists and humanists, people who believe that man is God, and that government, which is man's creation, is the answer to all of our problems?" (Baker 1986c, 1B). In addition to Adams's strong religious beliefs, his second wife had strong Christian right credentials as a member of the National Federation for Decency, an organization that campaigned against pornography and child abuse. She also was part of the Creation Health Foundation, which encouraged the teaching of creationism on an equal basis with evolution in public schools. Adams's wife was involved with anti-abortion groups as well (Baker 1986c, 1B).

In the runoff, Ted Adams was clearly the Christian right's candidate. Workman, with his different background and emphasis, was speaking to another constituency entirely. In this internecine partisan battle, it was clear who the party leaders were supporting. Twenty of twenty-three elected Republican officials in Greenville and Spartanburg Counties endorsed Workman in the runoff. There were also rampant rumors that gubernatorial candidate Carroll Campbell was actively aiding the mayor's campaign. Of course, Workman had considerably more money than Adams, yet Workman was still worried about his supporters coming back to the polls just two weeks after the initial vote. Workman understood the intensity of his opponent's supporters and knew they would return to vote in the runoff (Baker and Perry 1986b, 1C).

Table 5.2 shows the results of the Fourth District Republican runoff. Once again, Workman dominated in the city and Spartanburg County. He split the county precincts in Greenville and was defeated at Bob Jones but

Table 5.2. GOP U.S. House runoff results in 1986

Candidate	District-wide	City of Greenville	Greenville County[a]	Spartanburg County	Bob Jones Precincts[b]
Workman	**54.0**	**63.4**	49.4	**60.9**	40.0
Adams	46.0	36.6	**50.6**	39.1	**60.0**

Note: Numbers are percentages, and the data comes from the *Greenville News*.

[a] Not including the city.

[b] Residents of the Bob Jones University campus (which includes the homes and apartments for many of the faculty and staff).

not by an enormous margin. Workman's eight-point victory sent him to the general election and into an interesting matchup with the Democratic candidate, Liz Patterson, from Spartanburg. In one of the great coincidences of American politics, Patterson's father was Olin Johnston. Johnston was the man who defeated Bill Workman's father in the 1962 Senate race that helped spark a Republican resurgence in the Palmetto State. Now the children would conduct a rematch a generation later.

The 1986 General Election Campaign

Before the general election campaign even got under way, it may have been lost for Bill Workman. After the runoff, Ted Adams congratulated Workman but refused to endorse him. The Adams camp got involved in politics to change policy and bring some integrity back into public service. They disagreed with Workman on many of the issues, and they felt he lied and played dirty during the campaign. Plus, Adams and his followers did not get into the campaign to support business-as-usual politics.

Campbell was very irked with Adams, as were many other Republicans. A lot of the ministers who supported and encouraged Adams, when they found out he was not supporting Workman, characterized him as a "poor loser." According to Adams, a few dyed-in-the-wool Republicans and many religious elites defected and went with Workman. But most of the rank-and-file parishioners chose not to transfer over their support from Adams to Workman.

With a fractured party, Bill Workman took on the task of trying to defeat a popular state legislator from Spartanburg County. A historic rivalry between Greenville and Spartanburg Counties would play a role in this congressional race. In the first few decades of the twentieth century, Spartanburg dominated Fourth District politics and elected some national powerhouses to Congress. However, since the 1920s, the seat had always been represented by someone from Greenville. Greenville's economic boom, first through textiles and then through its attraction of BMW, Michelin, and other large corporations, gave Spartanburg a slight inferiority complex when it came to those across the county line. People from Spartanburg were proud to have a strong candidate in Liz Patterson, and the county was excited about the prospect of returning one of their own to Washington (Ron Romine, interview with author).

Patterson was a formidable candidate in her own right, regardless of her base. Many voters remembered her father and voted for him. In addition, she was popular with Republicans and Democrats alike for her moderate stands on fiscal issues. Even though the Fourth District voted 70 percent for Reagan in 1984, this would be a tough race for a Republican party that was united, let alone one that was severely divided in the aftermath of the Workman-Adams runoff. That said, the district had been won easily by a Republican since 1978 and, with the exception of 1976, had not gone Democratic in a presidential election since 1960—and that was by less than one thousand votes.

Neither observers nor participants remember issues playing a large role in the 1986 congressional election. The contest was fought mostly on personality, lineage, and geography. Workman made an effort to portray Patterson as a liberal on fiscal issues, but other than that there was not a focused debate on ideology. There was almost no mention of moral issues, such as abortion and school prayer, issues that had dominated the national agenda. The outcome was a 52 percent to 48 percent victory for Democrat Liz Patterson. Bill Workman was unable to avenge his father's defeat at the hands of Patterson's father twenty-four years earlier. Table 5.3 shows the voting breakdown, and later I will discuss these results and how they relate to my central arguments.

After any election, the losing side almost immediately begins to wonder why they came up short. There were several reasons offered for Workman's defeat. He blames, in part, Spartanburg Republicans who defected to Patterson for reasons of regional loyalty. Workman also credits Patterson for running a smart campaign and gathering large sums of PAC money. Other observers placed the blame at the Republican candidate's feet. Bob Taylor

Table 5.3. U.S. House general election results in 1986

Candidate	District-wide	City of Greenville	Greenville County[a]	Spartanburg and Union Counties	Bob Jones Precincts[b]
Patterson	**52.1**	45.7	45.2	**61.1**	18.7
Workman	47.9	**54.3**	**54.8**	38.9	**81.3**

Note: Numbers are percentages, and the data comes from the *Greenville News*.

[a] Not including the city.

[b] Residents of the Bob Jones University campus (which includes the homes and apartments for many of the faculty and staff).

of Bob Jones University thought Workman could have run a better campaign and specifically faulted his television commercials. "He ran a terrible general election campaign. Every time his ads went on television, the numbers dropped. The ads were seen as ridiculous" (Taylor, interview with author). Taylor also believes Workman was in an awkward position of running against a woman. According to the former dean at BJU, Workman ran a "gentlemanly" campaign that Patterson took full advantage of.

A reporter who covered Fourth District politics for the *Greenville News* spoke to me in detail about the city-county rivalry in Greenville and argued that this rift hurt Mayor Workman with voters who lived within the county but outside the city lines. Greenville's city-county rivalry has been around for decades. Ehrenhalt makes mention of it in his chapter on Greenville in *The United States of Ambition* (1991). The political reporter from the *Greenville News* believed that Workman's obvious association with the city of Greenville cost him votes in the county. He claimed county voters possess a lot of mistrust of city politicians. In discussing Fourth District political history, Taylor remembers there always being a few influential downtown businessmen in Greenville who believe they know what is best for the county. Outside the city lines, Taylor sees bitter resentment toward the powerful downtown business interests. As the pro-development mayor, Bill Workman was the powerful downtown business interest in 1986. Taylor believes that being the mayor of Greenville was not necessarily a good spot to run from county-wide.

On the other side, the Democrats were well aware of the city-county rivalry and sought to exploit it. Ron Romine was a high-level adviser to the

Patterson campaign. He tells of their desire to pit the county against the city. "We sent direct mail to the county folks using the Coliseum issue to place the county against the city and their candidate, Workman" (Romine, interview with author). Romine believes this strategy helped keep Patterson close in Greenville County. With Patterson likely to pile up the votes in Spartanburg, the key was not getting demolished in the more Republican areas of Greenville County. Sure enough, Table 5.3 shows how that strategy played out. Patterson won by twenty-two points in Spartanburg County and only lost by single digits in Greenville.[8] This combination led to a four-point victory district-wide.

Since the city-county rivalry was so important in this race, it makes sense to delve deeper and attempt to figure out what is at the heart of the enmity. Doing so will illuminate the role of religion and morality in this congressional election and also bring us back to the importance of Ted Adams's refusal to support his fellow Republican. When pressed further about the city-county rivalry in Greenville, several of my interviewees boiled it down to the same issues. The rivalry has really been a proxy for a cosmopolitan-traditionalist kind of dispute. The politicians and businessmen associated with the city group have continually attempted to modernize Greenville and make it attractive to young couples throughout the South. They want Greenville to shake off its small-town, parochial past and join the ranks of Birmingham and Atlanta as first-class, cosmopolitan urban centers. The cultural by-products of such development and progressivism directly challenge the religious traditionalism of the region. Greenville County is one of the most well-churched areas in the nation, and the majority of those churches espouse fundamentalist or at least a conservative form of Christianity. The development drive, in both an economic and a cultural sense, runs squarely into an inertia that makes the status quo of traditionalism quite powerful. Romine sees the rivalry stemming from "downtown development and sin. People out in the county look downtown and see corruption and drinking on Sundays. They see that the Peace Center (a Greenville arena) has Shirley MacLaine and God knows who else" (Romine, interview with author).

When asked what the city-county rivalry was all about, one of my sources at the *Greenville News* replied in the voice of the county folk, "The city of Greenville has Sunday liquor sales. It's an evil place, an evil place." The uneasy tension between the forces of progressivism and traditionalism can be seen behind every bar in the Greenville area in the form of hundreds of mini-bottles of alcohol. When liquor by the drink—that is, "free pour" out of normal-sized bottles—was being promoted, those who opposed it knew they did not have the votes to stop it. So they hoped to scuttle the transition by mandating that bars could not engage in "free pour." Instead, drinking establishments would be forced to provide mini-bottles of booze for their customers. The "drys" thought this would encourage pilfering and otherwise make it a hassle for bar owners to provide liquor by the drink. None of this happened, and in fact the unintended consequences of this legislation worked in favor of those seeking to imbibe their favorite spirits. The mini-bottles actually hold roughly two-and-a-half shots as opposed to the single shot one might receive from a free pour out of a normal-sized bottle. The mini-bottles have become so accepted that even after a law allowed "free pour," most bars have continued with the miniatures. One waitress I spoke with in Columbia, South Carolina, said her boss would not move to regular bottles because the shelving behind the bar was already built for the minis.[9]

The city-county rivalry is not just cultural, although that seems to be the driving force. Romine sees economic roots related to the cultural ones. Development costs money, and those in the county often see the city politicians as wanting to raise their taxes "and do the county in" (Romine, interview with author). Race also enters the equation as most of the public housing is inside the city limits of Greenville. According to Romine, race is always an issue in Greenville if only because a lightning rod for racial politics calls Greenville his home. "[Jesse] Jackson being from Greenville, when he comes in, the white folks in the county are that much more determined to vote against whatever he is for" (interview with author). Jackson was born and raised in Greenville, and while he has since built a national reputation, he often returns to the area and visits family. Whites and African Americans in Greenville County are acutely aware of his local roots.

The city of Greenville, according to Ehrenhalt, is a "small tail that wags a very large dog" (1991, 87). The county dominates in terms of population, and as Bill Workman found out, running for office district-wide from the city is very difficult. He was a city politician and not trusted by those in the county. In this case, one could substitute the terms "business Republican" for city politician and "Christian Republican" for those in the county. Workman was identified as an "old Republican," those who were not considered Republicans of the Christian Coalition variety. According to Romine, Workman was seen as the enemy of the right wing. He simply was not conservative enough. Adams had the support of the Christian right. This brings us back to the consequences of the divisive nominating campaign. Adams was from the county, and he defeated Workman in those precincts in the runoff (see Table 5.2). Since Workman's natural constituency was not the religious conservatives in the county, an endorsement from Adams was vital. It did not come, and many observers believe it may have cost the Republicans a seat they should have won. Ron Romine comments, "They had a fairly bitter primary fight so there was some lingering animosity, and I think that helped Ms. Patterson. There were people who either didn't go vote or might have voted for her out of spite or something like that" (interview with author). One reporter who covered the race believed the rivalry cost the Republicans a victory in 1986. "Any other Republican should have won that. Workman lost" (anonymous source, interview with author). Ehrenhalt's take on the 1986 election is as follows: "When Workman ran for Congress in 1986, he was challenged for the Republican nomination by three fundamentalist opponents and won the primary largely because the Bob Jones community did not unite behind any of them. Lingering skepticism about him among some of the Bob Jones loyalists held down his Greenville vote in the general election and provided a critical factor in his defeat" (Ehrenhalt 1991, 103).

In hindsight, Workman could have done more to appeal to the religious conservatives. In a relatively issue-free campaign, Workman only raised economic issues. He chose to attack Patterson as a liberal but an economic liberal. An attempt to separate the two on moral issues might have made the choice starker for Adams supporters who were unconvinced of Workman's conservative credentials. In the end, Workman failed to fully satisfy either wing of the Republican Party in the Fourth District, and the Democrat reaped the benefits. A district that by all rights should have been represented by a Republican would not be. Republicans were disappointed in Workman but angry at Ted Adams. Politicians and ministers alike were not pleased with Adams for remaining true to his principles and refusing to support the runoff winner. "Boy, were those ministers mad at me. [They said', 'because by withholding your 45 percent of the vote, she [Patterson] beat a Republican in a Republican district'" (Adams, interview with author). Indeed, Lee Bandy, in a column written early in the next election cycle, agreed with these ministers. "Greenville Mayor Bill Workman lost a cliffhanger to Ms. Patterson in 1986 because of a split between the party regulars and charismatic evangelicals, many of whom stayed home on Election Day" (Bandy 1988a, 1A).

Accommodating Another Group of Christian Republicans

Republicans had not seen the last of Ted Adams as he would run for Congress again in 1988. But before the 1988 campaign can be discussed, another influx of religious conservatives into national Republican politics was taking place that would have an impact on elections in the Fourth District and across the state. During the run-up to the 1988 election, a new group of religious conservatives was attempting to take over Republican state party organizations all across America. They were energized by the presidential candidacy of Pat Robertson. In South Carolina, the big battle began in Richland County in 1987. The Richland County seat is the state capital of Columbia. Robertson was a charismatic preacher, and his followers, while conservative Christians, were profoundly different than the Bob Jones activists who emerged in 1976 and had since been more or less integrated into the party structure upstate.[10] Robertson's followers began organizing precincts in hopes of wresting control of the party from the old guard. The battle was joined statewide between the charismatics and the party regulars. Robertson's people got organized and went to the precinct meetings just as the Bob Jones contingent had done twelve years earlier. The caucus meetings were generally not well attended, and the regulars took them for granted. Lee Bandy recalls, "They [Robertson's group] just went out and crashed the caucus meetings, and most of your regulars were out on the golf course" (interview with author). Bandy goes on to explain that the charismatics and Pentecostals were organizing behind the scenes, coming out of the churches, and nobody knew what was going on until it was too late. The impetus came from Robertson's home base in Virginia, but the foot soldiers were local churchgoers. This takeover mirrors the one in Sedgwick County. Bandy's characterization is eerily similar to that of Reverend Sloan from Chapter 4.

The rivalry between Robertson's forces and Republican Party regulars came to a head at the state convention in May 1988. Christian Republicans had enough delegates to control the floor. They were unified as well. The old-line party leaders still controlled the machinery going in, and they managed to disqualify some of the Christian delegations. The regulars barely held onto their power but only after a nasty fight. Some Christians who were uninterested in compromising left the party. But for the most part, the insurgents of 1987 and 1988 ended up working their way into the party structure and, paralleling the first influx of Christians, became assimilated into the party to the extent that they are now considered party regulars. According to Bandy, "The mainstream Republicans took them under their wings and taught them a few things" (interview with author). There were no more fights, and by the early 1990s, they had fully patched things up. While some suspicion might still linger between Christian Republicans and business Republicans, the two factions are united in purpose, and that purpose is electoral triumph. Religious conservatives realized they could be much more effective working within the party than as troublemakers. They became the backbone of the party throughout South Carolina and helped the GOP achieve incredible gains during the 1990s and in the early years of the new millennium.

According to most perceptive observers of modern South Carolina politics, Carroll Campbell was the person most responsible for dramatically improving the electoral fortunes of Republicans in the Palmetto State. An astute observer of South Carolina politics said this about Governor Campbell. "Carroll was a hell of an organizer. Carroll was a party builder. I mean if you get two Republicans together, Carroll would go talk to them" (anonymous source, interview with author). When Campbell took over as governor in early 1987, there were only a handful of GOP state senators, fewer than thirty state representatives, a few Republican sheriffs, and only a few county councils controlled by Republicans. Now in South Carolina, Republicans have strong majorities in both state houses. The changes at the state and local levels are striking, and Campbell is credited with setting up the organization to effect those changes. "Carroll was a strong governor. When you walked into his office, you had no doubt who the governor was. Power just oozed out of him. He worked areas of the state that hadn't previously been worked, and it all just came together very rapidly" (anonymous source, interview with author). It helped that Campbell had cultivated close ties with national Republican figures, such as George H. W. Bush and Lee Atwater. This gave the governor and his state party a stature that undoubtedly bolstered their local strength.

Campbell's biggest accomplishment may have been bridging the gap between the Christian conservatives and the Chamber of Commerce Republicans. Despite periodic spats, Campbell did a wonderful job keeping the party together amid infighting over platforms and delegate slates. According to my source at the *Greenville News*, having to deal with different types of Republicans did not bother Campbell, and he did a lot to bring them together. Referring back to the above quote, it did not matter if those "two Republicans" were Christian conservatives, or business Republicans, or one of each. "Carroll would go talk to them" (anonymous source, interview with author).[11]

Patterson Runs for Reelection

In the Fourth District, however, success did not come right away, and the fruits of Governor Campbell's work would not be immediately realized. After defeating Bill Workman, Liz Patterson sought to use the advantages of incumbency to make her seat safe despite its tendency to vote Republican for president. The 1988 GOP primary would be a repeat of the factional battle of 1986. The candidate associated with the Christian right was once again Ted Adams. This time he had name recognition and retained a strong cadre of dedicated supporters (Hoover 1988a, 2C). The business Republican closely associated with downtown Greenville was Knox White. White was a native of Greenville and had always wanted to be involved in politics. He worked for Carroll Campbell in Washington and hoped to follow in his footsteps by getting elected to Congress in the Fourth District. He fashioned himself as a moderate conservative and sought to cloak himself in Campbell's aura. As a result of his association with the governor, White had the support of the party establishment, leaving Adams as the outsider yet again. But the 1988 primary would be categorically different from the one two years earlier.

The biggest difference was the role played by religious and political elites. They were much warier of a divisive primary and much more interested in coordinating around a candidate that could be successful against Patterson. Van Hipp, South Carolina's GOP chair, said at the time, "We're not going to have the problems we did in 1986. We'll be more united this year" (Bandy 1988a, 1A). Of course, party elites certainly did not forget Adams's refusal to endorse Workman, and some blamed him for the loss in November. In fact, when Adams went around looking for support for his candidacy, he found that some who had supported him two years earlier were now very cold toward him. Early in 1988, Adams met with a big Baptist minister from Greenville, and the conversation went something like this:

Pastor: "Well. Ted, if you lose this time, are you going to shoot yourself in the foot again?"

Table 5.4. GOP U.S. House primary results in 1988

Candidate	District-wide	City of Greenville	Greenville County[a]	Spartanburg and Union Counties	Bob Jones Precincts[b]
White	57.3	66.4	53.3	56.6	57.3
Adams	42.7	33.6	46.7	43.4	42.7

Note: Numbers are percentages, and the data comes from the *Greenville News*.

[a] Not including the city.

[b] Residents of the Bob Jones University campus (which includes the homes and apartments for many of the faculty and staff).

Ted Adams: "Pastor, do you mean by not supporting the winner?"
Pastor: "Exactly."
Ted Adams: "Well, let me ask you this. Do you believe in telling the truth?"
Pastor: "Yes."
Ted Adams: "Well, I do too. Why would you support a candidate who would not tell the truth? That's what you asked me to do by supporting Workman. And now you want to do it again. Where are your principles?" (Adams, interview with author)

Adams was infuriated by this exchange, and it was a good indication of how the establishment viewed him. He was seen as not viable, in other words, unelectable. And many who might have been inclined to support Ted Adams based on the issues moved toward the candidate who had the best opportunity to win in November. Even the ultraconservative Bob Jones community abandoned Adams in favor of Knox White, who had worked hard to build relationships with the BJU folks while serving on the city council. The personal relationships White cultivated bore fruit on Election Day when he rather handily defeated Adams 57 percent to 43 percent. Interestingly, White's tally in the Bob Jones precincts mirrored the district-wide results, suggesting that personal contacts and viability trumped ideology and religious belief in the 1988 primary.[12] Table 5.4 presents the results in what should now be a familiar form.

There would be no runoff in 1988, and the primary itself was not nearly as nasty and divisive as the battle two years earlier. The most telling indication of the campaign's tenor was provided by Ted Adams—not exactly a team player. The former airline pilot endorsed Knox White in the days following the primary election. Adams was not attempting to curry favor with party elites; he simply felt that White had run a clean, honest campaign and did not "lie like Workman" or "pull up his signs" (Adams, interview with author; Bandy 1988b, 7C; Hoover 1988b, 1A).

Before moving on to the general election campaign and White's attempts to regain the Fourth District's seat for the Republican Party, it is worth closing the book on Ted Adams's career in two-party politics. Once again, his story is paradigmatic for how the major parties deal with candidates who are in some sense "too principled." Despite his endorsement of Knox White, Adams "was through with the Republican Party, and they were through with me" (Adams, interview with author). He would later join up with Howard Phillips in his Taxpayers' Party, which then morphed into the present-day Constitution Party. Adams had several bright young Christian politicos working for him in 1986 who abandoned him in 1988. He recalls that the really smart ones were hired away by the GOP. They were young and idealistic but became "neutralized" by the Republicans. They were pressured by Republican politicians, as well as by their own families, to leave the Adams campaign and join up with the party. "They became pragmatic," says Adams. According to Adams, he was sabotaged between 1986 and 1988, and lacked the money and support of the party insiders. The business crowd was with White, and they never would have supported Adams. Adams was stunned in 1988 that even members of his own church had supported White from the beginning (Adams, interview with author).

The qualitative difference between the 1986 and 1988 Republican nominating campaigns should have augured well for Knox White in his campaign against Liz Patterson. He still might have to overcome the city-county rivalry, but to the extent it was driven in 1986 by Adams's disgruntled supporters, he at least would not have to deal with that discord as he embarked on his journey to defeat the first-term incumbent.

Whereas the primary election differed considerably from 1986, the 1988 general election campaign was fought on similar issues as two years earlier. I had a lengthy discussion with Knox White in the mayor's office about the campaign against Patterson.[13] He outlined the campaign's emphasis on painting the incumbent as a big-spending, big-taxing liberal. White tried to pick apart some of Patterson's spending votes in particular. His campaign focused on internal spending items and argued that the Democrats, having been entrenched in power for so long, were taking advantage of the system and spending too much of the taxpayers' money. As far as moral issues were concerned, White had the following to say: "She was all over the board on abortion. But that didn't—really and truly—those were not the main issues that year. The main issues were economic and spending—some foreign policy issues" (interview with author). Late in the race, White ran several "Lefty Liz" television advertisements. One spot featured Patterson and Michael Dukakis, the Democratic presidential candidate, looking at each other while an announcer claimed the two were together on prison furloughs (a not-so-thinly veiled reference to Willie Horton, the subject of a controversial ad in the presidential race that year), high taxes, and support for organized labor. Patterson struggled to avoid too close an association with the more liberal national ticket. However, the problem for White and to some extent Workman before him was that Patterson was simply not a tax-and-spend liberal. She received passing grades from both the AFL-CIO and the U.S. Chamber of Commerce. In general, she did a very nice job during her first term of walking the fine line between satisfying her naturally liberal Democratic supporters and the Republicans and swing voters who found themselves on the conservative half of the ideological spectrum. She sided with Reagan on budget, tax, and defense issues and still managed to appease some of her more liberal friends with a vote or two (Bandy 1988c, 4B; Bandy 1988d, 1D).[14]

The 1988 race seemed to center on Patterson's ability to disassociate herself from the national party and the liberal presidential ticket. She was a delegate to the convention in Atlanta but only decided to go for one day when it became clear Dukakis would be the nominee.[15] Ron Romine admitted that Dukakis was a big problem for her. "She had to assure people she was still a good conservative" (Romine, interview with author). When the votes were counted, it was clear Patterson managed to pull off this feat.

Notably, the moral issue dimension was not pushed by White and his campaign. Only during the primary election, mostly driven by Ted Adams, were such issues as abortion and Patterson's views on them discussed. White was well positioned during the primary as a respectable moderate conservative on those issues, in the Carroll Campbell mold. During the general election, he neither had the disposition nor the pedigree to broach those issues in a way that might have pumped up his vote totals, especially in the areas outside of Greenville's city limits. This failure of Republican candidates to exploit the cultural liberalism of Democratic incumbents in the 1980s was also evident in Kansas's Fourth District (see Chapter 4).

Table 5.5. U.S. House general election results in 1988

Candidate	District-wide	City of Greenville	Greenville County[a]	Spartanburg and Union Counties	Bob Jones Precincts[b]
Patterson	**52.2**	49.8	45.1	**59.9**	21.2
White	47.8	**50.2**	**54.9**	40.1	**78.8**

Note: Numbers are percentages, and the data comes from the *Greenville News*.

[a] Not including the city.

[b] Residents of the Bob Jones University campus (which includes the homes and apartments for many of the faculty and staff).

Patterson defeated White by staying close in Greenville County and crushing him in her home county of Spartanburg and the mostly Democratic Union County. Table 5.5 shows the voting breakdown in this election. Moral issues, either White's conservative views on them or Patterson's liberal views, were simply not a big part of the campaign. White put forth an enormous effort, with lots of money coming from the national party, to brand Patterson as a liberal on crime and economic issues. It simply failed to work because the incumbent countered with a conservative enough record and the endorsements of the National Rifle Association and the American Medical Association (Bandy 1988e, 4B).[16]

After Two Tough Battles, a Respite for Patterson

In the aftermath of a hard-fought campaign in 1988, both parties agreed that Patterson could hold the seat as long as she wanted (Bandy 1988f, 1C). Patterson's perceived security made it extremely difficult for Republican candidates to gain support for a bid in 1990. David Thomas, a state senator from Greenville and a favorite of the fundamentalist crowd, got no early traction and had to withdraw before the primary owing to a lack of support. He failed to raise the sums of money necessary to challenge an incumbent. Republicans attributed his lack of fundraising success to the illness of Lee Atwater, while local Democrats blamed his association with the "Far Right" (Bandy 1990a, 4D). Thomas's withdrawal left the Republicans scrambling for a candidate, and a state representative named Terry Haskins stepped up to take the nomination. Haskins had graduated from Bob Jones and was well known for his conservative stances on religion and politics. Haskins's late start meant he was under severe pressure to put an organization together and raise money very quickly. Meanwhile, Liz Patterson was continuing to present herself as a moderate to her constituents. She was distressed when Molly Yard, the president of the National Organization for Women, showed up at a Patterson fundraiser. Congresswoman Patterson introduced all the dignitaries at the luncheon except Yard. A Patterson aide commented to the *Columbia State*, "The last thing we need in our conservative district is for voters to think Liz and Molly are old bosom buddies" (Warthen 1990, 4D).

Local politicos believed Haskins faced two problems in trying to upset a two-term incumbent. First, he started late and was therefore swimming upstream when it came to countering the built-in advantages of incumbency. Second, he had to convince business Republicans and old-line GOP conservatives that he was not a right-wing ideologue. He did not overcome either pitfall. Patterson spent three times as much as Terry Haskins, who raised just under $150,000. Contrast that figure with the war chests of White and Workman, who each collected over $630,000. There is little doubt that Haskins's difficulties raising money were related to his difficulty appealing to the business community—the so-called downtown crowd. In recent elections, religious conservatives provided the foot soldiers, and the downtown business interests provided the money. Predictably, the Bob Jones graduate and stalwart pro-life legislator had the volunteers but lacked the money.

The rift between religious conservatives and country-club Republicans once again played a role in 1990 and led to Patterson's easy victory in November. Haskins's campaign manager, Randy Mashburn, admitted as much in the days after the votes were counted. "The animosity was much deeper than I realized, and we're still paying the price. . . . Liz Patterson never won this seat. We have given it to her. Until the Republican Party mends its fences and gets out of its circular firing squad, it is going to be very difficult for us to win this seat" (Bandy 1990b, 4D).

In addition to the internal battles occurring in the Republican Party, Liz Patterson was now a three-term incumbent and steadily moving up in seniority. Republicans publicly feared she was entrenched. David Thomas remarked to Romine after 1990 that "you can't beat an incumbent" (Romine, interview with author). Patterson was also becoming quite popular in the Fourth. People enjoyed her personality and did not consider her issue positions out of line with district opinion. On economic issues, such as taxes and spending, they were correct. Patterson was far from a tax-and-spend liberal like many of her fellow Democrats. In fact, she routinely earned voting scores from business groups that were as high as those she received from organized labor. In addition, Patterson spent much of her congressional career on efforts to reduce the deficit and reform the budgetary process (Patterson, interview with author). On these issues, she was moderate to conservative and did indeed mirror constituent opinion. According to Ron Romine, the Democratic caucus wanted to kick her out because she was too conservative.

Despite her moderate reputation on economic issues, Patterson was anything but conservative on moral issues. While she attempted to hedge somewhat on the abortion issue, she was certainly seen as pro-choice. Her electoral successes in the Republican Fourth District stemmed mainly from her ability to appear conservative enough for the district. Her voting record on economic issues made this possible, but the job was made easier by her first two opponents, who both emphasized those subjects. Abortion and other moral issues played some role in 1990, but the Republicans were divided and the candidate was seen as too weak to be a legitimate threat to the incumbent. However, in the tight elections of 1986 and 1988, moral issues did not play a big enough role to showcase Patterson's liberal tendencies. This enabled her to win the election and then get reelected two more times. After the rout in 1990, many local observers on both sides of the partisan divide believed Liz Patterson would gain reelection for as long as she wanted. For this reason, nobody with any political stature sought the nomination in 1992. The formidable challenge of unseating Patterson fell to an unknown lawyer with no political experience and very little seed money.

A Virtual Unknown Makes It to Congress

Bob Inglis started his campaign with hardly any money but with a small, dedicated cadre of advisers. Inglis began by going door-to-door, introducing himself to voters in his home county of Greenville. In the beginning, it was the candidate and a group of close friends who formed the nucleus of his campaign operation. His people were mostly unknown campaign operatives with little experience in local politics. They would meet in his kitchen and thus were known as his "kitchen cabinet." His campaign manager was Jim DeMint who would go on to succeed Inglis in 1998 and ascend to national renown as a U.S. senator.

Before he could get a crack at Patterson in 1992, Inglis had to win his party's primary in August. Owing to Patterson's seeming invulnerability, Inglis's two opponents in the primary were even less known than he was. One was a libertarian and the other a party outsider. As we have seen, Republican primaries in the Fourth District can be brutal. In 1992, however, Inglis stood out as the Republican establishment's choice. Once again, a Republican congressional candidate claimed he could unite religious conservatives and business Republicans. Apparently, the money men believed him because Inglis far outspent his rivals in the primary campaign and defeated his competitors handily, garnering 71 percent of the vote (Fretwell 1992a, 1B; 1992b, 11A).

Emerging from the primary, Inglis had a distinct advantage relative to earlier challengers to Liz Patterson. Over 70 percent of Republicans had already cast their ballots for him. Bill Workman received only 49 percent and then 55 percent in the runoff, while Knox White garnered 57 percent of the vote against Ted Adams in 1988. In addition, there was no divisiveness that resulted from the nominating campaign. It was a relatively low-key battle that left Inglis without any battle scars.

During the two-month general election campaign, the candidates participated in several forums and debates. In early October, the conventional wisdom was that Patterson's moderate-to-conservative record, her strong constituent service, and her Spartanburg roots would carry her to another victory in November. There was some measure of surprise that Inglis was making his presence felt in the race despite no national GOP backing. Like Tiahrt two years later, Inglis could not get the national Republican Party to focus on a race that seemed from Washington to be unwinnable. Inglis was focusing on term limits and campaign finance reform (Fretwell 1992c, 3B).

Inglis's and Patterson's issue positions did not differ much, with the exception of their stance on abortion, and according to Romine, the Republicans went after Patterson on this issue. In the past, Republicans had challenged Patterson on fiscal issues. They claimed she was a typical tax-and-spend liberal. These attacks in 1986 and 1988 did not work because the Republicans could not point to enough of Patterson's votes to make the charges stick. Patterson was clearly not a tax-and-spend liberal. She was middle-of-the-road on economic issues and certainly to the right of the Democratic median. Abortion, however, was an issue on which she was vulnerable to the liberal charge. Patterson was 100 percent pro-choice, and Inglis felt abortion should only be legal in the cases of rape, incest, or endangerment of the mother's health. On the social issues, Patterson knew she was vulnerable to being portrayed as too far to the left. She tried to hedge on abortion, which only frustrated her liberal backers and certainly did not dissuade conservatives from believing she was anything but solidly pro-choice. She voted against family leave late in 1992, which infuriated many liberal women who had been longtime supporters. Romine believes those women were considerably less helpful in 1992 than they had been in elections past. So once again, Patterson was caught between a liberal national party and a very conservative constituency. She had walked the tightrope successfully in the past, but there was a possibility she might fall off in 1992.

In mid-October, Inglis finally received some money from the Republican National Committee. The check for $30,000 went straight into television advertising, and the Inglis campaign was at long last on the air. As the election drew nearer, Patterson still maintained a commanding lead in the polls. Both Democratic and newspaper polls showed the incumbent ahead by double digits going into the final week. On the final weekend of the campaign, more national assistance was provided for Inglis. This time, however, it was not from the RNC, and it did not come in the form of cash. The Christian Coalition dropped 200,000 voter guides into the district on the Sunday before the election. These pieces of literature were primarily distributed in Fourth District churches as part of a nationwide strategy to increase the turnout of pro-family voters. Ralph Reed and his organization did not just want these voters to go to the polls; they wanted them to be educated as to which candidates would further their particular interests if elected. Voter guides generally highlight the issue positions of the candidates contesting a particular race. Most often, the two candidates are placed side-by-side, and their respective policy prescriptions appear directly next to each other. In the case of the Christian Coalition's voter guides, the major issues were religious and moral in nature. The big one was abortion. According to the Christian Coalition's voter guides, Inglis supported abortion only in the "hard" cases (rape, incest, and to preserve the health of the mother). Patterson was listed as supporting abortion on demand. In addition to the differing issue positions of the candidates, these voter guides showcased photos of each candidate. As one might imagine, Patterson's picture was very dark looking and quite grainy. Inglis's was much clearer, and if one looked closely enough, one might have been able to make out a faint halo hovering over his head.[17]

The timing and magnitude of this activity was devastating to the Patterson campaign. There was no time to react to the onslaught and combat the supposed distortions. Not only were these voter guides important in mobilizing conservative Christians; they also helped to shift the basis on which the decision would be made. By highlighting such moral issues as abortion, school prayer, and contraception, these voter guides placed Patterson on the defensive on precisely the issues on which she was most vulnerable. Just as significantly, they brought those issue positions to the direct attention of the voters who would be most likely to disagree with her.

The extent of the damage would not be known until after the votes were tallied. Even on election night, Liz Patterson was confident of victory. Early evening news footage from the Patterson campaign's party showed the candidate smiling and dancing with supporters. By 10:00 p.m., however, the mood was significantly darker. The candidate looked nervous, and the numbers coming in were not easing her tension. The double-digit lead that Patterson had enjoyed just a week earlier had disappeared completely, and the race appeared to be very close. In the end, Bob Inglis had stunned the incumbent with 51 percent to 49 percent and regained the Fourth District's congressional seat for Greenville and for the Republican Party.

The Fourth was finally back in Republican hands, and the Christian right could claim a lot of the credit. All observers of this race that I interviewed credited the Christian Coalition with helping Bob Inglis to victory. The amount of credit assigned varied, but the work done by Reed and Robertson's group was mentioned by everybody as one of the reasons Inglis was successful in his upset bid. In his postelection analysis, Lee Bandy of the *Columbia State* offered the following insights into Inglis's surprising victory. He wrote that the religious right, traditional upstate Republicans, and President Bush's coattails combined to upset incumbent congresswoman Liz Patterson. "Credit has to be given to the mobilization of the religious right and the tradition of voting Republican up here. On Sunday before the election, the Christian Coalition distributed more than 200,000 voter guides to six hundred churches in the four-county district. The flier spelled out the positions of Patterson and Inglis on such hot-button issues as abortion, taxes, school prayers, and condom distribution in the schools" (Bandy 1992, 1A).

Years later, Lee Bandy recalled that the Christian Coalition did a lot to turn its people out in 1992. He remembers family issues mattering and Inglis being a pro-family candidate (Bandy, interview with author).

Another reporter also emphasized the role of religious conservatives, especially the Christian Coalition. "South Carolina's fourth in 1992 is an excellent example of the Christian right helping the Republican Party win a congressional seat that they might not have been able to win otherwise." He went on to speak of the thousands of pieces that went out the Sunday before the election. "In churches that allowed it, they would hand them out after services. In others, they would put the guides on a table. It had to be a major factor" (anonymous source, interview with author). Ron Romine, who had worked for Patterson's initial congressional campaign in 1986, elaborated on the effectiveness of the Christian Coalition's voter guides. "The fourth was a big target for direct mail through the churches—all across the district the Sunday before the election. She had a comfortable lead a week before the election, according to her polls. There was lots of movement that last weekend" (Romine, interview with author).

The voter guides helped mobilize religious conservatives to vote for Bob Inglis. They also highlighted the differences between the two candidates on moral issues. In addition, Inglis counted on evangelical parishioners to help him conduct a grassroots campaign that did not even run a television commercial until mid-October when national money finally began coming in. At this point, the reader should consider that the Christian Coalition did not participate until the weekend before the election, and the reason they did so was because they thought it would make a difference. Inglis's homegrown, grassroots campaign narrowed the gap sufficiently so as to alert Chesapeake, Virginia (the home of the Christian Coalition), that the voter guides might put the moral conservative over the top.

This type of grassroots campaign allowed Inglis to fly under the radar, and for that reason, he was taken very lightly by Patterson. Many of Patterson's campaign workers were helping Senator Fritz Hollings with his difficult reelection campaign, and Patterson did not spend the money that she had allotted for previous races. After 1990, it looked as if she had locked up the seat, and many observers believe she took it too easy in 1992. In the end, it ended up costing her dearly.[18] The notion that Patterson took Inglis for granted can also be linked to the Christian right, in particular the Christian Coalition. The infamous "stealth campaign" was an important strategy designed by Ralph Reed to help coalition-backed candidates win office. The idea was that if you can get your message to your followers through the churches and not the media, you would be able to turn them out without antagonizing the opposition. Inglis was able to do just that, and it was especially useful in relation to his moral conservatism.[19] Bob Taylor of BJU recognized the fruitfulness of this strategy. "[Inglis's] pro-life credentials were so solid that he didn't have to talk about it during the general election. ... Some who might have been alienated by a strong pro-life message never got that message from the media" (Taylor, interview with author). Most political watchers admit that they were taken by surprise by the stealth campaign and agreed that Inglis's backing from the Christian Coalition was very much under the radar. The timing of these voter guides, the Sunday before the election, took the Patterson campaign by surprise and helped turn a double-digit deficit in the polls into a two-point victory for Bob Inglis.[20]

Bob Inglis defeated Liz Patterson by just less than 5,700 votes. Considering that 200,000 voter guides were distributed in the churches on the Sunday before the election, it is likely that this grassroots effort provided Inglis with his margin of victory. If only one out of every thirty-five of those voter guides convinced someone who would otherwise not have voted to cast their ballot for Bob Inglis, then the grassroots blitz forty-eight hours before Election Day can be said to have delivered the election to Inglis and the Republicans. If only one out of seventy of those voter guides persuaded a Patterson voter to change their vote, that would also account for the margin of victory. Based on the numbers, it is not unreasonable to argue that these voter guides could easily have pushed Inglis over the top and sent him to Washington.

Knox White believed that the Christian Coalition might have boosted the electorate and turnout in the fundamentalist precincts—especially in Spartanburg County. "Bob [Inglis] had strong support from the Christian Coalition types to the extent they were here. ... First time for scorecards and they were out there for Inglis" (White, interview with author). As Mayor White recalled the influx of voter guides persuading voters to choose Inglis, one would not be surprised if he was feeling a bit wistful about the effect those pieces of literature might have had on his behalf four years earlier. White lost by only 7,441 votes. Even if he had been the beneficiary of only one-fourth of the 1992 effort, chances are he might have gathered the necessary extra votes to oust Liz Patterson in 1988.

As for the city-county rivalry, Inglis got around that by not having any real connection to the downtown community. However, he was able to get their support once the campaign got under way. His reputation as a religious conservative was unquestioned by his supporters, even though he did

Table 5.6. U.S. House general election results in 1992

Candidate	District-wide	City of Greenville	Greenville County[a]	Spartanburg, Union, and Laurens Counties	Bob Jones Precincts[b]
Inglis	**51.5**	**52.8**	**59.6**	42.2	**81.3**
Patterson	48.5	47.2	40.4	**57.8**	18.7

Note: Numbers are percentages, and the data comes from the *Greenville News.*

[a] Not including the city.

[b] Residents of the Bob Jones University campus (which includes the homes and apartments for many of the faculty and staff).

not emphasize that spirituality publicly. According to my anonymous source at the *Greenville News,* "He came across as a good family guy. Doesn't cuss, hardly drinks, tight with a dollar. His image dovetailed nicely with the religious right, even though he didn't wear his religion on his sleeve." That lack of in-your-face piousness no doubt appealed to business Republicans who had in the past been wary of supporting candidates connected overtly with the Christian right. Table 5.6 presents the election results for 1992. The patterns shown in the 1986 and 1988 general elections hold here. The Republican candidates won the city of Greenville by a smaller margin than they did the county. Patterson won easily in the other counties, and the Bob Jones precincts gave a large majority of their votes to the Republican. However, with the exception of Workman's strong showing in the city, Inglis did better across the board than the two city candidates. Table 5.7 allows for a closer comparison. This improvement made the difference between victory and defeat for the GOP.

An Important Reason Among Several

By no means were religious conservatives and their emphasis on moral issues the only reasons the Republican Party took hold of the Fourth District after three consecutive defeats. The anti-incumbency winds were blowing strong in 1992, and Inglis attempted to link Patterson to the House check scandal. The Republicans alleged Patterson's husband bounced a check, and that was enough to tie her to the more serious wrongdoing undertaken by some of her congressional colleagues. Inglis also ran on a

Table 5.7. Republican candidates running against Liz Patterson

Candidate	District-wide	City of Greenville	Greenville County[a]	Other Counties	Bob Jones Precincts[b]
Bob Inglis (1992)	**51.5**	52.8	**59.6**	**42.2**	**81.3**
Knox White (1988)	47.9	50.2	54.9	40.1	78.8
Bill Workman (1986)	47.9	**54.3**	54.8	38.9	81.3

Note: Numbers are percentages, and the data comes from the *Greenville News*.

[a] Not including the city.

[b] Residents of the Bob Jones University campus (which includes the homes and apartments for many of the faculty and staff).

term-limits platform, which galvanized many voters in 1992. During the campaign, he limited himself to six years in office. Finally, Patterson had the unenviable task in 1992 of running on the Clinton-Gore ticket in South Carolina. Despite her continued efforts to fashion sufficient distance between her and the national Democrats, having Clinton on the ballot had to damage her electoral chances. The Friday before the election, President Bush came to Spartanburg to campaign for Bob Inglis. Of course, Bush did outstandingly well in the Fourth District, carrying it 54 percent to 33 percent over Bill Clinton, and Patterson believes the presidential visit was an important reason for her defeat (Patterson, interview with author). Clinton was seen as the devil incarnate by many Fourth District voters. Ron Romine observed that area Democrats always have a harder time in presidential years when they have to carry the burden of a national ticket (interview with author).

So the Fourth District returned to the Republican column after a three-term departure. There were many reasons why Liz Patterson could not continue to defend her tenuous hold on that congressional seat. The check scandal, anti-incumbency, the Republican advantage in the district, Clinton, complacency, and the Christian right all combined to oust her from office. It appears from my interviews and archival research that all of these reasons were necessary and most likely none were sufficient alone. In such a close race, removing one or two of these elements probably would have allowed Patterson to remain in Congress for one more term. With the national trends breaking the way they did in 1994, it is extremely difficult to imagine Patterson holding off her next challenger. It is entirely possible she might have followed other endangered Democrats and retired rather than face the unenviable challenge of holding onto a conservative Southern district in the Republican year of 1994.

Catching Up with Fourth District Politics

Over the next two elections, Bob Inglis went on to solidify the Republicans' hold on the Fourth District. He fulfilled his pledge to leave office after three terms and was replaced by Jim DeMint in 1998. DeMint was one of the small group of advisers that helped Inglis win in 1992 and was a candidate cut from the Inglis mold. He was relatively inexperienced in politics and relatively unknown to most voters. He was respected by religious conservatives but did not go out of his way to trumpet his moral conservatism. In the Republican primary runoff, DeMint defeated a popular state senator named Mike Fair. Fair had the fervent support of many religious conservatives, including Bob Taylor of Bob Jones University. Fair won the original primary but was defeated by DeMint in the runoff when Fair's supporters failed to turn out in the numbers they did in the original contest. DeMint won easily in November and was barely challenged over the next two elections. In 2004, he left the House and defeated Inez Tenenbaum in a race for Fritz Hollings's U.S. Senate seat. After Patterson's defeat, the closest a Democrat came to winning back the seat was a 58 percent to 42 percent loss in the 1998 open seat contest with Jim DeMint. The Fourth District is solidly Republican from top to bottom now, and it is one of the congressional seats that Republicans do not have to worry about defending. It is also one of the at-risk seats wrested from the Democrats in the early 1990s that was vital to them gaining control of the House after forty years in the minority.

Interestingly enough, DeMint's successor in 2004 was also his predecessor, Bob Inglis. Proving that there are second acts in politics, Inglis returned to the House, although he had moderated during his time out of politics. He described himself as much more pragmatic and willing to see the other side of certain issues. In the ultraconservative Fourth District, this did not hurt him, at least not right away. Inglis won the open seat in 2004 and this time did not pledge to limit his service to three terms. However, a hard-charging conservative U.S. attorney from Greenville did, in fact, limit Inglis once again to six years of service. Trey Gowdy challenged Inglis in the Tea Party year of 2010, claiming correctly that Inglis had tacked to the left on a number of issues. Gowdy did not run with overt Tea Party support but certainly benefited from being an outsider in 2010. He came in first in the primary with 39 percent to Inglis's 27 percent and soundly defeated the incumbent in the runoff, 71 percent to 29 percent. Gowdy breezed to victory in the general election and would go on to become a thorn in the Obama administration's side as he publicly called for Attorney General Eric Holder's resignation after the controversial "Operation Fast and Furious" gun-tracking program came to light. Like Pompeo in Kansas's Fourth, Gowdy did not stress social conservatism to gain entry into the U.S. House, but he also voted to defund Planned Parenthood in 2011 and received a 78 percent rating from the Family Research Council during his first term (Barone and McCutcheon 2013, 1493).

Gowdy played an important role in the 2016 presidential election as he was the personification of the Republican obsession with Benghazi and Hillary Clinton's alleged role in the tragedy. Gowdy conducted hours and hours of hearings on this explosive issue but could not come up with any firm charges against Secretary Clinton. Gowdy remained very popular at home, winning reelection easily in 2016 and once again finding the spotlight during the very public and very controversial inquiry into possible Russian collusion with the Trump campaign. Gowdy likely would have had this seat for as long as he wanted it as South Carolina's Fourth is among the most Republican in the nation, but alas, he did not want it anymore. On January 31, 2018, he announced that he would be leaving politics at the end of his current term. Despite the retirement, this seat stayed in Republican hands after the 2018 midterm election.

Chapter 6

Overcoming the Past

A Neighborly Battle for the U.S. Congress

The two main challengers for the 1994 Republican congressional nomination in Tennessee's Third District grew up as next-door neighbors in Chattanooga. They both went to the same Lutheran church. Although they were a few years apart, both were raised in the same neighborhood—in the same environment. Both had a strong Christian faith and were heavily involved in civic groups and activities. Both belonged to the Chattanooga Jaycees and joined the Young Republicans during the 1980s. However, by 1993, when they both officially announced their candidacies for the Republican nomination, they had vastly different resumes.

One candidate became a member of the Tennessee state house in 1991 after defeating an eighteen-year Democratic incumbent. He quickly distinguished himself in Nashville with his aggressiveness and legislative acumen. In 1992, the Democratic-led legislature redistricted him in with a twenty-four-year Republican incumbent. He shocked everyone by defeating his more senior challenger and easily rode to victory in the general election. When this candidate made the race in 1994, he could already boast of several stunning electoral victories and significant legislative experience in his short career. One might say he was the total embodiment of Gary Jacobson's challenger quality variable (Jacobson 2001, 174).

His childhood friend and neighbor was a college dropout and had never held public office. The extent of his political career was a brief stint as Hamilton County Republican Party chair. In addition, as a young adult, he developed a drug habit and had a few run-ins with the law. These indiscretions were made public two years earlier when he first ran for Congress. By any objective standards, his qualifications for office paled in comparison to his opponent.

Not surprisingly, the primary election was no contest. The Republican nominee defeated his childhood neighbor by a six-to-one margin. He outspent him, outcampaigned him, and was able to gain the widespread support of party activists. The only surprise was the identity of the winner. It was not the two-term incumbent from the state legislature. Indeed, it was the candidate with the checkered past and thin political resume. Here was a case where the less experienced candidate easily defeated a much more qualified rival. Furthermore, he went on to defeat his Democratic opponent in November and seize an at-risk district for the Republican Party in 1994.

Zach Wamp defeated Ken Meyer in the 1994 primary because he had the full support of party activists and the backing of an increasingly powerful bloc of religious conservatives. These two Republican Party factions united behind Wamp and helped him defeat a far more qualified challenger in the Republican primary. With their continued support, he was able to capture a congressional seat that the GOP had not held since 1974.[1] The former group consisted of the richest and best-connected members of the local community. They were led by men who had helped build the Republican Party in Southeast Tennessee during the 1960s and 1970s. In past chapters, I have referred to these types of Republicans as business, or Chamber of Commerce Republicans. In Hamilton County, this faction did not always operate within the formal party structure, but by recruiting candidates and controlling nominations, they were extremely influential in local Republican politics. The latter group consisted of individuals who were very religious and relatively new to politics. They first got involved in local politics during the 1980s but met tremendous resistance. They came from different backgrounds than the old-guard, business Republicans, and their fervent emphasis on moral issues did not mesh well with a group that was more concerned with economic issues. By the early 1990s, however, these socalled Christian Republicans had gained in numbers, toned down their rhetoric, and became much more sophisticated in their political activism. The group developed into a powerful player in Third District politics and had a tremendous influence on the outcome of the 1994 congressional campaign.

That contest highlights the electoral importance of local political and economic elites, as well as the incredible clout wielded by a tightly organized and highly intense group of Christian right Republicans. It produced yet another Republican conquest of an at-risk district formerly held by Democrats and was one of many seats that swung to the GOP during the midterm election of 1994. For that reason, it is the centerpiece of my third case study. However, before getting to the details of that race, I will trace the development of both the business and Christian Republicans in Tennessee's Third District and examine the impact of the two groups on past congressional elections.

Building the Republican Party in Southeast Tennessee

In the decades following Reconstruction, the Republican Party was nonexistent throughout most of the South. Tennessee Republicanism was centered in the eastern third of the state. These were "mountain" Republicans who did not own slaves and did not want to secede. East Tennesseans voted in 1860 to stay in the Union, while Middle and West Tennessee voted to secede. The state as a whole was strongly Democratic during the Jim Crow period, but the first two congressional districts (both in Northeast Tennessee) had always been solidly Republican. The Second District is the longest consecutively held U.S. House district in the country. Centered in Knoxville, current congressman John Duncan Jr. is the latest in a long line of Republicans to represent this area.[2]

Of course, the face of Southern politics changed dramatically during the 1960s. The civil rights revolution began to make Republicans out of many of the state's traditional Democrats. These were people who, before this new era, were much more concerned about the Tennessee Valley Authority and the price of farm commodities than about race. As a consequence of the increased salience of racial concerns, normal Democratic majorities were cut statewide. Lyndon Johnson won only 55 percent against Barry Goldwater in 1964 (Barone and Ujifusa 1973, 756). And in the Third District, a young Republican named Bill Brock easily won reelection after winning the seat against a moderate-to-liberal Democrat two years earlier.

The Third District is centered on Hamilton County, which contains roughly half of the district's population. Chattanooga, along the Georgia border in the southeastern corner of the state, is the major urban center in Hamilton County and had always been less Republican than the rest of East Tennessee (Barone and Ujifusa 1973, 755). Bill Brock's family ran a very successful candy business in the Chattanooga area, and the candidate was able to raise sufficient funds for his first congressional run in 1962.

In addition, according to a political science professor at the University of Tennessee, Chattanooga, Brock benefited from the defection of large numbers of conservative Democrats who were unhappy that year with their party's nominee. Brock held the Third District seat for four terms before going on to the U.S. Senate after defeating the incumbent, Al Gore Sr., in a bitter race in 1970. Brock would lose six years later to Jim Sasser, but his and his family's imprint on Tennessee politics would resonate far beyond his fourteen years as an elected official. In the wake of his rise to power emerged a vibrant, well-organized Republican Party that changed the region's political landscape. For this reason, it is worth examining that rise to power and its consequences.

According to the same university professor, Bill Brock was instrumental in building the Republican Party in the Third District and the "modern" Republican Party across the state. Brock was part of the Goldwater movement and one of the new, aggressive, small-business type of Republicans. Brock was extremely conservative on fiscal matters and a terrific organizer. Along with his brother Pat, Bill Brock organized Hamilton County at the grassroots level. They realized races were won block by block and precinct by precinct. Tom Griscom, a former staffer to Senator Howard Baker, credits the Brocks for reviving the Republican Party in the area and drastically diminishing the historical advantage held by the Democrats. Before the organizational efforts of the Brocks, a candidate could win just because he was a Democrat. Before the Brocks, there really was no Republican Party in Hamilton County (Griscom, interview with author).

While Bill Brock was the successful candidate, his brother Pat was an excellent strategist. Pat Brock focused heavily on grassroots organization and party building. For the man behind the scenes, it was all about turnout—targeting friendly voters and getting them out to vote. The Brock organization worked extremely hard at the more mundane aspects of politics in an effort to vault the Republican Party into a position of prominence. During Bill Brock's four terms in the U.S. House, the organizational efforts in the Third Congressional District intensified and expanded, eventually spawning a statewide Republican network. Brock used this network in his senatorial race against Al Gore Sr. in 1970. Brock did a masterful job of linking Gore to Washington elitism, charging that he was out of touch with the concerns of everyday voters back in Tennessee. During that election cycle, LaMar Baker, a rather uncharismatic candidate who owned a janitorial service, won the vacated Third District congressional seat. Baker was very conservative and benefited from the Brock organization. Other well-known Tennessee Republicans did as well. Howard Baker first was elected to the U.S. Senate in 1966 with the help of the Brock organization, and future governor Don Sundquist was one of the early Brock people (Griscom, interview with author).

Ideologically, Brock Republicans were quite conservative. Other prominent Tennessee politicians, such as Howard Baker and Lamar Alexander, were seen as a bit more moderate. However, social issues were never that important to Bill Brock and his supporters. Such issues as abortion, school prayer, and gay rights had not yet assumed their central role in the political debate. When the Brocks built the party, religious conservatives were not active in Republican politics. The local Republican Party during the 1960s, 1970s, and early 1980s was dominated by businessmen—some corporate types, others small-business owners—who mostly concerned themselves with economic issues. There were some party leaders who did not come from the corporate world. Ken Meyer recalls a school principal who was a friend of Howard Baker becoming very active in the party. However, according to Meyer, most of the movers and shakers in the Republican Party came from the business world. They had strong educational backgrounds in free-market economic principles and became involved in party politics through such organizations as the Chattanooga Jaycees, the Chamber of Commerce, and local chapters of the Young Republicans (Meyer, interview with author).[3]

Like Goldwater, Brock and his fellow business Republicans would not identify with the religiously conservative wing that currently wields such tremendous power within the Republican Party. This fact is of great importance considering Pat Brock remained an extremely important figure in Hamilton County politics. Still operating behind the scenes for the most part, Brock and his followers exerted considerable influence on Republican activity in the area all through the period of study.[4]

Watergate Takes Its Toll on the Third District

While Bill Brock was winning election to the U.S. Senate, LaMar Baker kept the Third District in the Republican column by defeating a Hamilton County councilman 51 percent to 46 percent (Barone and Ujifusa 1973, 763). The Third District was the most marginal in Tennessee during this time, and Brock's handpicked successor was by no means a stellar campaigner. In fact, Baker only received 55 percent of the vote two years later, running a disappointing seventeen points behind President Richard Nixon (Barone and Ujifusa 1975, 945–46). Baker had failed to make the Third District safe, and Nixon's emerging difficulties would soon prove damaging to the Republican incumbent.

Throughout 1974, it appeared as if LaMar Baker would be challenged by a local television anchor by the name of Mort Lloyd. Lloyd was a strong candidate with good name recognition. Tragically, he died in a plane crash during the campaign, and local party leaders offered the nomination to his widow, Marilyn. It was a polite gesture that most thought would be declined by Mort Lloyd's wife. Surprisingly, she accepted and went on to capitalize on the sympathy she derived from the death of her husband as well as from the strong Democratic winds powered by the ruinous scandal in the White House. Marilyn Lloyd, listed on the ballot as Mrs. Mort Lloyd, defeated the Republican incumbent LaMar Baker 52 percent to 46 percent. The Third District would be represented by a Democrat for the first time since 1962 (Barone and Ujifusa 1977, 800).[5]

Marilyn Lloyd's victory in 1974 was a huge upset. The Associated Press did not even have a biography for her. Most observers felt that it was a fluke wholly attributable to Watergate and her husband's death. They assumed she would be a one-term congresswoman, easily defeated two years later when the scandal and plane crash receded into memory. However, Marilyn Lloyd and her staff had a different idea. They immediately worked to build a strong constituency service organization and to take advantage of Lloyd's natural strengths as a campaigner. Lloyd also did a good job of getting on committees where she could be an effective advocate for her home district. As a result, she had an extremely successful first term in Congress.

Lloyd Builds a Base and Solidifies Her Hold on the District

One of Marilyn Lloyd's legislative assistants during the early part of her congressional career explained to me the political strategy in the months after the upset victory over LaMar Baker. Lloyd's advisers looked to increase minority voting in Chattanooga and improve turnout among traditional Democrats. They also wanted to improve the candidate's standing with women, which was one of her weaknesses in 1974. To implement the strategy, the campaign opened several district offices that were led by young, politically savvy administrative assistants. Each had sizable staffs of case workers. These offices kept the congresswoman very well informed and maintained a visible presence for her while she was in Washington.

According to her legislative assistant, Lloyd exhibited a real gift for campaigning during her first term. She was a "people person" who possessed all of the attributes of an effective and successful politician. Lloyd was adept at working a room. She had a good memory for names, made good eye contact, and left everyone believing that "Marilyn was his or her best friend." Finally, Lloyd selected her first committee assignments with an eye toward helping her constituents. Her most useful committee was Public Works and Transportation. One of the key issues in the 1974 campaign was a severe flood that did significant damage to the Brainerd area of Chattanooga. Another major issue was a serious traffic choke point in Hamilton County created by the lack of adequate bridge space over the Tennessee River. Her position on Public Works enabled Lloyd to deliver badly needed, high-profile projects to deal with these two problems. The first-term Democratic incumbent procured money for the construction of the Brainerd Levee, which would prevent future flooding, and for the construction of a new six-lane bridge over the Tennessee River. Her constituents were very appreciative and many years later remembered what Marilyn Lloyd had done for the district.[6]

The strategy for increasing Marilyn Lloyd's appeal paid off dramatically in 1976. When LaMar Baker tried to recapture his old seat in the House, he could only muster 32 percent of the vote. In 1978, the Republicans did not even put up a challenger in a district that had been held by Republicans for twelve years before Lloyd's Watergate-aided win. Marilyn Lloyd received high marks during her first few terms for constituency service, campaigning skill, and committee assignments. However, she was never known as a policy expert. According to her legislative assistant, nobody really considered Lloyd an issue-oriented candidate. She had strong views but was focused more on helping the district than on learning the intricacies of a particular policy. Ideologically, Lloyd was quite conservative for a Democrat and even found herself to the right of many Republicans. This served her well as the Reagan Revolution swept the nation.

In 1980, Ronald Reagan defeated Jimmy Carter by fifteen points in the Third District, yet Lloyd's Republican opponent could only manage 39 percent of the vote. Undoubtedly, her conservative voting record appealed to a district that was steadily moving to the right. Marilyn Lloyd was pro-defense and anti–gun control, and she walked a tightrope between labor and business, managing to appease both. She was, however, more liberal than Republicans on job training, unemployment measures, and education. As for moral issues, she opposed the Equal Rights Amendment and was against abortion except in the cases of rape, incest, and to protect the life of the mother. These stances managed to placate different groups of voters and blunted Republican attempts to tie her to the liberalism of the national Democratic Party. Her challenger in 1980 ran again in 1982 and did three points worse. However, a high-profile legislative failure and the presence of an enormously popular Republican president at the top of the ticket ensured that Marilyn Lloyd would face a difficult race in 1984.

Congresswoman Lloyd's First Real Electoral Challenge

Democrats all across the country had to reckon with Ronald Reagan's coat-tails in 1984. The popular president had recovered from a difficult first two years, and it was indeed "Morning in America" to many. Southern Democrats representing conservative districts suffered the additional burden of having to distance themselves from their party's liberal standard-bearer, Walter Mondale. Mondale acknowledged that he might raise taxes if he won the presidency, and Reagan was clearly the stronger candidate on foreign affairs. Additionally, the Democratic Party was now firmly associated with the cultural and racial liberalism that emerged during the 1960s. The national picture did not bode well for Marilyn Lloyd.

But Lloyd had always counted on a high-quality constituency service operation and a knack for delivering for her home district. Unfortunately for her, as the election of 1984 approached, she showed weakness in this area as well. For years she had worked hard, with the help of Republican senator Howard Baker, to save the Clinch River breeder reactor, which was located in the northern part of the district. It was an important project for the local economy but was finally eliminated in 1983. This damaged Lloyd politically and eroded her image as a highly effective member of Congress with the power to produce for the district.

The national and local tides were working against the Democratic incumbent, which spurred a Republican businessman named John Davis to return home from Washington and run for the Third District's congressional

seat. Davis was originally from Roane County but had moved to Chattanooga. He was young and single, and had previously worked in advisory
roles for President Ford and Senator Baker. Davis was encouraged to run by
Governor Lamar Alexander, Senator Baker, and Bill Brock (Casteel 1983, C4).
Davis attacked Lloyd's lack of clout in Washington and her inability to fully
use her position to help the district maintain the Clinch River breeder reactor.
On the issues, Davis indicated he was a conservative but that he would be
somewhere to the left of Lloyd's previous Republican challenger who was
seen by many as too extreme. In a February article in the *Chattanooga Times*,
Davis described his political lineage. "There's no doubt I'm a conservative,
but the people who gave me my political education, like former President
Ford, Howard Baker, and Lamar Alexander, are pragmatic conservatives.
That's the best way to describe me" (Casteel 1984, B1).

It is pretty clear which faction of the Republican Party John Davis
emerged from. Davis was the classic 1980s business Republican who
stressed the ineffectiveness of the Democratic incumbent and focused on
economic issues at the expense of social issues such as abortion (Frank
1984, B4). Bill Workman and Knox White of Greenville, South Carolina,
come to mind. Pamela Rudd, a conservative Catholic and pro-life activist
living outside Chattanooga, was unhappy with both congressional candidates in 1984. Lloyd may have been pro-life with exceptions, but according
to Rudd, she did not care about the social issues that drove voters like
herself. And Davis was no better. "He was the classic John McCain type,
who says we have to have a strong economy, but who gives a flip what
people do with their personal lives. Their only human 'rights' issue is free
trade and a high GNP" (Pamela and Robin Rudd, interview with author).
Dave Flessner, onetime political reporter for the *Chattanooga Times-Free
Press*, agreed that Davis, despite being pro-life, had no special appeal to
religious conservatives (Flessner, interview with author).[7]

The national GOP isolated Lloyd-Davis as one of the ten most important races in the country. Senator Connie Mack from Florida and Guy
Vander Jagt, a congressman from Michigan and head of the Republican
National Congressional Committee, visited the district to campaign for the
challenger. Lloyd refused to debate and was criticized for accepting large
PAC contributions. In the end, the election turned out to be closer than
anyone expected. John Davis lost by just over 9,200 votes (Barone and
Ujifusa 1985, 1259). The Lloyd campaign did not take him seriously,
according to her legislative assistant, and underestimated the "Reagan"

effect. He recalled Davis's numbers generally tracking Reagan's except in the more liberal northern county of Anderson. It was this area of the district that narrowly maintained Lloyd's tenure. After his defeat, Davis vowed to run again. Considering his near-upset and the strong support he had from prominent Republicans within the district and across the state, he appeared to be the overwhelming favorite to gain the GOP's nomination in 1986.

The Christian Right Enters Third District Politics with a Flourish

Before 1986, religious conservatives had not gained any political traction in Hamilton County. Moral issues, such as abortion, school prayer, and the Equal Rights Amendment, played very minor roles in congressional campaigns. At the presidential level and during the 1984 senatorial race between Democrat Al Gore Jr., Republican Victor Ash, and independent candidate Ed McAteer, these issues were front and center. McAteer, formerly of Colgate-Palmolive and a cofounder of the Religious Roundtable, made moral traditionalism the centerpiece of his long-shot third-party candidacy. His campaign galvanized pro-life activists and religious conservatives across the state, but he could only muster 5 percent of the vote on Election Day. John Davis failed to tap into this intensity because he did not stress these types of issues in his congressional race with Marilyn Lloyd. As stated in the previous section, pro-life activists such as Pamela Rudd, who was part of Tennessee's state chapter of National Right to Life, were decidedly unimpressed.

Religious conservatives would not have to wait long for their champion to emerge at the congressional level. That candidate was Jim Golden, and the year was 1986. Golden was raised in Bradley County and received his bachelor's degree from Lee College, a Christian school in Cleveland, Tennessee. He went on to study law at the University of Tennessee and then joined the Christian Legal Foundation—an organization that catered to Christian clients and issues. Golden was also a member of the fundamentalist Church of God, which is headquartered in the Third District (Hanshaw 1985, A1).

Jim Golden was a relative newcomer to politics when he decided to run for the Republican congressional nomination against John Davis. In 1984, he was motivated by the abortion issue to assist Reagan's reelection campaign (Gardenhire, interview with author). Other than that bit of activism,

Golden had no real political experience and clearly was a party outsider. He was also clearly an underdog in his attempt to defeat the previous Republican nominee. "From a speakers' platform laden with Republican dignitaries, Bradley County GOP chairman John Ratcliff extolled the virtues of John Davis as a candidate for Congress in 1986 and as an opponent of Democrat Marilyn Lloyd. After Davis spoke, Ratcliff returned to the podium only to mispronounce the name of 'that other Republican running for the seat.' That other Republican, attorney Jim Golden, took the mistake in stride. He pointed out that at the same point two years earlier John Davis was not very well known either" (Hanshaw 1985, A1). Golden may not have been widely known as the campaign kicked off, but he did have a strong base of supporters in the religious community. His credibility with the religious right was enhanced significantly when Pat Robertson spoke at a fund-raiser for Golden in November 1985. Robertson opined, "[Golden's] the kind of man that would be a credit to this region as a representative, and he shares the values I share, both the social values and the economic values" (Hanshaw 1985, A1).

Golden's primary campaign would revolve around moral issues and actively seek the backing of the many religious conservatives who lived in the district. Tennessee's Third was an area with numerous churches comprising several evangelical and independent fundamentalist denominations. There was a strong pro-life movement in the area that had been conducting regular protests at what was the only abortion clinic in Chattanooga.[8] Golden, in his heart and soul, was part of that movement and sought to transfer some of this energy and activism to his congressional campaign. Indeed, his supporters were extremely conservative on moral issues, and some were entirely motivated by abortion (Flessner, interview with author). Several observers noticed that Golden made "Christian values" the focal point of his campaign. Pamela Rudd, the pro-life activist who had been so disillusioned with John Davis in 1984, was ecstatic when Jim Golden decided to run in 1986. According to Rudd, who became quite friendly with the candidate, Golden did not want to run on a "yuppie platform" like John Davis. Abortion was going to be the driving force for Golden's candidacy, not an embarrassing side issue as it had been for so many Republican candidates over the years.

Rudd attended an early planning meeting at the home of another conservative Christian activist named Doug Daugherty. Daugherty helped start the Christian Action Council and signed on as Jim Golden's campaign manager. At the very first meeting, the principals realized that the local powers in the Republican Party would be with Davis. The only other option was to conduct a grassroots campaign that appealed to the social conservatism of the rank and file. The idea was to go to civic groups and churches and tell people who Golden was. The candidate would answer their heartfelt questions, and the campaign hoped word of mouth would spread, enabling Golden to gradually erase the name recognition advantage enjoyed by John Davis (Pamela Rudd, interview with author).

Golden's membership in the Church of God would potentially be quite helpful since its members comprised roughly 15 percent of the district. While his fellow congregants would be likely to support one of their own, getting them to participate would be difficult considering the particular kind of religious doctrine that was taught in this denomination. Holiness is most important, and that translated into avoiding worldly things. Participating in elections was seen as worldly, and the congregants would have to be prodded to get involved because Church of God members traditionally did not vote (Daugherty, interview with author).

So Doug Daugherty came up with a plan to reach these potential voters and bring them into the political process as supporters of Jim Golden. He explained, "We really went after the Christian conservative vote. We created a fifteen-minute cassette tape with Jim just explaining his position on different issues" (Daugherty, interview with author). To get this group to vote, they needed a longer message than could be contained in a letter. Plus, Daugherty told me, they were accustomed to listening to tapes—sermons on tapes, music on tapes, and so on. The campaign included voter registration forms with the tapes. These were particularly useful in Tennessee since anybody can register to vote by mail. Eventually, they expanded the operation and mailed the tapes to 15,000 people whose names they culled from church rolls. These were conservative churches that supplied the campaign with their directories. Daugherty recalls the tapes creating a lot of talk and not costing large sums of money. Further, they also helped to raise money, which began to come in at a good clip from religious conservatives across the district.

Golden's cassette tapes contained a strong right-to-life message that was clearly targeted to those voters who would be friendliest to that appeal. The public campaign was centered on other issues. Golden was a strong fiscal conservative and did not dwell on moral issues in public statements. The local paper did report his support of voluntary prayer in schools and his stance against legalized abortion, but they were not presented as being more important than Golden's beliefs on other issues (Hanshaw 1985, A1; Casteel 1986, B1).[9]

A Factional Battle for the Republican Congressional Nomination

The first debate between Golden and Davis was held in May and hosted by the Pachyderm Club, a local Republican organization. They discussed a wide variety of issues, agreeing on a potential restructuring of the Tennessee Valley Authority, balancing the budget, and gun rights. As for the moral issues, Golden was clearly the more conservative of the two candidates. While both supported voluntary prayer in schools, Golden sought to get rid of pornography while Davis only would support people's right to protest against it. On abortion, Golden argued strongly for a constitutional amendment to prohibit abortions and produced an old newspaper clipping containing a quote from Davis in which he told a reporter that he did not believe the U.S. Constitution was the place to deal with the abortion issue. Davis replied that he was opposed to abortion but thought the Constitution should be the court of last resort (Casteel 1986, B1).

The primary campaign pitted two competing Republican factions against each other. According to Todd Gardenhire, who was very active in the Republican Party at the time, John Davis had the Brock organization behind him (Gardenhire, interview with author). Pamela Rudd recalls the "Republican machinery" in the city was supporting Davis, so Golden was forced to "honeycomb underneath the Republican status-quo" (Pamela and Robin Rudd, interview with author). He was an embarrassment to many in the Republican Party because of his devout religiosity, but he could count on the support of religious conservatives who were becoming more active in politics across the country and were being spurred to participate in the Third District by Golden himself. In the end, the newcomer with the superior grassroots organization defeated the more experienced candidate with the backing of the local political and economic elites. In fact, it was no contest. Golden received 65 percent of the vote district-wide and a few points more than that in Hamilton County. Golden attributed his stunning victory to straight talk, hard work, and prayer (Wann 1986, A1). Pamela Rudd agreed. She attributed Golden's win in the primary to his tireless interactions with the people in which he conveyed his spirituality and how that would inform his political decision making. He went door-to-door. He went to the churches. According to Rudd, it was old-fashioned, "work your ass off" politics. "Golden was part preacher, part politician." On the other hand, Rudd's husband Robin thought Davis believed that "he could just stay up at the Pachyderm Club, go to a few Young Republican meetings, and win the nomination" (Pamela and Robin Rudd, interview with author). This assessment of the aloofness with which many business Republicans approached politics in the 1980s echoes Reverend Sloan's opinion in Chapter 4 and Lee Bandy's in Chapter 5. Christian Republicans had the intensity and were willing to work hard to gain power. However, the reader will see in the next few sections that a willingness to work hard sometimes is not enough.

Golden Finds It Difficult to Move Toward the Political Center

Since primary elections are often low-information contests decided by more committed ideologues within each party, candidates are forced to appeal to their base when seeking their party's nomination. As a result, they often find themselves too far from the district median when contesting the general election. Sometimes it can be difficult to moderate one's policy positions to avoid being seen as too extreme in November. For Jim Golden, this task was that much more difficult considering the type of primary campaign he ran. A professor at the University of Tennessee, Chattanooga, characterized the Golden primary campaign as divisive. His overt religious appeals offended many inside and outside of the Republican Party. He certainly would have great difficulty uniting the GOP behind his candidacy. A Republican operative I spoke with recalls the Golden cassette tapes as being a bit "freaky" and off-putting.

Doug Daugherty, Golden's campaign manager, immediately realized the necessity of moving back to the center against Marilyn Lloyd since they had tacked far to the right to win the primary. They shifted their focus to the need for a change. The Golden campaign could not attack Lloyd personally or attack her character since she was perceived as a nice Southern woman. They also would find it difficult to attack her on the issues since her conservative philosophy fit nicely with district opinion. Daugherty recalls combing over Lloyd's voting record with an eye toward picking out particular votes to hit her on. He conceded that this was a difficult task, and they had little success in doing so. In the meantime, they did receive $50,000 from the RNC and added two graduates from a conservative campaign school in Washington. They also continued the grassroots, door-to-door activity that served them so well in the primary campaign (Daugherty, interview with author).

Meanwhile, the incumbent vowed not to be caught off guard by another Republican challenger as she was with John Davis two years earlier. This meant a more aggressive fund-raising strategy and get-out-the-vote effort. Lloyd trumpeted her success in securing federal funding for new roads, bridges, and developments, such as the Trade Center in Chattanooga and the Hamilton County Riverport Industrial Park (Flessner and Kopper 1986, A1).[10] Golden countered on the campaign trail that Southeast Tennessee trailed most of the country in economic growth. Golden advertised his support for a constitutional amendment to balance the budget, a presidential line-item veto, cutbacks in foreign aid, and the abolition of the Department of Education. Lloyd disagreed on the line-item veto and the Department of Education, but did vote for across-the-board spending cuts as presented in the Gramm-Rudman bill. She also emphasized a list of 228 budget cuts that she voted for (Flessner and Kopper 1986, A1).

As with Liz Patterson and Dan Glickman, Marilyn Lloyd was adept at deflecting charges that she was too liberal for the district on fiscal matters. Even though Golden often criticized Lloyd for being one of the biggest spenders in Congress, and seemed to be supported by a National Taxpayers Union's survey that placed the Third District incumbent in the top 20 percent of all congressional representatives in her support for spending bills, the Republican challenger seemed to get very little traction on economic issues. Both Patterson and Glickman, however, were vulnerable on social issues such as abortion when their Republican challengers finally decided to make them a central part of the debate. Lloyd's relatively conservative position on abortion, school prayer, and the Equal Rights Amendment made her much less susceptible to Republican attacks on these moral issues than her colleagues from South Carolina and Kansas. Even still, Jim Golden did carve out a position to the right of Lloyd on abortion. While both candidates said they opposed abortion, Lloyd clearly made exceptions for when the mother has been a victim of rape or incest or when her life was in danger. Golden said he would grant exceptions in a constitutional amendment on abortion, but he refused to detail those exceptions for fear of undermining overall support for a potential amendment. Lloyd was not in favor of amending the constitution to ban abortions (Flessner and Kopper 1986, A1).

With a Republican candidate so closely associated with the religious right, it was inevitable that the role of religion in politics would be a major theme of the campaign. A week before the election, an article in the *Chattanooga Times* focused on the role religion was playing in the Third District race. It is clear from the article that Golden was employing the same dual campaign strategy in the general election that he used in the primary. He continued to send out cassette tapes to voters that emphasized his Christian faith and how that affected his political beliefs. "When talking to civic groups or to reporters at press conferences, Golden has consistently hit at his opponent on economic issues. . . . On the tape, Golden says he opposes abortion, pornography, and giving greater rights to homosexuals and focuses on other moral issues" (Sher 1986, A1). As the media glare grew brighter, more details regarding these tapes surfaced.

> The 30-minute tape is titled "Justice and the Children." The tape features nineteen references to God, several to Jesus, six quotations from the Bible, references to three other Scripture verses, two parables of Jesus, Golden's own personal testimony about his conversion as a born-again Christian, and an exhortation for the listener to "pray and repent." He mentions secular humanism and calls the federal government a "new God." After introducing his personal background, including his family, Golden says, "I guess the other thing I ought to tell you that is most important of all and that is that I'm a Christian. I'm a believer in Jesus Christ and I have accepted him as my personal Lord and Savior. That's the most important thing about my life." (Sher 1986, A1)

With minor differences, the tape is identical to the one Golden's campaign sent out in the weeks before the Republican primary. That offering mobilized a large number of conservative Christians during the primary. In Hamilton County, fourteen precincts ran out of ballots when an unexpectedly large number of people showed up to vote for Golden. In the general election campaign, the religiously infused tapes seemed to have a similar effect. Sher writes, "More than 250 people were registered as voters in the Highland Park Precinct since the primary. . . . The precinct includes the

Highland Park Baptist Church and its affiliated school, Tennessee Temple University" (Sher 1986, A1).

The danger of this emphasis on conservative Christianity was that it would turn off moderate Republicans and those who were less religious in nature. Despite the need for the Golden campaign to at least make an effort to get back to the center, it also needed to mobilize the base to have any hope of beating a relatively popular incumbent. Overtly religious candidacies had proven disastrous in other districts, including earlier in the year when Republican congressman Mark Siljander from Michigan, who had won in the past by mobilizing Christian conservatives, lost his primary contest after sending a letter to ministers saying that by supporting him "we can break the back of Satan."[11]

When the votes were counted on election night, Marilyn Lloyd had successfully beaten back another serious challenge. She defeated Golden 54 percent to 46 percent to retain her seat in Congress. According to the *Chattanooga Times*, "Most of the campaign centered on Golden's attempts to portray Congresswoman Lloyd as a wavering and ineffective representative who, though she voted conservative on some issues, still had ties to liberal Democrats in Washington" (Sher and Flessner 1986, A1). The less visible part of the campaign—the one with religious overtones that sought to mobilize conservative Christian voters—may have come back to haunt Golden, as some Republicans were turned off and Democrats charged that Golden was attempting to inject religion into politics (Sher and Flessner 1986, A1).

Republicans Turn on One of Their Own

It is fair to assume that more moderate Republicans and those in the party less concerned with moral issues were especially likely to desert Golden in the general election. Todd Gardenhire recalled a clear division between the different wings of the Republican Party. They all agreed on the social issues; it was just a question of salience. They all went to church, but the Christian Republicans did not care about anything else except the moral issues (Gardenhire, interview with author). Doug Daugherty realized the downside of playing so strongly to the religious conservative base. Golden's campaign manager believes that the candidate turned off a lot of people in the middle during the general election campaign because he went after the religious vote so strongly. They thought he was dangerous. Daugherty admits that it might have helped if they had not been so connected with an extremely conservative moral message, but he does not know how else they would have won the primary without that strong appeal to religious conservatives (Daugherty, interview with author).[12]

Rank-and-file Republicans were not the only ones dismayed by the religious overtones of Golden's campaign. The local political and economic elites, still led by Pat Brock, were extremely unhappy that Golden defeated their chosen candidate in the primary and took the party too far to the right in the general election campaign. In fact, the Davis backers appeared to be involved in the primary campaign more to stop Golden than to get Davis elected (Gardenhire, interview with author). They failed but did not quit trying to defeat Golden once he received the nomination. A local Republican operative believed Pat Brock and others in the party leadership abandoned Golden. Their actions strongly suggest that many of the powerful business Republicans that helped build the party in Hamilton County would rather have seen Democratic incumbent Marilyn Lloyd get reelected than have Jim Golden win.

A few days before the election, letters were sent out to Republicans in Hamilton County imploring them not to vote for Golden because he was dangerous. The recipients of these mailings were encouraged to vote for Lloyd and do anything they could to make sure she was victorious. Indeed, several Republicans visited Lloyd's headquarters on election night, one remarking to reporters that he never thought he would be working for a Democrat (Sher and Flessner 1986, A1).

Doug Daugherty believes the letters were incredibly damaging to his candidate's chances. The Golden campaign hit their vote target in every county except Hamilton, which was home to many of the Chamber of Commerce Republicans targeted by the anti-Golden letters (Daugherty, interview with author). They lost 51 percent to 48 percent there, running almost six points behind Winfield Dunn, the defeated Republican gubernatorial candidate. If Golden had run evenly with, or slightly ahead of Dunn, he would have outpolled Lloyd. It is entirely plausible that the letters may have made the difference between victory and defeat for Jim Golden.

When Daugherty first mentioned the anti-Golden letters to me, he said that "some influential Republicans" sent them out. Others agreed. Pamela Rudd blamed the "Republican status quo" in Chattanooga. She referred to them as the Lookout Mountain power structure, named for the neighborhood in which many wealthy and powerful Republicans live. Lookout

Mountain literally looks out over, and down on, the city of Chattanooga from the south. Rudd contacted Jim Golden and asked him about the letters.[13] Golden said extremely powerful members of the GOP wrote the letters to mid-level and high-level movers and shakers of the community. He emphasized that the letters did not go out to the general public (Pamela and Robin Rudd, interview with author). Others, including David Fowler, a current state representative from the area, heard about the letters. Fowler understood that some people were afraid Golden was too Christian or too pro-life and had pressured others into writing the letters (Fowler, interview with author).[14]

Based on the combined recollections and opinions of several individuals closely connected to the 1986 campaign, it appears likely that elements within the Republican Party deliberately set out to sabotage their own candidate because they did not approve of his message and style. Obviously, they were willing to tolerate Marilyn Lloyd rather than risk Jim Golden winning the seat and becoming the de facto head of the local Republican Party. The extent of the split within the Republican Party between the so-called business and Christian Republicans was evident during Golden's Election Night festivities. The reception was at the Chattanooga Choo Choo, a local hotel and popular tourist spot. As the party was going on, the "traditional" Republicans were in one room with an endless stream of hors d'oeuvres and free-flowing beer and wine. The Golden people were in another with considerably less food and no alcohol. These Christian Republicans were the moral crusaders, while the "traditional" Republicans were the business types who had been active in the party for a long time. They were clearly distinct groups that night and throughout the campaign. Golden's people were extremely conservative on moral issues, with some supporters entirely motivated by the abortion issue. Most of these activists came in with Golden, and some probably left with Golden as he decided not to seek public office in the future. Their segregation at the party was a fitting coda to an election campaign that never managed to speak to both groups.[15] The powerful old-guard business Republicans not only decided to refrain from aiding the Golden campaign; they actively went about trying to disrupt it. Marilyn Lloyd was a formidable candidate, and she may have won even if the Republicans had been united. Without that unity, however, Jim Golden's candidacy was doomed. Golden ran outside the party structure in the primary, and he paid for it in the general election.

The Hamilton County Republican chair lamented the infighting and lack of unity that marked the 1986 congressional campaign. Ray Albright, a veteran lawmaker who served as chair of the Hamilton County legislative delegation, suggested the need for Republicans to nominate a candidate with deep roots in the party structure. "We haven't had a great number of team players run for the 3rd district congressional seat in the last few years, and that's been a weakness. I think this district is very winnable, and I think if we had a candidate who has done his duties to the party and the community then we have a real chance to win. Everybody has got to start somewhere, but you don't usually jump up as an unknown and run for Congress" (Flessner 1986, B1). Albright, who is from the Chamber of Commerce wing of the party, went on to say that he hoped to play a stronger role in recruiting Republican candidates for the congressional race. Both comments suggest a concerted effort to regain full control of the party apparatus in an effort to nominate a business Republican to go against Marilyn Lloyd in 1988.

Lloyd Coasts in 1988 and 1990

After deciding to retire in July 1987, Marilyn Lloyd changed her mind and sought an eighth term in the House of Representatives. She planned to run on her experience and seniority, and as an incumbent, she would possess significant advantages over the Republican candidate (Flessner and Sher 1988, A1). For the GOP, the big concern was avoiding the type of bloody primary that most likely prevented them from capturing the Third District seat in 1986. In February 1988, three candidates were thinking about running for the Republican nomination. One was the aforementioned Ray Albright, a fiscal conservative associated with the business wing of the party. He was joined by Gene Hunt, a favorite of the Brock organization, and Harold Coker. Coker was the closest of the three to the religious right. Albright led in early polling, but Coker had begun to organize and raise money earlier than his potential opponents. According to a report in the *Chattanooga Times*, a meeting was set up to discuss avoiding a costly, divisive primary (Sher 1988, A1). Apparently, the get-together was successful as Harold Coker faced no competition in the August primary. According to Todd Gardenhire, the old guard wanted Ray Albright to run against Harold Coker, but Albright realized that the rank and file of the Republican Party had recently become more conservative and more focused on social issues. Coker outflanked Albright on the right, and since he knew he did not have the support of the primary electorate, he passed on the race.

Gardenhire also speculated that Gene Hunt was only involved because Pat Brock wanted to hurt Harold Coker's campaign. When the nomination seemed certain to go to Coker, there was no need for Hunt to stay in the race (Gardenhire, interview with author).

Harold Coker had no trouble raising money in his race against Marilyn Lloyd. He was a county commissioner and his wife, Lil, was very active in the state Republican Party. However, owing to Lloyd's conservatism, he had great difficulty distinguishing himself from the Democratic incumbent on the issues. The only issue on which they totally disagreed was the line-item veto. So Coker worked hard to associate himself with the Bush-Quayle ticket and, by extension, to tie Marilyn Lloyd to Michael Dukakis and his Massachusetts liberalism. This would be a tough task considering Lloyd had always managed to shy away from open identification with the more liberal national Democratic leadership. For good measure, she stayed away from the Democratic National Convention to film commercials and campaign in the district (Meacham 1988, A1).[16]

Coker was scoring points with some RNC ads that attacked Lloyd on social issues. However, Coker's daughter, who ran the campaign, pulled the ads after some evangelicals complained that they were too harsh. According to a Republican operative, this was a mistake, and Dave Flessner, who covered the race for the *Chattanooga Times*, believes Coker ran a poor campaign that was consistently outmaneuvered by Lloyd and her team. After pulling the social issue ads, Coker was left attacking the incumbent on her effectiveness, her oversight of the Tennessee Valley Authority, and her acceptance of speaking fees from defense contractors. Lloyd countered by citing her experience and saying she possessed the clout to help the district. She portrayed Coker as a negative campaigner who did not understand how the federal government worked (Rawlins and Flessner 1988, A1).

Coker's attacks on Lloyd's effectiveness and his continued attempts to paint her as a big-spending liberal were falling on deaf ears. Two weeks out, Lloyd led by twenty points, even while Dukakis trailed in the Third District by seventeen. Thirty-four percent of Bush voters said they would support Congresswoman Lloyd. These are the ticket splitters that created the at-risk districts that kept the Republicans in the minority throughout the 1970s, 1980s, and early 1990s. Lloyd led in all seven counties, including an impressive 52 percent to 35 percent in all-important Hamilton County. She was favored by nearly all types of voters, but gleaned her greatest support from African Americans, women, and older voters. Even among voters who called themselves conservatives, Coker only led by a margin of 43 percent to 42 percent. This last result provides clear evidence that Marilyn Lloyd was able to sidestep the charges that she was a liberal Democrat (Flessner 1988a, A1).

The poll numbers presented in the previous paragraph proved to be a fairly accurate gauge of the final results. The Democratic incumbent easily defeated her Republican challenger 57 percent to 42 percent. Lloyd managed to win all seven counties, and her victory was boosted by ticket splitters. Coker tried to link Lloyd to Dukakis and failed miserably. "During the campaign, Rep. Lloyd endorsed Dukakis but kept her distance from the Democratic presidential nominee, differing with Dukakis on a host of defense and social issues. She has held her seat in the Republican-leaning 3rd District by voting the wishes of her constituents and consistently providing people with help in getting government aid" (Flessner 1988b, A1).

This formula had indeed worked for Marilyn Lloyd since her first term. She had beaten every type of candidate the Republicans put up against her, and she did it in years where Democrats fared poorly in the district at the state and national levels. By 1990, she seemed unbeatable. The Republicans, recognizing this fact, hardly put up a fight in that year's election. A staunch Republican with a moderate background named Grady Rhoden would be the token candidate. Rhoden did not seek campaign contributions or even adopt a platform (Hicks 1990, B2). Interestingly enough, Marilyn Lloyd's biggest challenge came from the left in the form of an independent candidate by the name of Pete Melcher. A teacher at a prestigious private high school, Melcher criticized Lloyd for "voting like a right-wing Republican" (Flessner 1990a, A1). He criticized Lloyd for her stands on the environment and abortion. He promoted strong environmental laws and supported cuts in military spending (Flessner 1990a, A1). The National Organization for Women and the League of Conservation Voters surprisingly endorsed Melcher in 1990, and he received 6 percent of the vote district-wide and almost 9 percent in Hamilton County. Lloyd barely achieved a majority (53 percent) across the district and won only a small plurality over Rhoden in Hamilton County. Pundits blamed the anti-incumbent sentiment that swept the country that year as well as near record-low turnout for Lloyd's disappointing performance against competitors who raised tiny sums of money and hardly campaigned (Flessner 1990b, D1; Kopper 1990, A3).

Interestingly, the noncampaign of 1990, as it was widely referred to, had some important political consequences for the race that followed in 1992.

First, Todd Gardenhire, a well-connected Republican activist for many years, believed the Lookout Mountain power structure did not want Marilyn Lloyd to face a serious challenge in 1990. He argues that the local economic elites were quite satisfied with having a business-friendly member of the majority party with plum committee assignments representing them in Washington. In addition, they reasoned that if they pressed Lloyd, she would have to respond by spending lots of money to aggressively turn out her base of union workers, women, and minorities. This would be detrimental to the electoral fortunes of Republicans running winnable statewide races (Gardenhire, interview with author).[17] Second, Pete Melcher embodied the danger Democrats who try to run away from the liberal label in conservative districts face. Melcher attacked from the left and picked off thousands of votes that otherwise would have gone to Marilyn Lloyd. In 1990, it did not affect the race. In a closer contest, though, it could mean the difference between retaining one's seat and being forced into early retirement. For Lloyd, that difficult election was right around the corner because Todd Gardenhire, mindful that the local Republican power structure would not actively back a congressional challenger, decided that this was a perfect time to make a run himself.

The Lookout Mountain Power Structure Flexes Its Muscles Again

Todd Gardenhire came to politics in a decidedly different way than many of his peers. As a student at Tennessee's Cleveland State Community College in 1970, Gardenhire could not have been less political. One day after a typically long commute from Chattanooga to attend a science class, that all changed. Antiwar protesters were picketing outside the science building, causing the canceling of the class Gardenhire was scheduled to attend that afternoon. Gardenhire did not have too much of an idea what the issues were behind the protest; he just knew that he had wasted a trip up to Cleveland. Todd and his friends were very angry and decided to "break up" the protest. The dean of students made Gardenhire go to the hospital and apologize to the kids who were hurt in the confrontation. One of them was wearing a "Gore for Senate" button. Right then, Gardenhire decided that he was going to be for Gore's opponent—whoever he might be. He went home, found out that the Republican candidate was Bill Brock, and immediately volunteered for his campaign.[18]

After transferring to the University of Tennessee, Gardenhire joined Young Americans for Freedom, and they took over the student senate. In 1976, Gardenhire became involved with Reagan's insurgent campaign against incumbent president Gerald Ford. Many prominent Tennesseans backed Ford, including both U.S. Senators—Howard Baker and Bill Brock. Gardenhire eventually worked his way up to state chair of the campaign and ended up procuring more delegates for Reagan than Ford received. Four years later, Reagan ran for the nomination again, and this time a Tennessean was one of his main rivals. Gardenhire stuck with the governor from California instead of backing Howard Baker, and Reagan won not only Tennessee's primary; he went on to win the Republican nomination and then the presidency.

Reagan's win cemented Gardenhire's position in the party hierarchy, and he gained a place on the state executive committee. Gardenhire then moved to Washington, D.C., working in the White House from 1984 to 1989. When Gardenhire returned to the Third District, the religious right had gained considerable power within the party structure. In addition, the economic elites had become accustomed to Marilyn Lloyd and preferred to have her remain in Washington. Pat Brock and his fellow Lookout Mountain residents were satisfied with the token candidacy of Grady Rhoden in 1990, and they wanted Lloyd to have another free ride in 1992.[19]

Todd Gardenhire had bucked powerful local leaders before, and he decided to do it again by throwing his hat into the ring for the Republican congressional nomination. His campaign theme was health care. "People are living longer. . . . I care about the problems this brings, and, most important, I care about the people that these problems touch" (Meacham 1992b, B1). Gardenhire touted his experience in civic affairs and business and stressed his longtime involvement with the presidential campaigns of Reagan, Bush, and Jack Kemp, as well as with a host of state and district races. In late February, he was ahead in fund-raising and steadfastly refused to take PAC money or attack his fellow Republicans. An article in the *Chattanooga Times* described his platform as follows: "His platform is conservative. Gardenhire supports term limits, less federal regulation, controlling government spending, and internal congressional reform" (Meacham 1992b, B1).

The Brock organization on Lookout Mountain saw the potential strength of a Gardenhire campaign and decided if there was going to be a serious challenge to Marilyn Lloyd in 1992, it might as well be from a candidate they preferred. So they went about recruiting a candidate, promising to provide all necessary resources—most important, money—for a legitimate congressional run. After being spurned by two potential candidates, they approached Zach Wamp, who was the Hamilton County Republican Party chair at the time (Gardenhire, interview with author). Wamp accepted the offer, and the Lookout Mountain power structure finally had a horse to back.

Zach Wamp was an interesting choice because he had never run for public office and had an extremely checkered past. He failed to graduate from college mostly owing to a cocaine habit he had developed during his junior year. After returning home, the drug abuse worsened, and he eventually had to check himself into a drug rehabilitation center in Chattanooga. After a successful stint in rehab and a rededication to the Christian faith, Wamp overcame his problems with drugs, went to work for his father's real estate company, and got involved in local Republican politics.[20] Wamp would run as a conservative Republican on a platform of fiscal responsibility, cutting federal bureaucracy, and taking a tough stance on crime (Meacham 1992a, B1).

Like Gardenhire, Wamp also pledged not to take PAC money. However, thanks to his wealthy benefactors, he did not have to worry too much about raising sufficient funds to run a competitive race. Gardenhire, on the other hand, was doing a respectable job raising funds through his business and personal contacts. However, now that Wamp was in the race with the full financial backing of the Brock organization, Gardenhire realized that he potentially had to face two high-intensity, expensive elections; the primary and the general. Without PAC money, and with a presidential and statewide race sucking money out of the district, Gardenhire was far from sanguine about his ability to compete. The candidate needed some more friends, and he sought out Jim Golden to see if the former congressional candidate could drum up some support in the Christian conservative community. Gardenhire expected some assistance considering he was one of the few high-level Republicans in Hamilton County to help Golden during the 1986 general election. A meeting was convened, and Gardenhire recalls sitting at a table with Golden and some other members of the local Christian right community. They said they wanted someone to carry the banner on abortion. Gardenhire replied there were other issues that were more important and abortion was not his only concern as a congressional candidate. According to Gardenhire, Golden then got up and came across to where he was sitting. Golden pounded on the wooden table, stuck his finger in Gardenhire's face, and said, "It is the only issue!" With that, any hope Gardenhire held of gaining the religious right's support drifted away (Gardenhire, interview with author).

Without the support of either of the two main Republican factions, Gardenhire made a "business decision" and dropped out of the congressional race in June 1992. According to Gardenhire, after the local religious right declined to support him, they went to Zach Wamp and gave him the same ultimatum. As with the Brock people, Wamp dutifully accepted and assured Golden the abortion issue would be front and center in his campaign. In a circumstantial way, my newspaper research corroborates this story. Throughout the spring, neither Republican candidate was stressing the types of moral issues that had become more and more relevant to the political discourse in America. Both Gardenhire and Wamp were focused on fiscal issues and reforming Congress. This seemed particularly odd in a year when Marilyn Lloyd might finally be seriously vulnerable on moral issues. During the previous term, Lloyd had supported a bill allowing American servicewomen and military dependents access to abortions in military facilities overseas. This was one of the few "pro-choice" votes she had made during her tenure in Congress up to that point. In past races, Lloyd was often endorsed by national right-to-life organizations. Whether she sincerely altered her views or felt the pressure from Pete Melcher on the left is pure speculation and not particularly relevant to this discussion. The fact remains, if the Republicans chose to make abortion an issue in 1992, there would finally be some real differences between the candidates, and a strongly pro-life opponent might seriously hurt Marilyn Lloyd in this socially conservative district.[21] Despite the shift in the district dynamic on abortion, this and other moral issues were simply not being stressed by Gardenhire and Wamp during the early stages of the campaign. However, at the end of July, after Gardenhire had departed the race (and after Golden delivered his ultimatums to both candidates), Zach Wamp made his first lengthy public statements on family values and religious principles, and the *Chattanooga Times* noticed for the first time the degree to which Wamp and Lloyd differed on the abortion issue (Powell 1992, A1; Meacham 1992c, A1).[22]

With Todd Gardenhire out of the race, Zach Wamp cruised to victory in the primary, garnering 77.5 percent of the vote. "In his victory speech, Wamp called for a basic return to values in an apparent effort to pick up support from socially conservative voters who may be angered by Rep. Lloyd's move toward the center on issues like abortion. He noted that references to God are sprinkled throughout public life, but have been banned from the public schools for more than thirty years" (Kopper 1992, B1). With issues of moral traditionalism assuming a prominent role in his campaign and Pat Brock as his finance chairman, Zach Wamp had married two factions of the Republican Party—albeit in a convoluted way—which had been bitter enemies only six years earlier. The fact that Wamp was even in the race is a testament to the power and influence wielded by a local group of elites who exercised a great deal of control on Republican politics despite operating outside the formal party structure.

Increased Polarization Leads to a Close and Bitter Contest

Marilyn Lloyd and Zach Wamp did not disagree on everything during the 1992 election. They both were against the savings-and-loan bailout and for the Brady Bill, the Persian Gulf War, and campaign finance reform.[23] However, they sharply differed on the two issues that aroused the greatest passion in the electorate: crime and abortion. Marilyn Lloyd supported the Democratic crime bill while Zach Wamp opposed the proposed legislation, calling it pro-criminal and anti–law enforcement. On abortion, they not only disagreed on allowing military personnel overseas to get one; they also diverged on the so-called gag rule that prohibited family-planning clinics that obtain federal funds from discussing abortion with their clients.[24]

During their first debate in mid-October, Wamp accused Lloyd of being on both sides of the abortion issue by saying she would support a woman's right to an abortion but that she was personally pro-life. Lloyd responded that she believed all women had a right to the best health care available and hoped all women would choose life. The two candidates also clashed over taxes, economic growth, education, and AIDS research funding, with Wamp taking the more conservative position on all four issues (Meacham 1992d, A1).

The reporter covering the debate recognized the new polarization evident in the Third District race in 1992. "That is perhaps the most interesting element of this campaign. For years, Republicans have been confounded by Rep. Lloyd's image of Southern conservatism. But, Wamp says, she has now moved away from the votes she cast in the 1970s and 1980s, moving left of center" (Meacham 1992d, A1). Perhaps this was due to pressure from left-wing schoolteacher Pete Melcher, who ran as an independent in 1990 and grabbed 6 percent of the vote. He threatened to run again in 1992 but backed out, endorsing Lloyd in late October and urging his supporters to vote for the Democratic incumbent. This was extremely important for Lloyd in a race that figured to be closer than any of her previous reelection battles. Predictably, Wamp howled that Melcher and Lloyd "cut a deal." According to Wamp, Lloyd would end her opposition to abortion rights and make more of an effort to protect the environment in return for Melcher's withdrawal and his subsequent attacks on the Republican challenger. Of course, Lloyd and Melcher both denied any collusion (Meacham 1992e, A1).

As the race neared its final days and the outcome remained in doubt, the focus shifted (thanks mostly to the Lloyd campaign) to Zach Wamp's past personal problems. Lloyd began hitting Wamp hard for lying on a sworn deposition that he finished college, denying he had legal problems in college when he was convicted of bouncing two twenty-dollar checks, and a recent lawsuit where he and his family were accused of selling substandard apartments (Meacham 1992e, A1). The negativity reached its crescendo only days before Election Day when the Lloyd campaign got its hands on a mug shot taken of Zach Wamp after a barroom brawl in the early 1980s and broadcast it as part of a campaign ad. Wamp angrily countered, "When you're at the bottom of the sewer, you can't get any lower. And she's at the bottom. She's fired every bullet she's got—and now she's firing blanks" (Meacham 1992f, A1). Bill Brock spoke out against Lloyd's tactics, and Wamp received public support from Vice President Dan Quayle, former U.S. senator Howard Baker, and former Tennessee governor Lamar Alexander (Meacham 1992f, A1).

Lloyd Barely Survives Against a United Republican Party

Marilyn Lloyd's ninth reelection campaign was by far her closest. She won by only 2,917 votes and lost Hamilton County for the first time since her upset victory over LaMar Baker in 1974.[25] Wamp benefited considerably from the anti-incumbency trend that was sweeping the nation in 1992. Further, Al Gore's place on the national ticket changed the dynamics of Tennessee politics. Lloyd found it that much more difficult to distance herself from the national ticket, and it cut down significantly on the number of ticket splitters. Republican ticket splitters, particularly those in Hamilton

County—which Bush also won—were Bush-Wamp voters this time (Meacham 1992h, A1). Undoubtedly, this was in large measure due to the support Wamp had from the Lookout Mountain power structure and his ability to also gain the backing of pro-life activists and other religious conservatives. Jon Meacham, who covered the campaign for the *Chattanooga Times*, marveled at Republican unity. "Wamp energized Republican activists from across the party's spectrum. Older Bill Brock supporters from the 1960s moved easily with conservative evangelicals and young, mainstream Republicans" (Meacham 1992g, A1). Although it is just speculation, I imagine that the Wamp party on election night 1992 looked very different from Jim Golden's party in 1986. In fact, one might say that Zach Wamp combined the appeal of John Davis and Jim Golden into one unified Republican campaign. Regardless of the reasons, the two main factions in the Republican Party put aside their differences in 1992 in common cause and made Wamp a significantly more formidable challenger to Lloyd than he otherwise would have been.

However, despite everything Wamp had going for him in 1992, he still could not defeat Marilyn Lloyd. Even though he had solid financial support, his fund-raising was no match for a well-connected incumbent such as Lloyd. He was outspent by a greater than two-to-one margin, and his get-out-the-vote effort was not as effective as it could have been. After the campaign ended, rather than being discouraged, Wamp was strongly hinting at another run. He wrote an editorial in the *Knoxville News Sentinel* two weeks after the election to thank his supporters. The following excerpt does more than simply leave the door open for a possible run in 1994. It also reasserts the religious tinge that marked much of his campaign. "This great nation must turn from many of its ways and seek God's face if we are to solve our problems. I have been encouraged by countless supporters to run again and will be seriously considering this in the next few months" (Wamp 1992, A9). In fact, many observers that I spoke with considered Wamp's 1994 campaign to have begun the day after his defeat in 1992.

Wamp Goes After an Open Seat

In 1992, Zach Wamp came within a few thousand votes of becoming a U.S. congressman. Two years later, his prospects were even brighter. He had additional time to build a more extensive and efficient grassroots operation. In addition, his name recognition was much greater after competing in such a high-profile race. In the 1992 race, he had fully addressed and owned up to his past personal problems and also had survived a barrage of nasty attacks. Future assaults on his character based on the same concerns would likely be seen as mean-spirited and repetitive. The most important reason for Wamp's enhanced probability of winning a congressional seat, however, was Marilyn Lloyd's retirement. Lloyd was always a formidable candidate and had never lost an election. Moreover, winning an open seat is almost always much easier than beating an incumbent. If he could secure the Republican nomination again, Zach Wamp would get that chance. And another reason he would benefit from running for the second time was the widespread feeling within the local Republican Party that he deserved another chance, considering how close he came to winning in 1992. Many believed the nomination was Wamp's to lose and that he should be the presumptive nominee in 1992. However, there was one person in particular who did not share this feeling. His name was Ken Meyer, and he decided to swim against the tide and challenge Wamp for the Republican congressional nomination in 1994.

A Rising Star Is Pulled Back to Earth

In this chapter's opening anecdote, I chronicled the brief but wildly successful political career of Ken Meyer. He broke onto the scene in 1990 by defeating an eighteen-year Democratic incumbent in a state legislative race. Meyer was heavily involved in the Jaycees and the local Chamber of Commerce. He got into politics through the connections he made and networks he tapped into as a result of his membership in these civic organizations. Because he was raised Christian, it was assumed he was part of the religious right. Though he shared many of the values espoused by Christian conservatives, he was not a part of this faction of the Republican Party. Meyer's background was economics, and he ran on economic issues. He aligned himself more with Newt Gingrich than with those in the so-called religious right. Meyer was involved with GOPAC, and that organization was very supportive of him in his legislative races. In addition, Meyer's political connections largely were with business-type Republicans in the area (Meyer, interview with author).

During his first term in Nashville, Meyer stepped on many toes—both Democratic and Republican. He infuriated Democrats by being the biggest thorn in the governor's side, and his fellow Republicans resented all the publicity he was receiving for his efforts. The Democrats got back at him by redistricting him in with David Copeland, a twenty-four-year state legislator who was enormously popular with Republican elites. Meyer was implored by the local power structure not to run against Copeland. He was told to wait his turn and not upset the apple cart by taking on a legislator who had built a long, distinguished career in the party and in Nashville. Meyer rebuffed these entreaties and took on Copeland with the same vim and vigor, not to mention skill, as he did the longtime Democratic incumbent he defeated two years earlier. Meyer won the primary and coasted to victory in November. However, the party never forgave him, and they were displeased once again when he decided to challenge Zach Wamp for the congressional nomination in 1994 (anonymous Republican operative, interview with author).

As I intimated at the beginning of the chapter, on paper, Meyer was clearly the better candidate going into the primary election campaign. This appeared to be the case even considering Wamp's nearly successful run against Marilyn Lloyd in 1992. In Jacobson's terms, Meyer would have been considered a quality challenger while Wamp would not. Despite this, Ken Meyer was soundly defeated and absorbed the first loss of his young career. There is much circumstantial evidence that suggests Meyer was beaten so badly because he was in disfavor with the local power structure and, conversely, Wamp had earned their respect and trust. There is much hard evidence, however, that the increasingly powerful religious right in the area was behind Wamp 100 percent and actively worked for him against Ken Meyer. In the next section, I will address both of these assertions.

Meyer Fails to Gain the Support of Either Major Republican Faction

In May 1993, it was reported that none other than Pat Brock may have tried to discourage Meyer from running (Sher 1993a, B1). Obviously, Brock did not get his way, and Todd Gardenhire and Jim Golden could both testify to the electoral pitfalls that await a candidate who crosses Pat Brock and the Lookout Mountain power structure. Wamp's list of donors included both Pat and Bill Brock as well as many of Hamilton County's other traditional big GOP benefactors. It was widely known in the district that the big money in the county looked to Pat Brock when deciding which candidates to support financially. Indeed, many had given money to Wamp *after* Meyer expressed interest in the seat (Sher 1993b, B3).[26] Meyer was essentially frozen out by the big-money donors. After raising $65,000 by the end of 1993, his fund-raising efforts slowed to a crawl, and he only showed $83.11 in the bank at the end of the first quarter of 1994. By May 1994, Meyer could only boast of four paid staff members while Wamp had eight. Wamp had money for television and lawn signs; Meyer did not (Gabel 1994c, A1). Meyer himself seemed to recognize what he was up against. "Meyer is used to being an outsider, even in his own party. Meyer says Republican Party leaders like Mayor Gene Roberts, County Commissioner Harold Coker, and Zach Wamp, now his opponent, tried to talk him out of running against Democratic lawmaker Paul Starnes (in 1990). "They were afraid that I would win. I don't fit into their little club. I get along with them fine. But I've never been one who is someone who can be told what to do" (Gabel 1994d, A8).[27]

Without much financial support, Meyer hoped to rely on a door-to-door campaign. But he had problems in this area as well. Meyer had only a hundred volunteers while Wamp had ten times as many (Gabel 1994c, A1). This discrepancy in manpower was no doubt related to the religious right's backing of Wamp and their rejection of Meyer. Even though both candidates were Christians and held conservative viewpoints on moral issues, Ken Meyer could not cut into the support and goodwill Wamp had engendered with the religious conservative community during his last race.[28] Wamp's story of personal redemption through Jesus Christ held special resonance with an electorate laden with born-again and evangelical Christians (Flessner, interview with author). Ken Meyer related to me his frustration on this score during our interview. He recalled little old ladies coming up to him during the campaign and saying, "Well, you know, I'd love to support you, but he's more Christian than you." Meyer had no scandals in his past and lived a relatively clean life, but it did not play. It did not have the impact and was not as important as Wamp's life story. People would tell Meyer that he did a good job in the legislature, but they had to support Wamp "because he's Christian," implying that Meyer was not a Christian when he most certainly was (Meyer, interview with author).

In addition to relating how his personal conversion helped him overcome past problems, Wamp emphatically played to the Christian conservative constituency in other ways. Wamp said at a local meeting of the Christian Coalition in May that Republicans more than Democrats seek to uphold "Christian ideals," which is the only way to solve the nation's problems (Silence 1994a, A4). In July, he was quoted as saying that politics is not important, "but God and relationships are most important" (Silence 1994b, B1).

Having the Christian right in his corner was very important to Zach Wamp since religion and morality were front and center in races at every level in Tennessee in 1994. Born-again Christian Steve Wilson infused the GOP U.S. senatorial primary with religious conservatism by talking of a "war raging in America as our faith and values are under attack. Liberals have made it illegal to pray in public schools. But they use our classrooms to teach radical sex education, even homosexuality" (Sher 1994, A1). David Fowler, the former chairman of a foundation committed to a vision of "Chattanooga as a community for God," challenged longtime moderate Republican incumbent Ray Albright for his state senate seat in 1994. State GOP chairman Randle Richardson welcomed the Christian activists into a party he described as "inclusive." The intensity of religious conservative activism was extremely high, and Zach Wamp was clearly benefiting from it. Ed McAteer, who was one of the first candidates in the area to gain most of his support from this bloc of voters, said enthusiasm levels were triple what they were ten years earlier when he ran as an independent for the U.S. Senate. Lynn Ray, a Tennessee Volunteers for Life lobbyist, said, "There was no movement like there is today" (Sher 1994, A1). Wilson estimated the religious right movement in Tennessee was a hundred thousand strong.[29] The Tennessee chapter of the Christian Coalition conducted a candidate survey sent to roughly three hundred candidates for state and federal office. Based on the results of this survey, they hoped to pass out 750,000 voter guides statewide before the primary elections. Moral issues, such as the state lottery, abortion, school prayer, and no-fault divorce, dominated the survey, but there were also questions on guns, welfare, and education. Ken Meyer believes he was hurt by these Christian Coalition voter guides because they suggested that Meyer was not as "pro-life" as Wamp. Indeed, he was not: Meyer believed in exceptions for rape, incest, and the life of the mother while Wamp only backed exceptions to protect the life of the mother.[30]

General Election Polarization on Abortion

The unequivocal support of the local party elites and the area's religious conservatives made Wamp impossible to beat in the Republican primary.

He crushed Meyer, his boyhood friend and neighbor, defeating him by a whopping forty-three points.[31] His support from both factions of the Republican Party also made him the favorite going into the general election campaign against a property assessor and former Roane County Democratic Party chair named Randy Button. Button began his campaign focusing on retaining and recruiting jobs for the district, bringing the deficit down, and coming up with affordable health care (Gabel 1994a, C1). Button presented himself as at least a moderate Democrat, if not a conservative one. He agreed with Wamp on term limits, repealing the crime bill, opposing an American invasion of Haiti, and not increasing funding to mothers who have additional children while on welfare. Button said he would be obligated to vote in the interests of his constituents, even over party leaders. While there were some differences between the candidates on health care and special-interest funding of campaigns, the main issue on which the candidates diverged was abortion. "On abortion, the two candidates are far apart. Wamp holds the view that abortion is unacceptable under any circumstances; including rape or incest. . . . Abortion can be justified only to save the life of the mother. Button believes abortion is wrong, but he says he does not want to push his view on others. He says alternatives like adoption and abstinence should be emphasized to young people. But he says he will uphold the laws of the country and follow court decisions" (Gabel 1994f, A1). While Button's position certainly was not on the far liberal end of the spectrum on this important issue, Wamp was almost as far right as one can get. There was clear polarization on this issue and by far the subject the candidates disagreed on most. It was also an issue that retained enormous salience for many religious conservatives across the country. And in Tennessee's Third District, they were out there working hard for Zach Wamp.

Conservative Christian Activists Display Sophistication and Intensity

Many religious conservatives were brought into the political process by Jim Golden's congressional campaign in 1986. Some left when Golden lost, but others remained active. One of those was Doug Daugherty, Golden's campaign manager. Daugherty joined the Chattanooga Resource Foundation in 1990 and added a political component to its other activities.[32] The CRF was started in 1983 by several prominent Christian leaders and businessmen in the Chattanooga community. It was a Christian organization committed to the welfare of the city. Its members identified problems in the city and tried to come up with faith-based solutions. In the early years, there were no employees: the board did all the work. It engaged very little in politics until Daugherty joined. A parallel does emerge between Daugherty bringing politics to the CRF in the early 1990s and David Gittrich, who masterminded the political operation for Kansans for Life during the same period. While national organizations such as the Christian Coalition received all the headlines for their political activism in 1992 and 1994—and they were an important presence in many congressional districts—local groups such as the CRF and KFL did much of the work at the grassroots level and were extremely valuable to Republicans who espoused morally conservative messages.

Politically, the Chattanooga Resource Foundation did five things in 1994. First came the Salt and Light Update, a leaflet that would be distributed at churches focusing on a particular issue and what people could do about it. They printed up to forty thousand per month to give out. Issues included the state lottery, a parental notification law, and local pornography. According to Daugherty, they were very successful. The Salt and Light Update on local pornography helped shut down several stores in the Chattanooga area that sold pornographic material.[33] Second, when elections came up, the foundation sent out surveys to local candidates to get their issue positions on the record. Questions included ones on prayer in schools, which was considered a local issue by Daugherty. They surveyed anyone running for anything, and then they would print the results and distribute them at no cost to local churches. Daugherty felt this gave voters the information to make good choices when going to the polls. The questions were not limited to issues of moral traditionalism, Daugherty says, but they were the heart and soul of the effort. Third, the CRF published a monthly prayer letter that went out to people who wanted to pray for Chattanooga. It went out to forty-five thousand people and did not endorse candidates. However, it asked people to pray for the election, pray for the candidates that tell the truth, and pray that the most important issues will be addressed in the campaign. It told people to pray for the candidates' families to be protected and to pray for the right person to get elected. However, it did not take a position on who that might be. According to Daugherty, the newsletter was not overtly political, but it kept politics in the minds of the people as something they should be thinking about.

Fourth, the foundation ran a leadership program that mentored roughly twenty to twenty-five students every six months. For two to four weeks, they would spend time on the importance of law in a culture and how this touches on politics. Daugherty told me that several local candidates came out of the leadership school. Fifth, the CRF once used an automated dialing machine that called people and alerted them to activities relating to an issue that they had registered an interest in. For example, if an important vote was coming up on abortion, they would call everyone who had expressed an interest in that issue and explain to them what was going on and what they could do to help.

Before 1990 and Doug Daugherty joining the CRF, the organization was not very political. The number-one goal of the foundation was to look out for the welfare of the city, and Daugherty felt this made it necessary to get people in the city involved and aware. It was important to the foundation that those in the religious community not have such low turnout rates. Daugherty believed these candidate surveys were a responsible use of the foundation's resources. "We knew that the community was a conservative community. But what we also knew was that people did not make a connection between an issue and a candidate. And because of that, a lot of them didn't vote for the candidate that most represented their issue. They voted for Marilyn because she was perceived to be a conservative Democrat. People weren't connecting how she felt on the issues. We thought if we could connect issues to candidates, it would be a good idea. We thought that would help to do that" (Daugherty, interview with author). David Fowler also spoke positively of the political aims of the foundation. "[CRF] has encouraged political leaders locally to consider the moral and social aspects of the communities (e.g., pornography at a local level, abortion, marriage, etc. at a state level) in which they serve instead of only the economic aspects" (Fowler, personal communication).

The two quotes in the previous paragraph nicely encapsulate the role played by local Christian conservative activists in congressional elections beginning in the early 1990s. Moral issues had become more and more salient over the past decades, but the voters had not been able to vote on the basis of these issues because they either did not know what the candidates thought about issues of moral traditionalism or because there was no difference between the major party candidates. The CRF through their Salt and Light Updates and candidate surveys, much like the automated phone calls done by KFL, helped take care of the first obstacle. Other religious conservative activists, along with candidates Todd Tiahrt and Bob Inglis, took care of the second by taking strong stands on such issues as abortion and gay rights.

All the sophistication and effort in the world cannot help a candidate if the public does not respond and get involved—whether it is simply voting, giving money, or volunteering for a campaign. Zach Wamp benefited greatly from an energized and active religious conservative community in Tennessee's Third District. There are roughly eight hundred churches of varying size in the Chattanooga area. Many are fundamentalist or independent evangelical in nature. During the 1994 general election campaign, their congregants were out in full force for one of their own. Billy Linville was Randy Button's campaign manager, and he still remembers the intensity of Wamp and his supporters. "[Zach] had a fundamentalist-type of intensity to him and his campaign. It was very urgent and it fit with his personality. He had developed a core group of supporters that had the same personality. They were spreading the gospel." Linville recalls Wamp having an "unbelievable grassroots network going on. They were soldiers in his army" (Linville, interview with author). According to Linville, they were focused and willing to do whatever it took to win—all in the name of God. Most of the volunteers came from the socially conservative wing of the party, and many had not been involved in politics before but were motivated by Wamp and his campaign.

Linville laments the way the race took shape and how it turned out for his candidate. Despite his moderate positions, Button was tarnished by the "D" beside his name when trying to gain support from voters and interest groups. The National Rifle Association endorsed Wamp despite the fact Button was a hunter and that he supported every gun-friendly policy advocated by the NRA. Button also tried to focus on health care and the economy, which was in excellent shape. However, these topics could not compete with the social issues.[34] Linville remembers Hillary Clinton being an issue in the race, and according to Button's campaign manager, in 1994 in Tennessee's Third District, "Hillary" was code for "gay." For Linville, liberals, Clinton, guns, God, and gays were the issues that drove everything in that year.[35] Linville also noticed the unity among Republican factions that had feuded in the past. "Three things brought the old guard Republicans together with the religious conservatives: 1) hatred and fear of President Clinton, 2) liberalism, 3) the real possibility of becoming a majority in Congress" (Linville, interview with author).

Tennessee's Third Adds to the Republican Congressional Landslide of 1994

In the end, Zach Wamp's ability to unite the old-guard moneyed elite and the newly active Christian conservatives behind his candidacy helped him defeat Randy Button. Wamp won by just under 11,000 votes (52 percent to 46 percent). He spent just over $700,000, roughly $200,000 more than Button (Barone and Ujifusa 1995, 1240). Wamp boasted of Democratic defections. "I had a lot of Democrats come up to me today. Richard Jones at the Soddy-Daisy precinct [approached me]. He said, 'I'm a labor man. Today I voted a straight Republican ticket'" (Gabel 1994h, A1). Every observer of the election that I spoke with mentioned the role played by religiously conservative activists and moral issues in Zach Wamp's win. Assessments of how important they were varied. Dave Flessner did not believe the race necessarily broke on social issues but that they are always an undercurrent. Bob Swansbrough admitted religious conservatives were a major force in Wamp's campaign, but he did not think they were running the show. Billy Linville argues that the dynamic by which Wamp won was the effective organization and strategy of the social right. Christian conservatives may not have won the election for Zach Wamp by themselves, but most agree they were certainly pivotal to his victory. Without their money, time, and energy he could not have won. The real key to Wamp's win and the Republican Party's takeover of this at-risk district was the symbiotic relationship that developed between the business Republicans informally led by Pat Brock and the Christian Republicans coming out of the churches. The partnership was not there in the 1980s, and the GOP suffered for it. Billy Linville gives the so-called religious right a great deal of credit for making this happen. "The social right, prior to the 1990s, was less organized, less savvy, and much more passive. Thanks to the Christian Coalition and other similar organizations, the social right became very adept at message, organization, intimidation, and setting the tone of local and congressional campaigns. They became political experts. Of course, at the same time, the Democratic Party became emasculated and timid, defensive and hesitant. It all came together in 1994—the perfect storm" (Linville, interview with author).

No More Risk in Tennessee's Third

In 1994, Wamp said he would serve only twelve years in the House, and in 2004, he spent months traveling the state with an eye toward running for the Senate seat that Bill Frist vacated in 2006. But Chattanooga mayor Bob Corker said he was running and within two months had raised $2 million. Seeing this, Wamp decided not to run. He did not keep his term limits promise and instead successfully sought reelection in 2006. Twelve years after vanquishing the Democrats in the watershed election of 1994, Wamp had made this seat his own. As with Kansas's Fourth and South Carolina's Fourth, Tennessee's Third went from being an at-risk district held by Democrats in the early 1990s to being a no-risk district held by the GOP in the first decade of the twenty-first century. It was also one of the districts that contributed to the Republican takeover of the House in 1994.

In 2010, Wamp finally decided to jump into a statewide race seeking the Republican nomination for governor. A second-place finish seemed to end his political career. The primary to replace Wamp was spirited as personal injury lawyer Chuck Fleischmann barely bested Robin Smith, a health care consultant and former chair of the Tennessee Republican Party. Fleischmann won by two points and in the general election largely ignored his Democratic opponent, steering clear of debates and candidate forums. In this safe district, there were no negative repercussions from that strategy as Fleischmann outpolled his opponent by a two-to-one margin. Despite the intensity of Tea Partiers in 2009 and 2010, Fleischmann, along with Pompeo and Gowdy, did not seek out the support of the myriad number of groups associated with the movement. Fleischmann also steered clear of social issues in his first campaign but voted to defund Planned Parenthood and received a healthy 95 percent rating from the Family Research Council (Barone and McCutcheon 2013, 1540).

Fleischmann proved to be an extremely loyal Republican during his first few terms in Washington. He is known as a strong opponent of gun control and, as a freshman, snagged a seat on the Energy and Water Development subcommittee of Appropriations where he has faithfully looked after his district's interests. Fleischmann's only electoral worry would come from the GOP primary, but after squeaking by two strong challengers, including Zach Wamp's son, Weston, in 2012, he has seemingly made this seat one of the safest in the nation. In 2018, he won 79 percent of the vote in the Republican primary and 64 percent in the general election.

Shifting Gears

Chapters 4, 5, and 6 delved deeply into three congressional districts that share many characteristics, shedding light on the role of the Christian right in U.S. House elections. Local grassroots activists fought hard to get candidates nominated who would stress the issues of moral traditionalism that they cared about. After some initial failures, they eventually prevailed, first within the Republican Party and then against the Democrats. These districts flipped to the GOP during the early 1990s, helping the Republican Party fashion a majority that with the exception of 2006–2010, remained until 2018. The importance of moral issues to U.S. House voters and the increased polarization on these issues helped create the conditions necessary for the Republican takeover of Congress and subsequent solidification of their majority. In Chapters 7 and 8, I will undertake a quantitative analysis of this phenomenon using American National Election Studies survey data and my candidate placements. I hope that the empirical work that follows provides a firmer grounding for the conclusions I have drawn thus far.

Chapter 7

Issue Polarization and Voting Behavior in U.S. House Elections

Connecting Issues to Candidates

The Chattanooga Resource Foundation (CRF) was started in 1983 by several prominent Christian leaders and businessmen in the medium-sized Tennessee community. It began as a Christian organization committed to the welfare of the city. Its members would identify problems and try to come up with faith-based solutions. At first it was mostly apolitical, but in the early 1990s, it began to involve itself in local campaigns and other political activities. Doug Daugherty, a former congressional campaign manager, joined the CRF in 1990 and stressed engaging and informing the public about which candidates took religion and morality into consideration when making public policy decisions. He sought to increase voter turnout rates and create a connection between voters, candidates, and issues of moral traditionalism. The main vehicle for doing this was the publication and dissemination of candidate surveys. The CRF would query candidates running for office about their views on the issues and then print the results and distribute them at no cost to local churches.

In the early 1990s, Chattanooga was represented in the U.S. House by a moderate Democrat named Marilyn Lloyd. Lloyd had been in office since 1974 when she ran in place of her deceased husband, Mort Lloyd. Daugherty was frustrated that Chattanooga continued to reelect a Democrat who, while no flaming liberal, appeared to be left of the district on many issues, including abortion. "We knew that the community was a conservative community. But what we also know was that people did not make a connection between an issue and a candidate. And because of that, a lot of them didn't vote for the candidate that most represented their issue. They voted for Marilyn because she was perceived to be a conservative Democrat. People weren't connecting how she felt on the issues. We thought if we could connect issues to candidates, it would be a good idea. We thought that would help to do that" (Daugherty, interview with author).

My Congressional Vote Model

Connecting issues to candidates did indeed turn out to be a good idea, and not long after Doug Daugherty and the CRF started distributing candidate surveys, the Republican Party had wrested Tennessee's Third District seat from the Democrats. For an issue to influence a voter's decision at the polls, it is necessary for a citizen to know where the candidates stand on that issue and for the candidates to differ in some way on that same issue. Then, and only then, can the issue have an impact on the voter's decision-making process. In this chapter, I will be creating voter knowledge and issue polarization variables in an effort to assess the relative salience of moral issues in the congressional voting calculus. Chapter 2 covered the placement of candidates on an ideological continuum, and in this chapter, using American National Election Studies (ANES) data, I specify a model that will seek to quantify how much predictive power moral issues can have on voting for the House of Representatives.

I will be employing a communications-based interaction model that accounts for voter ideology, voter knowledge, and district issue polarization. In a presidential voting model where the messages are very intense and widespread, a simple interaction model without an estimation of voter knowledge would likely be sufficient.[1] In U.S. House elections, where message intensity varies considerably among candidates and therefore districts, an effort must be made to interact ideology and polarization with the probability that people will become aware of these factors. The estimation process will take place in two stages. The first stage will predict the likelihood of a voter "receiving" campaign messages. Variables determining this likelihood include campaign spending, incumbency, media coverage, and an individual's level of political information. The values on these measures will vary in three ways. Each voter will have a different level of political information while the party of the candidate and the particular district will also contribute to a computation of what I am calling "knowledge of the Democratic candidate" and "knowledge of the Republican candidate." In the second stage, I will use average voter knowledge calculated from stage one to

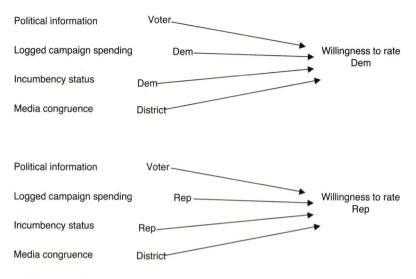

Figure 7.1. Stage one of my communications-based interaction model estimating message reception

run separate regression analyses on those voters with below-average and above-average knowledge of the candidates. I will be predicting congressional vote choice with voter ideology and district issue polarization on three broad issue domains: moral traditionalism, economics, and race and ethnicity. In addition, I will include a term that interacts voter ideology with district issue polarization on each of the three issue dimensions. Standard demographic and political control variables along with year dummies round out the model. Figure 7.1 diagrams stage one of the model while Figure 7.2 shows stage two.

Using the coefficients produced in the stage-one regression, I have calculated two probabilities for each voter: one for the likelihood that they have received the Democratic message (Knowledge $_{Dem}$) and one for the likelihood that they have received the Republican message (Knowledge $_{Rep}$). In stage two, the average of these two knowledge variables will be used to split the data into two separate regressions to assess the direct and interactive effects of voter ideology and district polarization on the probability of voting Republican for the U.S. House. Splitting the data is a way of determining how knowledge interacts with all of the variables in the regression.[2]

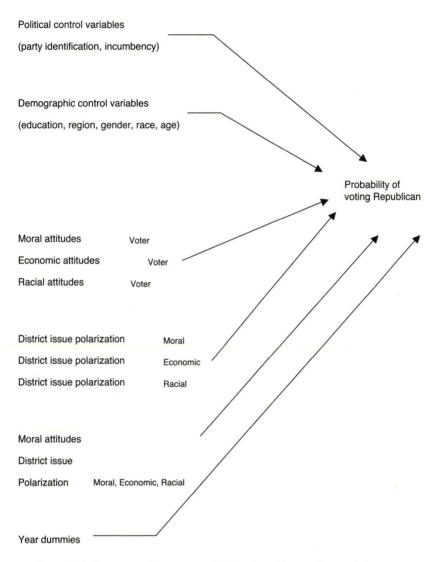

Political control variables
(party identification, incumbency)

Demographic control variables
(education, region, gender, race, age)

Probability of
voting Republican

Moral attitudes   Voter
Economic attitudes   Voter
Racial attitudes   Voter

District issue polarization   Moral
District issue polarization   Economic
District issue polarization   Racial

Moral attitudes
District issue
Polarization   Moral, Economic, Racial

Year dummies

Figure 7.2. Stage two of my communications-based interaction model
estimating U.S. House vote

Six groups of independent variables will be included in my model. The first set consists of the standard political measures that must be included in any congressional voting model. Both party identification and incumbency have strong bivariate correlations with congressional vote (0.611 and 0.464, respectively). The second set includes standard demographic variables, such as education, region (South), gender, race, and age. Education, race, and gender are positively correlated with Republican vote choice while age and South show no significant correlation. The third group consists of voter ideology on each of the three issue dimensions. The fourth set includes district issue polarization on each of the three issue dimensions. The fifth set consists of voter ideology interacted with district polarization for each issue dimension. Finally, there are year dummies included in the model. An equation estimating the Republican U.S. House vote provides the reader with the complete model specification of stage two,[3] and the next three subsections of this chapter elaborate on the variables I am most interested in: voter ideology, voter knowledge, and district issue polarization.

Three Issue Dimensions

To run my vote choice model, I make use of two data sources. For voter attributes, I rely on the ANES. For candidate placements, I mine the *Almanac of American Politics*. While the earlier analysis of candidate positions presented in Chapter 2 includes all cycles from 1978 to 2012, the period of study for the congressional voting model exhibited in this chapter is more limited. There are three reasons for this. First, the key independent variable I will be employing to measure voter morality was not included in the ANES until 1986. Second, in 2002 the ANES conducted an abridged study that excluded several essential variables. Finally, there were no time-series studies at all in 2006 and 2010. Despite these limitations, the ANES is particularly helpful in this analysis because they code voters by their congressional district. The number of districts sampled by the ANES varies from year to year and ranges from a minimum of 121 in 1990 to 434 in 2012. There is also variation in the number of individuals questioned in each district. For the years included in the current analysis, the average number of respondents per district is 10.7, with the minimum being one respondent surveyed in multiple districts over multiple years, and the maximum being 81 from Tennessee's Fourth District in 1988. These small Ns and a lack of randomness at the district level would be problematic except that my analysis involves an aggregation of respondents across districts across years.

I chose to include three broad issue dimensions in my analysis. The first deals with moral or cultural issues, the second with economic or fiscal issues, and the third with racial or ethnic issues. I will now relate how I chose to operationalize voter positions on these three dimensions. Issues of morality are some of the most controversial subjects in current American politics. Abortion, LGBTQ rights, women's rights, and school prayer are just some of the issues known for their moral tenor debated publicly in modern American political life. They are often the most bitterly contested issues because they strike at the core of many Americans' most cherished beliefs. In the era of the "culture wars," moral appeals are widely believed to cross traditional religious barriers. Gone are the days of the tripartite classification of Protestant-Catholic-Jew (Herberg 1960). What we see now are evangelical Protestants, conservative Catholics, and Orthodox Jews on one side of the divide, in a cultural struggle with mainline Protestants, liberal Catholics, and reformed Jews on the other side (Hunter 1991). Therefore, I wanted to find a measure of an individual's stance on moral issues that was tied neither to one particular topic or issue, since there are many that can be important, nor to a particular denomination or religious tradition, considering the limitations of those categories in determining how someone feels about these hot-button cultural issues. And for practical purposes, I wanted a variable that was asked consistently by the ANES for as much of my period of study as possible. In fact, I settled on combining multiple questions into a four-item moral traditionalism scale. These four questions were asked every year the ANES was conducted between 1986 and 2012 with the exception of 2002. Respondents were asked the following questions and were instructed to either (1) agree strongly, (2) agree somewhat, (3) neither agree nor disagree, (4) disagree somewhat, or (5) disagree strongly:

1. The newer lifestyles are contributing to the breakdown of our society. (VCF0851)
2. The world is always changing and we should adjust our view of moral behavior to those changes. (VCF0852)
3. This country would have many fewer problems if there were more emphasis on traditional family ties. (VCF0853)

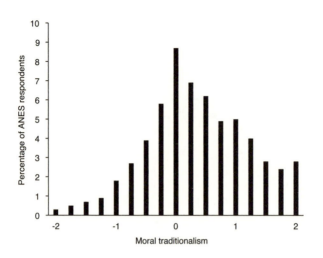

Figure 7.3. Distribution of U.S. voters on the moral traditionalism scale

4. We should be more tolerant of people who choose to live according to their own moral standards, even if they are very different from our own. (VCF0854)

To create the moral traditionalism scale, I recoded the four variables above so higher numbers indicated a morally traditional viewpoint and then averaged the respondents' score. The resulting scale ranged from a minimum of 1 to a maximum of 5. These values were then transformed so the minimums and maximums matched the candidate scale presented in Chapter 2 (i.e., a minimum of –2 and a maximum of 2). The frequency distribution for the moral traditionalism variable is presented in Figure 7.3, and the means for each year are shown in Figure 7.4.

The frequency distribution for the moral traditionalism scale resembles the normal distribution but is skewed slightly toward the right, which is the more conservative end of the scale. This skew is also represented in Figure 7.4, which shows the means on that moral traditionalism scale over time. In every year during the period of study, the mean is positive, which denotes the conservative leanings of the country on this scale. However, when looking at the time trend, it is clear that after a peak in 1994, the nation has been trending in a liberal direction when it comes to these questions. But we are interested in this scale not for its own sake but as a proxy

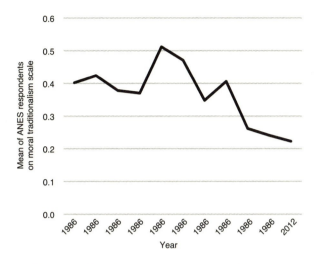

Figure 7.4. Mean moral traditionalism of American public over time

Table 7.1. Moral traditionalism and attitudes toward abortion

Moral Traditionalism	Mean Abortion Attitudes[a]	N
−2	1.14	69
−1	1.55	486
0	2.14	2,413
1	2.34	1,392
2	2.99	774

[a] Abortion attitudes range from 1 to 4, with higher numbers denoting a more pro-life stance.

and a representation of how voters might feel about various hot-button moral issues. For this measure of voter morality to be valid, it would have to predict attitudes on moral issues. For it to be reliable, it would have to be supported by other surveys taken during the past thirty years.

The correlation between moral traditionalism and abortion attitudes is 0.318 ($p < 0.001$). Table 7.1 displays an almost perfect linear relationship between the two variables. On the low end of the moral traditionalism scale, the mean response corresponds most closely to the following attitude toward abortion: "By law, a woman should always be able to obtain an abortion as a matter of personal choice." The high end of the moral traditionalism scale represents the following attitude toward abortion: "The law

Table 7.2. Moral traditionalism and attitudes toward school prayer

Moral Traditionalism	Mean Attitudes on School Prayer[a]	N
-2	1.49	36
-1	2.08	295
0	2.33	1,623
1	2.43	952
2	2.58	554

[a] Attitudes on school prayer range from 1 to 4, with higher numbers denoting a more pro–school prayer stance.

should permit abortion only in case of rape, incest, or when the woman's life is in danger."[4] On school prayer, the correlation is 0.169 (p < 0.001). Table 7.2 also shows a fairly linear relationship (although slightly weaker) between moral traditionalism and attitudes on school prayer. And finally, on gays in the military, the moral traditionalism scale correlates at 0.255 (p < 0.001). Of those who scored –2 on the moral traditionalism scale, 100 percent of them believed gays should be allowed to serve in the military. Of those who scored 0 on the moral traditionalism scale, 73 percent agreed with that proposition. Of those who scored 2 on the moral traditionalism scale, only 39 percent believed gays should serve in the military. In addition, the voter morality variable does a nice job of predicting religious behavior, correlating with church attendance at 0.355 (p < 0.001), as well as predicting religious doctrine, correlating with attitudes toward the Bible at 0.308 (p < 0.001).

Concerning reliability, several studies have found that Americans show evidence of high levels of religiosity and are fairly conservative on moral issues. Lyman Kellstedt and his colleagues found that over 60 percent of the population exhibits high levels of religious commitment (1996, 184). They conclude the following: "Even minimal measures of religious affiliation and involvement show impressive relationships with political attitudes and behaviors, quite apart from other social and demographic characteristics" (Kellstedt et al. 1996, 187). Furthermore, the relationships are quite consistent, with higher levels of religious commitment correlating with conservative positions on abortion and gay rights. In addition, the demographic characteristics of moral conservatives in my research correspond to those in other studies. Age is positively correlated with religious and moral

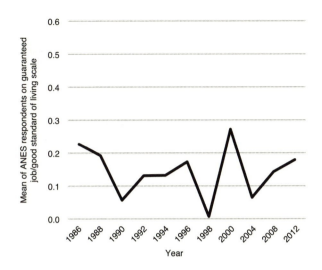

Figure 7.5. Mean economic attitudes of American public over time

conservatism while education is negatively correlated. In addition, South-erners are much more likely to be religiously and morally conservative than residents of other regions.

To measure voter attitudes on economic issues, I chose to use the guar-anteed job and standard-of-living question asked by the ANES in all years from 1986 to 2012 with the exception of 2002.[5] Of course, this question does not address every conceivable economic issue that might come before the voters and enter into the public policy debate. However, I believe it is representative of broader economic ideas about the role government should play in the economy and on economic issues more generally. Plus, it has the benefit of being asked consistently throughout the period of study. This 7-point scale was recoded to a 5-point scale and transformed to fit the −2 to 2 candidate message scales introduced and presented in Chapter 2. Fig-ure 7.5 displays mean economic attitudes over time. The numbers are somewhat choppy, and if any trend can be reported, it is only a slight liberal trend over the period of study. That said, the average in all years is still positive, meaning the country leans to the conservative end of the spectrum on the issue of whether the government should provide a guaranteed job and a good standard of living.

To measure racial attitudes, I have selected the question concerning aid to blacks and minorities, which is also asked from 1986 to 2012 with the

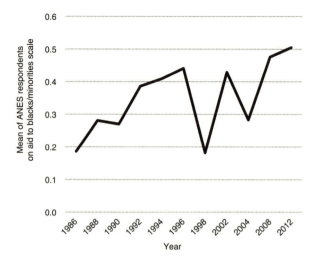

Figure 7.6. Mean racial attitudes of American public over time

exception of 2002.[6] As with the economic variable, there are such issues as busing, affirmative action, and illegal immigration that are not directly represented by this question, but I believe it serves the general purpose of getting a sense for how respondents feel about the government's role in helping African Americans and other minority groups. Therefore, it is a good proxy for the other issues that the ANES does not always ask about. Figure 7.6 shows mean racial attitudes over the period of study. As with moral and economic attitudes, the country is slightly right of center, but this is the only dimension that exhibits a conservative trend from 1986 to 2012. The year 2012 accounts for the most conservative value on this measure.

The expectation, of course, is that there will be a positive relationship between voter ideology and U.S. House vote. Figure 7.7 shows the bivariate relationship between each of the three issue dimensions and Republican vote. On moral issues, the relationship is positive and fairly strong. On economic issues and racial issues, there is a similar trend, but we do not see very conservative voters significantly more likely to vote Republican then their less conservative counterparts. There appears to be a problem with only looking at the simple bivariate relationships between issue distance and congressional vote. Obviously, there are important control variables missing, but more important than that is the lack of a measure of

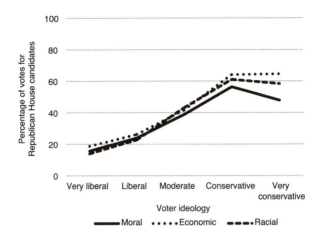

Figure 7.7. Bivariate relationships between voter ideology and Republican votes for the U.S. House

whether the voter actually knows where the candidate stands on the issues. Remember, this is not a presidential election where tons of information are foisted on the American electorate. Congressional candidates are much less known to the public, and there needs to be a way to take this into consideration in any congressional voting model. Furthermore, a lack of polarization on a set of issues would render even the most attentive voter unable to decide based on those issues. In the next subsection, I will model voter knowledge, and after that, I will discuss how I measured district issue polarization.

Measuring Voter Knowledge

In studies of issue voting, we look for how predictive a particular issue position is of the ultimate vote choice. This type of model is, however, easier to implement for presidential vote decisions in which both candidates are fairly well known than in congressional vote decisions where one, both, or neither candidate may be well known. For example, how can a citizen vote on the basis of the issues when one or both candidates are largely unknown to him or her? The standard issue voting model does not capture this complexity.

My approach is to conduct a two-stage logistic regression analysis with the first stage serving to estimate and compute knowledge of the Democratic and Republican congressional candidates. Those predicted knowledge values will be the probability of the voter "receiving" the message of each candidate and will be used to split the data in the second stage of the regression, which will estimate and compute the probability of voting for the Republican candidate. The dependent variable in stage one is whether or not the respondent is willing to rate the candidate on a one-hundred-point feeling thermometer. Respondents are given the option of saying they do not recognize the candidate's name or saying they do not know enough to rate. So, in essence, this thermometer variable serves as a measure of whether the voter recognizes the candidate's name and feels he or she has enough information to place them on the feeling thermometer scale. This is my proxy for whether or not a voter has "gotten the message" from a particular candidate, and I have selected four independent variables that figure to be strong predictors of this. The first measure, political information, varies by voter. This is the respondent's level of political information reported by their ANES interviewer. It ranges from 1 to 5 with a mean of 3.15 and a standard deviation of 1.1, with higher numbers indicating greater political information. Of course, the expectation is that higher levels of political information will increase the likelihood of receiving both candidates' message. The second measure, campaign spending, varies by candidate. The more money a candidate spends, the more likely voters are to hear the message coming from the campaign. In the model, campaign spending is logged and adjusted for inflation. The third measure, incumbency, also varies by candidate. An incumbent will be better known than a challenger with all other things equal. And finally, there is media coverage, which varies by district. This variable was created by counting up the number of Nielsen television media markets that cover a particular district and then dividing that by the total number of districts covered by those media markets. Maximum convergence, or coverage, would take place when a television market has the identical geographical shape as a congressional district. The value on this variable would be 1/1 or 1. There is no actual instance of this perfect level of convergence. The theoretical minimum would be zero if a district was not covered by any media markets, but there is no real-world instance of this either. So to illustrate how this variable works in practice, I will give some examples of districts with varying degrees of convergence. Districts in urban areas will generally have low levels of convergence. Consider the Los Angeles metro area. It is covered by one media market (Los Angeles), but there are currently twenty-nine congressional districts within that market. So each district gets 1/29 of the coverage. That computes to 0.034 and would suggest that each of those L.A.-area districts is getting very little coverage. However, Massachusetts's First District also has one media market covering it (Providence, Rhode Island–New Bedford, Massachusetts), but only two districts share that media market. In this case, the media coverage value would be 1/2, or 0.5. Another way to get relatively sizable amounts of coverage would be to have more than one media market covering the district. Mississippi's Third District is covered by five media markets, and those five markets touch on sixteen total districts. The value would be 5/16, or 0.313. When predicting how much knowledge a voter will have about those who are running to represent them in the U.S. House, we would expect media coverage as measured here to have a positive and statistically significant effect. As shown in Figure 7.1, I will be estimating this "knowledge model" for both the Democratic and Republican candidates. Two equations, one estimating knowledge of the Republican U.S. House candidate,[7] and the second estimating knowledge of the Democratic U.S. House candidate,[8] represent stage one of my voting model. Here I am estimating the probability of a voter receiving a candidate's message measured by the individual's ability to rate said candidate on a one-hundred-point feeling thermometer. Their willingness to rate the congressional candidate is the dependent variable in stage one, and the independent variables are the voter's political information as estimated by the ANES interviewer, candidate spending, incumbency status, and media coverage.

Tables 7.3 and 7.4 show the logistic regression coefficients for stage one. All four independent variables have positive and significant effects on voter knowledge as measured by their willingness to rate the candidates. These coefficients do not have intuitive meaning by themselves, so in Figures 7.8, 7.9, and 7.10, I present the predicted probabilities of Republican name recognition, varying spending, incumbency status, and media coverage, respectively. The effects of respondent political information can be gauged by looking across each of the three figures from left to right.

The first thing to notice from these three graphs is the strong, independent, and direct effect of political information on a respondent's willingness to rate the Republican candidate. Regardless of which of the other three variables is manipulated, as political information rises, so does the probability of

Table 7.3. Model coefficients for estimating knowledge of Republican U.S. House candidate

Independent Variables Dependent Variable: Willingness to rate Republican candidate	Beta Coefficients (Standard Errors)
Political information	0.543 (0.017)
Republican spending	0.181 (0.007)
Incumbency status	0.847 (0.039)
Media coverage	0.972 (0.154)
Constant	−2.573 (0.077)
N	17,420
Adjusted R-square	0.191

name recognition and, with it, presumably message reception. However, political information does not seem to interact with any of the other three variables as the gaps between the lines in each of the three figures are relatively stable regardless of the value political information takes.

Figure 7.8 shows the impact of spending on name recognition. The difference between high and low spending, defined here as one standard deviation above and below the mean, amounts to about twenty-five percentage points. Figure 7.9 displays the effect of incumbency on name recognition. The difference between being a challenger and an incumbent is about fifteen percentage points. And finally, the impact of media coverage is much smaller as represented by the tiny gap between the two lines in Figure 7.10. High media convergence only gets a candidate four percentage points more likelihood of name recognition than a district with low media convergence. As one would expect, Republican knowledge is positively and significantly correlated with Republican vote while Democratic knowledge is negatively and significantly correlated with Republican vote (0.377 and −0.338, respectively). However, I will gauge the impact of this important

Table 7.4. Model coefficients for estimating knowledge of Democratic U.S. House candidate

Independent Variables Dependent Variable: Willingness to rate Democratic candidate	Beta Coefficients (Standard Errors)
Political information	0.473 (0.017)
Democratic spending	0.193 (0.008)
Incumbency status	1.109 (0.039)
Media coverage	2.044 (0.167)
Constant	−2.626 (0.084)
N	17,874
Adjusted R-square	0.177

variable, both directly on the vote and in interaction with voter ideology and district polarization, by averaging Republican and Democratic knowledge and splitting the data set into two groups based on those values. The first will consist of voters with below-average knowledge, and the second will consist of those with above-average knowledge. This avoids the need for a cumbersome triple interaction model (see note 2).

Operationalizing District Issue Polarization

Finally, I will be measuring district issue polarization by coding candidate messages on all three issue dimensions and subtracting the Democratic value from the Republican value. This procedure is discussed in great detail in "Increasing Polarization on the Issues" in Chapter 2. The reader will recall that the theoretical range of this variable goes from −4 (very liberal Republican, very conservative Democrat) to 4 (very conservative Republican, very liberal Democrat). Obviously, the theoretical minimum is very unlikely to occur, and in fact, Tables 2.3 to 2.5 show that from 1978 to 2012 there were no districts that took a value of −4. The theoretical maximum is

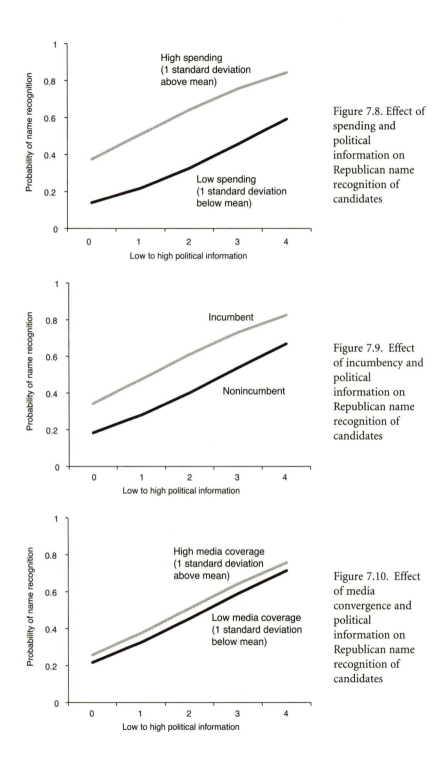

Figure 7.8. Effect of spending and political information on Republican name recognition of candidates

Figure 7.9. Effect of incumbency and political information on Republican name recognition of candidates

Figure 7.10. Effect of media convergence and political information on Republican name recognition of candidates

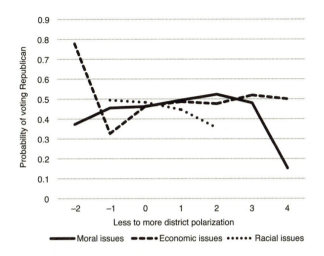

Figure 7.11. Direct effects of district polarization on the Republican U.S. House vote

also unlikely as this denotes extreme polarization. There were instances of this in the data but not many, as one can see from looking back at Tables 2.3 to 2.5. This variable would not figure to have a direct effect on vote choice in the aggregate. Variations in district issue polarization should induce some voters to vote Republican and some to vote Democratic. Sure enough, Figure 7.11 is consistent with this supposition. Issue polarization then would seem to depend on a voter's position on the issues in question. That is why I focus so much attention in the final section of this chapter on the interaction between those two variables.

Interactions Among Voter Ideology, Voter Knowledge, and Issue Polarization

Table 7.5 presents the logistic regression coefficients from stage two of my model. The middle column presents results for those voters with below-average knowledge, and the right-hand column shows results for those with above-average knowledge. Splitting the data set in this fashion allows me to estimate the interactive effects of voter knowledge on Republican U.S. House vote. For now, I will analyze only the direction and statistical significance of the model's variables. In Chapter 8, I will tackle substantive significance and quantify the different effects through the use of various simulations. As expected, party identification and incumbency have positive and highly significant effects on vote choice regardless of voter knowledge. As for the demographic variables, education is positive and significant for those with below-average knowledge of the candidates but not significant for those with above-average knowledge. Living in the South is important only for those with above-average knowledge. Gender is never significant, while race is significant in both data sets. Finally, older Americans are significantly more likely to vote Democratic when they have above-average knowledge. As for the direct effects of voter ideology, moral traditionalism is the only issue dimension that shows a positive and significant effect, and it holds for both highly knowledgeable and less knowledgeable voters. The other two issue dimensions are never significant. This is an interesting finding as it leads us to believe that even without polarization and regardless of knowledge levels, moral issues remain very important to voters. Now, all issues should be more important when there is indeed polarization and greater knowledge among the voters. This will be assessed when examining the interaction terms. Before we get to that, as expected, district issue polarization is indistinguishable from zero for all dimensions in both segments of the data set. It is positive for all three issue dimensions but not significant for any of them. Polarization in and of itself should not be expected to affect vote choice. Finally, we examine the coefficients for the three interactions included in this study. If polarization does increase issue salience, the coefficients should be positive and significant. If knowledge is also a factor, the effects should be larger in the right-hand column of Table 7.5. First, let us examine moral issues. Among below-average knowledge voters, the main interaction is positive but not significant. Among higher-knowledge voters, it is both positive and significant at high levels. This suggests knowledge is important for voters where moral issues are concerned. For economic issues, it is actually negative—not quite significantly so for less knowledgeable voters but positive and significant for above-average voters on knowledge. Knowledge really matters for voters on what may rightly be thought of as more complicated economic issues. On racial issues, there is very little difference between the two subsets, with both regressions giving us positive and significant coefficients on that final issue dimension. Even without a good amount of knowledge of the candidate's position on race, these issues still affect vote choice,

Table 7.5. Logistic coefficients predicting Republican U.S. House vote

Independent Variables Dependent Variable: Republican House vote	Beta Coefficients for Below-average knowledge respondents (< 0.636)	Beta Coefficients for Above-average knowledge respondents (> 0.636)
Party identification	2.071 (0.125)	2.215 (0.080)
Incumbency	1.270 (0.102)	1.058 (0.055)
Education	0.196 (0.089)	0.034 (0.058)
South	0.071 (0.189)	0.244 (0.111)
Male	0.010 (0.154)	0.014 (0.095)
White	0.879 (0.229)	0.680 (0.152)
Age	−0.038 (0.044)	−0.092 (0.030)
Moral traditionalism	0.380 (0.103)	0.272 (0.061)
Guaranteed job	0.198 (0.102)	0.096 (0.070)
Aid to blacks	0.016 (0.085)	0.162 (0.062)
Moral issue polarization	0.010 (0.102)	−0.157 (0.056)
Economic issue polarization	0.100 (0.112)	0.039 (0.063)
Racial issue polarization	0.232 (0.132)	0.093 (0.106)
Moral issue interaction	0.117 (0.109)	0.187 (0.052)
Economic issue interaction	−0.164 (0.089)	0.140 (0.061)

(continued)

Table 7.5. (Continued)

Independent Variables Dependent Variable: Republican House vote	Beta Coefficients for Below-average knowledge respondents (< 0.636)	Beta Coefficients for Above-average knowledge respondents (> 0.636)
Racial issue interaction	0.207 (0.106)	0.222 (0.122)
Constant	−1.470 (0.461)	−0.725 (0.337)
N	1,855	4,628
Adjusted R-square	0.486	0.451

Note: Standard errors are shown in parentheses.

especially when there is polarization in the district. These are just preliminary interpretations of the model's coefficients. Chapter 8 begins with interpreting the size of these effects and attempts to quantify the importance of moral issues relative to other impactful variables when determining congressional vote choice.

Chapter 8

The Importance of Being Moral

Bibletown, USA, Versus Sodom and Gomorrah

The American experiment has historically been likened to a melting pot where individuals of different races, ethnicities, religions, and cultures have assimilated and learned to live together. This notion has been challenged in recent decades as it has appeared that we resemble more of a salad bowl—one that has not been tossed very well. Political and demographic research has shown that we have sorted ourselves quite completely, creating islands of blue counties in a mostly red sea. On many dimensions, the country is deeply divided, and more often than not, we live among people who are like us on many political, demographic, and socioeconomic variables. On the moral and cultural issue dimension, there is the Bible Belt as opposed to the most cosmopolitan of areas in the big cities on either coast. Obviously, the appetite for candidates stressing moral traditionalism would vary depending on where the politician is running for office. My congressional voting model can simulate the electoral impact of moral issues in different types of districts. We can imagine two hypothetically extreme districts and name them Bibletown, USA, and Sodom and Gomorrah.[1] Stressing moral traditionalism in the former should bring an electoral advantage to the Republican candidate who does so. Doing the same in the latter district would seem to hurt that candidate's chances. But how much and under what circumstances might it make the difference between victory and defeat? This chapter opens with two simple simulations of this nature and then delves deeper into the substantive, statistical, and causal significance of the findings stemming from the model specified in Chapter 7.

The hypothetical Bibletown is a Southern district with 75 percent of the voting population scoring 2 on the moral traditionalism scale, 20 percent scoring 1, and 5 percent scoring 0. That electorate is very conservative on moral issues. In 2012, a Republican challenger running against a Democratic incumbent in Bibletown can win despite being outspent by the Democrat only if they are considered very conservative on moral issues. With all of the other variables set at their means and the Democrat positioned as a moderate on moral traditionalism, the Republican candidate will win 52.3 percent of the vote. If the candidate is seen as only marginally conservative, he or she will fall short, winning just 48.3 percent of the vote. If the candidate is seen as moderate or does not stress moral issues at all in the campaign, he or she will lose, taking only 44.3 percent of the vote. The difference of four points does not sound like a lot, but all other things equal, it can easily make the difference between a Republican pickup and a Republican defeat in a hotly contested U.S. House seat.

Conversely, we can simulate the impact of a strident, morally conservative campaign message in an extremely liberal district such as Sodom and Gomorrah. Sodom and Gomorrah would be the mirror image of Bibletown when it comes to moral traditionalism, with 75 percent scoring a −2 on that scale, 20 percent scoring a −1, and 5 percent scoring 0. In this instance, in 2012, a Republican incumbent can lose his or her seat to a big-spending, moderate Democrat if the incumbent espouses a very conservative moral message. This kind of Republican will win 44.2 percent of the vote. If the incumbent adopts only a conservative moral message, he or she will capture 55.8 percent of the vote; if the Republican is seen as moderate, he or she will win convincingly with 67.1 percent. These effects are not small, and as I demonstrate in this section, they can be pivotal. In addition, as I will show in the following section, they fare quite well when compared with the effects of economic and racial issue positions.

Operationalizing Issue Importance in U.S. House Elections

The three case studies chronicled in Chapters 4 through 6 present significant and persuasive qualitative evidence for the importance of moral issues in flipping three congressional districts from Democrat to Republican during the early 1990s. I believe these particular instances are emblematic of what has happened across the country over the past thirty-five years. To

Table 8.1. How each dimension stacks up on the three aspects of issue importance

Aspects of Importance	Effect on Vote	Polarization	Partisan Congruence
High	Moral, racial	Economic	Moral
Moderate		Moral	Economic, racial
Low	Economic	Racial	

begin to tackle this question more systematically and with quantitative evidence, I specified a model in Chapter 7 to test the relative effects of moral, economic, and racial issues on congressional vote choice. The beginning of this chapter highlights some basic simulations designed to show the substantive significance of moral issues in U.S. House elections. But to build a more complete case for the importance of moral issues, both in their own right and relative to the other two issue dimensions, I need to go beyond simply the effect on the vote that moral-issue distance is found to have. Issue distance can potentially have a large impact on a voter's calculus, but if there is no polarization on the issue, there is no logical way for that impact to be realized. In other words, if there is no public difference between the two major candidates on a particular issue dimension, then no matter how much importance a voter ascribes to it, it cannot affect that voter's decision-making process. And a candidate, or a party for that matter, cannot benefit from a set of issue positions without being closer to the voters' values on that dimension. In sum, there are three elements that combine to produce issue importance: (1) an issue dimension's effect on the vote choice, (2) an issue dimension's polarization, and (3) partisan congruence with the voters on an issue dimension. In the next section of this chapter, I will address how the three dimensions I include in my research fare on each of the three criteria listed above. Table 8.1 previews my conclusions. Quantifying the differences between the three issue dimensions will follow.

Effect on Vote

When arguing for the importance of issues in elections, one would need to demonstrate that at the individual level a voter's position on the issue in question predicts his or her vote choice. A more conservative ideology should produce a greater probability of voting for the Republican candidate. Since we are directly interacting voter ideology with issue polarization and indirectly interacting those two variables with knowledge (by splitting the data set), the best way to assess effect on the vote is through a series of graphs. Figures 8.2a to 8.2c graphically represent these effects for voters with below-average knowledge, while Figures 8.3a to 8.3c do the same for voters with above-average knowledge. On the y axes lie the individual-level probabilities of a voter choosing the Republican candidate, while the x axes plot voter ideology. The solid lines depict cases where there is no polarization on the particular issue dimension. The dotted lines represent instances where the Republican is more conservative on that dimension. Taken as a whole, these six graphs give us a sense of the impact of the three variables we are most interested in on each of the three issue dimensions included in the study. We can compare issue dimensions by reading down each set of graphs, which tell us what we need to know about the effect of voter ideology. Comparing Figure 8.2 to Figure 8.3 gives us the effect of voter knowledge. Comparing the slopes of the solid and dotted lines within each graph shows us the effect of district polarization. For moral issues, voter ideology has a huge effect regardless of knowledge or polarization. People are going to the polls, and their placement on the moral traditionalism scale has a large impact on their vote choice. For economic issues, knowledge appears to be a key factor when assessing the impact of voter ideology and district polarization. Among voters with below-average knowledge, polarization actually has a negative effect on the vote, meaning that the more conservative they are, the more they vote for the Democrat when the Republican is demonstrably more conservative on those issues. On the other hand, among voters with above-average knowledge, the expected effect is found, but the reader will notice that the magnitude is smaller than for moral issues. For racial issues, polarization is necessary for voter ideology to matter among voters with below-average knowledge. Among voters with above-average knowledge, polarization creates as great an effect for racial issues as it does for moral issues.

These are potentially large effects, especially in tightly contested congressional races. As shown in the opening of this chapter, the impact of moral issues can make the difference between victory and defeat in certain circumstances. But how do these effects compare with those of other political and demographic variables estimated in the voting model? Table 8.2 presents the marginal effects of selected variables included in the model explicated in the previous chapter. Of course, party identification and incumbency exhibit the largest and most significant effects in the model. Much of

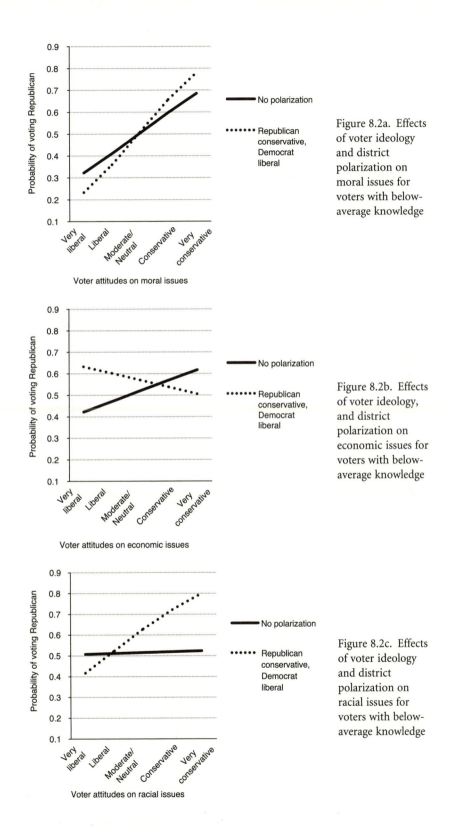

Figure 8.2a. Effects of voter ideology and district polarization on moral issues for voters with below-average knowledge

Figure 8.2b. Effects of voter ideology, and district polarization on economic issues for voters with below-average knowledge

Figure 8.2c. Effects of voter ideology and district polarization on racial issues for voters with below-average knowledge

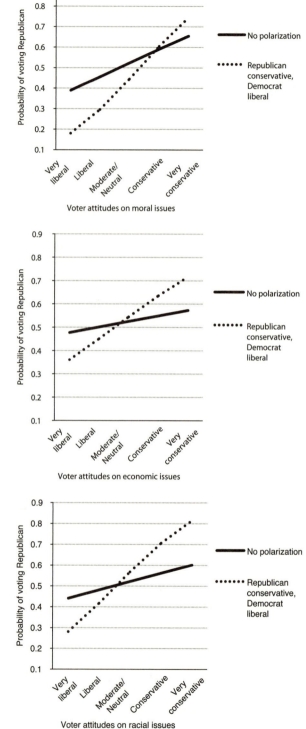

Figure 8.3a. Effects of voter ideology and district polarization on moral issues for voters with above-average knowledge

Figure 8.3b. Effects of voter ideology and district polarization on economic issues for voters with above-average knowledge

Figure 8.3c Effects of voter ideology and district polarization on racial issues for voters with above-average knowledge

Table 8.2. Marginal effects of selected variables on Republican U.S. House vote

Variable	Range	Size of Effect for Below-Average Knowledge Voters (%)	Size of Effect for Above-Average Knowledge Voters (%)
Party identification	Strong Democrat vs. strong Republican	+76.2 (0.000)	+79.9 (0.000)
Incumbency	Challenger vs. incumbent	+45.5 (0.000)	+47.7 (0.000)
Education	Least educated group vs. most educated group	+14.5 (0.028)	+2.5 (0.556)
Region	Non-South vs. South	+1.7 (0.706)	+6.0 (0.028)
Gender	Female vs. male	+0.2 (0.950)	+0.3 (0.886)
Race	Nonwhite vs. white	+21.6 (0.000)	+16.8 (0.000)
Age	Youngest cohort vs. oldest cohort	−5.4 (0.392)	−13.6 (0.002)

Note: P-values are in parentheses; all other variables are set at their means over the period of study, and the year is set at 2012.

congressional voting can be explained by these twin pillars of electoral prediction, and both matter regardless of knowledge. But there is still some variation left to explain. Race is also a reliable predictor regardless of knowledge levels, although not to the extent of party id and incumbency. Among those with less knowledge, education is a significant predictor of the vote, and among those with more knowledge, living in the South and age are significant predictors as well. The rest of the effects, as shown in Table 8.2, are much smaller and do not achieve standard levels of statistical significance.

Table 8.3 quantifies the total impact of the three variables I am most interested in. These are some of the numbers used to generate Figures 8.2a to 8.2c and 8.3a to 8.3c. Greater knowledge leads to larger effects for issues in five of the six scenarios. The exception is economic issues with no polarization. Economic issues stand out for another reason. In the below-average knowledge subset of the data, a conservative Republican candidate in a polarized district is less likely to be the choice of conservative voters. Even though

Table 8.3. Marginal, total effects of voter ideology, voter knowledge, and district polarization on Republican U.S. House vote

Issue dimensions and highlighted scenarios	Voter ideology	Size of Effect for Below-Average Knowledge Voters (%)	Size of Effect for Above-Average Knowledge Voters (%)
Moral issues, no polarization	Liberal to conservative	18.8 (0.0002)	23.5 (0.0000)
Moral issues, Republican conservative, Democrat liberal	Liberal to conservative	29.7 (0.0002)	30.9 (0.0000)
Economic issues, no polarization	Liberal to conservative	9.9 (0.2022)	4.8 (0.0008)
Economic issues, Republican conservative, Democrat liberal	Liberal to conservative	−6.3 (0.2022)	18.4 (0.0008)
Racial issues, no polarization	Liberal to conservative	0.8 (0.0225)	8.1 (0.0014)
Racial issues, Republican conservative, Democrat liberal	Liberal to conservative	19.8 (0.0225)	28.9 (0.0014)

Note: F-values from a joint test of significance are in parentheses; all other variables are set at their means over the period of study, and the year is set at 2012.

the F-test does not achieve standard levels of significance, it is still a notable finding. Moral issues are strong with or without polarization and with or without knowledge. Racial issues seem to need district polarization to really affect the vote. A quick comparison of Tables 8.2 and 8.3 shows that moral and racial issues come in a solid third to party identification and incumbency when it comes to predicting vote for the U.S. House of Representatives. Economic issues lag behind the other two issue dimensions.

Issue Polarization

The individual-level effects of each issue dimension on vote choice, once established, do not fully make the case for the absolute and relative importance of these issues. There must be a difference between the candidates on

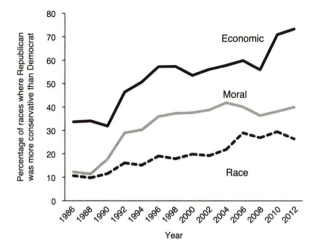

Figure 8.4. District polarization on the three issue dimensions

the issue dimension in question. In other words, polarization is a prerequisite for issues to influence the electoral choice of an individual voter. As noted above, that is especially the case for issues of race and ethnicity. Furthermore, to the extent that issue polarization is widespread, there is more potential for that issue to influence the wider political landscape. In Figure 8.4, the reader can see that all three dimensions show increased polarization over the period of study. But clearly there are more instances of polarization on economic issues than on issues of moral traditionalism or race. In 1986, there were about three times as many contests with economic issue polarization as there were with moral or racial issue polarization. In 1994, 50 percent of contested elections included economic polarization, 30 percent moral issue polarization, and 10 percent racial issue polarization. And in the most recent year included in the study, 2012, economic issue polarization soared to 73.3 percent, while moral issue polarization rose again to 40.0 percent and racial issue polarization came in at 26.4 percent. In 2012, that amounts to 286 contests where the voters had a choice between a more conservative Republican and a more liberal Democrat on economic issues. On moral issues, they had that same choice in 156 contests and on racial issues, the corresponding number of contests was 103.[2] Now everyone who follows House elections knows that a small minority of seats are competitive to begin with. Estimates in recent cycles have put that figure at about 15 percent. But referring back to the percentages above can give us the number of in-play seats where different issue dimensions might affect the choice of the voter. Fifteen percent of 435 gives us around 65. If we assume similar proportions of polarized contests for competitive and noncompetitive seats, then we get approximately 49 competitive seats with economic issue polarization, 26 competitive seats with moral issue polarization, and 19 competitive seats with racial issue polarization. Since the current GOP majority stands at 45 seats, 23 switches would give the Democrats control of the House in 2018. Polarized seats could easily produce enough change to imperil the Republican majority. But that would mean Democrats would have to be well positioned in these districts to take advantage of the polarization. They would have to find themselves closer to the voters' preferences on the issues than the Republicans. The next section shows that on none of the three issue dimensions studied is that the case.

Partisan Congruence

The first two criteria analyzed above establish the means by which an issue or set of issues might affect House elections both at the individual and aggregate levels. What the third criterion considers is how these issues might help one party or the other. Naturally, if one party is closer to the voters on a particular issue dimension with effects on the vote and polarization established, that party figures to benefit electorally. Using my candidate placement scores and ANES data on voters, we can take a look at where the parties sit in relation to the general public. Figure 8.5 provides this look for moral issues, Figure 8.6 for economic issues, and Figure 8.7 for issues of race and ethnicity. On all three dimensions, the Republican Party is closer to the voters throughout the period of study. However, the congruence between the GOP and the electorate is most striking on moral issues, especially since 1992. From 1986 to 2000, the Republicans are also fairly close to the voters on economic issues. But then they veer off to the right while voters continue on a relatively moderate trajectory. The result is that since 2000 the voters have been pretty much right in the middle between the two parties. And finally, the voters are consistently more conservative than the two parties on race, but the Republicans once again are closer to the voters. When you compare the two parties on the three dimensions, it appears that Republicans would seem to have the potential to benefit the most from the polarization that exists on moral issues. Furthermore, this seems to be the

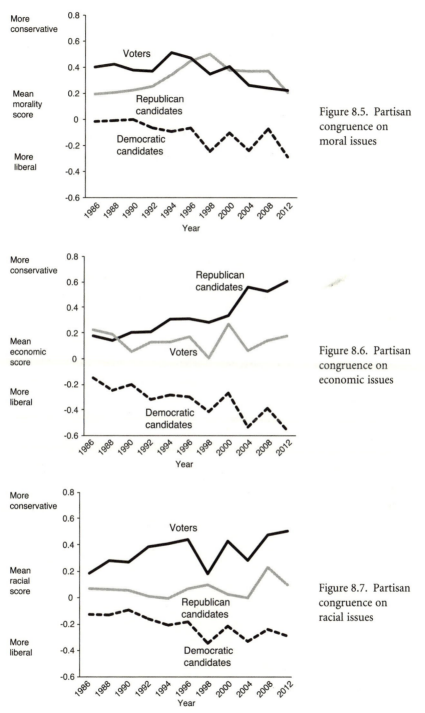

Figure 8.5. Partisan congruence on moral issues

Figure 8.6. Partisan congruence on economic issues

Figure 8.7. Partisan congruence on racial issues

case since the early 1990s, which jibes quite nicely with the stories that emerge from my three case studies.

Pulling It All Together

When one pulls together the results from these three assessments, it is clear that there is the potential for all three issue dimensions to matter in congressional elections. While incumbency and party identification still dominate House elections as we might expect, there is still room for moral, economic, and racial issues to matter. Moral issues exhibit a large effect on the vote and account for significant levels of polarization across the country. Furthermore, there currently exists a Republican Party well positioned with respect to the voters to capitalize on the polarization on and salience of such issues as abortion and gay rights. Economic issues cannot claim as large an effect on an individual's vote choice, but there is more widespread polarization on the issue. However, the GOP as it is currently constituted does not find itself much closer to the voters on such issues as taxes and spending than are the Democrats. Finally, racial issues can have a large effect on the vote, but there is less polarization on these issues. And the reader should not forget that especially for racial issues, polarization seems to be a prerequisite for those issues to affect vote choice. The Republican Party is closer to the electorate on such issues as aid to minorities and illegal immigration than the Democratic Party, but the real challenge for the GOP to capitalize on racial issues seems to be the unwillingness of many Republican candidates for the U.S. House to stress these issues publicly. Sadly, one needs to look no further than Donald Trump's openly ethnocentric, race-baiting presidential campaign to see the twenty-first-century potential for such an appeal.

Chapter 9

Moral Victories and a New GOP Majority

Two Twenty-First-Century Faces of the "New" Republican Majority

In 1984, eight years before Mark Gietzen engineered a pro-life takeover of the Sedgwick County Republican Party and two years before contentious primaries doomed the Republican Party in South Carolina's Fourth District and Tennessee's Third, Trent Franks began his political career by winning a single term in the Arizona state house. Franks was known for wearing a tie tack in the shape of the feet of a fetus, reminding everyone of his singular focus on stopping abortion. In 1992, while associated with James Dobson's Focus on the Family, Franks led an unsuccessful effort to limit abortion rights by statewide ballot initiative. In 1994, he lost to John Shadegg in the Republican primary for the U.S. House of Representatives. Franks and Shadegg were both strong conservatives, but the eventual winner was buoyed by the public endorsements of conservative icons Paul Weyrich, Phyllis Schlafly, and William F. Buckley Jr. (Parish and Brinkley-Rogers 1994, A10). Despite the loss, Franks was undeterred. He ran again in 2002 for the seat of Republican Bob Stump, who was retiring from Arizona's Second District. Stump finished a twenty-six-year congressional career and promptly endorsed his chief of staff in the Republican primary. Franks was not in the top tier of candidates early on, but with the help of his Christian conservative base and a healthy infusion of his own cash, he won the primary over Stump's choice by 797 votes. The general election in this safe Republican seat was anticlimactic. During the pivotal primary campaign, Franks benefited greatly from voter guides sent out by the Center for Arizona Policy, which billed itself as "fighting for conservative, traditional views on gambling, homosexuality, and pornography" (Barone and McCut-cheon 2011, 94). For his part, Franks called for overturning *Roe v. Wade* and for constitutional protections for fetuses during the campaign. After getting to Washington, Franks consistently began receiving the most con-servative ratings on social issues from *National Journal,* and in the after-math of the 2008 election, he called Barack Obama "the most dangerous president the country has ever had" (Barone and McCutcheon 2011, 94). Franks represented Arizona in the U.S. House until December 2017 when he was forced to resign after being accused of asking multiple female aides to carry his child as a surrogate mother.

In 2008, another strong social conservative was elected to the House of Representatives from Mississippi's Third District. Like Arizona's Second, this district in the heart of the Bible Belt is strongly Republican, with John McCain winning 61 percent of the vote against Barack Obama. For this reason, the real drama was in the GOP primary. There were three serious candidates: state senator Charlie Ross, a wealthy businessman named David Landrum, and Gregg Harper, a county party chairman who despite never having run for office before had lots of experience working for other candi-dates. Harper is a born-again Christian who had his conversion experience in high school. He met his wife at a church function (Barone and McCut-cheon 2011, 857–58). Ross had endorsements from local party leaders and the Club for Growth. And both Ross and Landrum outspent Harper. But Harper went door-to-door and had a significant number of young volun-teers working hard to get his name out there.[1] Ross and Harper finished first and second in the initial round of voting, but a runoff was in the cards as neither candidate came close to securing the 50 percent required by Mississippi law. Charlie Ross emphasized his vast legislative and military experience, while Harper countered with strongly conservative views on abortion and same-sex marriage. In this real-life Bibletown, U.S.A., moral traditionalism won 57 percent to 43 percent over experience (Barone and McCutcheon 2011, 858). In June 2017, Harper cosponsored a bill to strengthen parental notification and intervention requirements for un-emancipated minors seeking an abortion (U.S. Congress 2017). His reli-gious affiliation and church membership are quite prominent on the biographical section of his official website (Gregg Harper 2017).

Both Trent Franks and Gregg Harper had to win contested GOP pri-maries in order to make their way to Washington. They did so behind a strong moral message that resonated with Republican primary voters. In both cases, they outpolled candidates with more institutional support and, in Harper's case, considerably more money. They went on to represent heavily Republican districts in the House of Representatives for over a decade. These are two more examples of the kinds of candidate that burst onto the scene as far back as the early 1980s. They have helped contribute to the Republican majority that held control of the House for all but four of the previous twenty-four years.

Two Tea Partiers Turned Morally Traditional Stalwarts

Of course, this modern-day majority was born in 1994, and that watershed election has been well documented in this book. But an extremely unpopular George W. Bush allowed the Democrats to regain control of both houses of Congress in 2006. That Democratic majority was short-lived, however, as the Republicans rode another wave back into power four years later. The 2010 surge was powered in large part by the Tea Party movement, which I discuss in Chapters 1 and 2. The Tea Party was widely reported to be all about fiscal issues with nary a hint of moral traditionalism in the message of Republican candidates in that midterm election. And sure enough, my candidate data mostly verifies the conventional wisdom on that front (see Figure 2.5). However, as I also chronicle at the beginning of Chapter 2, the freshman class of 2011–2012 embarked on an ambitious campaign to defund Planned Parenthood and forged strongly conservative ratings from the Family Research Council. In this section of my concluding chapter, I want to zoom in on this phenomenon by briefly sketching the congressional careers of two Tea Partiers who turned out to be morally traditional stalwarts once in office.

Diane Black was a state senator in Tennessee when she threw her hat into the ring to succeed longtime conservative Democratic congressman Bart Gordon. The Sixth District was solidly Republican, and Gordon had held it for twenty-five years owing to his being significantly to the right of most Democratic members of Congress. Black was an across-the-board conservative, who while in the state legislature, pushed for a traditional definition of marriage, for allowing Tennessee residents to opt out of Obamacare, for a balanced budget amendment, and for a zero-tolerance policy for illegal immigrants. Black survived a bruising three-way primary, winning by only 283 votes. In the general election campaign, she received the vocal support of local and national Tea Party groups along with the endorsements of Senator Lamar Alexander and Sarah Palin. She won easily with 67 percent of the vote (Barone and McCutcheon 2011, 1504).

Her economic message during the campaign was quite conservative, and the Tea Party support she received was undoubtedly due to those attitudes she publicly pronounced. However, her first piece of legislation on Capitol Hill was a bill to deny federal funding to Planned Parenthood because of the organization's involvement with abortion. Black ended up introducing six more abortion-related bills during her first term (Barone and McCutcheon 2013, 1550). In subsequent terms, her actions on moral issues picked up considerably. In 2013, she sponsored a measure to give any individual or group that opposes contraception an automatic exemption from the requirement in the health care law that employee health insurance plans provide birth control. And in 2015, she filed a bill to block Title X federal funding to organizations that perform abortions, including Planned Parenthood. Finally, Black was a strong proponent of the House-passed bill barring most abortions after twenty weeks, citing growing evidence that fetuses feel pain at that point in the gestation process (Cohen and Barnes 2015, 1692). While these efforts did not make it through the Senate, much less become law, this kind of aggressive activity in the House has kept the pro-choice movement on the defensive in Washington.

Diane Black was swept into office in part by a fiscally driven Tea Party movement. The congresswoman from Tennessee's Sixth District may not have gotten to Washington by stressing her anti-abortion views, but once there she has seemingly made it her number-one priority. Flipping a Democratic district in 2010, the GOP's representative here is a strong moral conservative and emblematic of the recent Republican majority. And she is not alone.

Like Representative Black, Blake Farenthold became a freshman member of Congress in 2011 when he was sworn in as the representative from Texas's Twenty-Seventh District. And like Black, Farenthold barely survived a close primary election, this time winning in a runoff by 246 votes. But unlike Black, Farenthold had to defeat a Democratic incumbent, Solomon Ortiz, in November. Farenthold's campaign message focused entirely on economic issues. He was especially opposed to Obamacare, which he deemed a bad case of government intrusion into the private sector. The Republican newcomer was an underdog to the Democratic incumbent, finding himself outspent two to one. However, his campaign picked up steam late in the race with the support of local Tea Party activists. Farenthold led on election night, but the tally was close enough that a recount was ordered. Ortiz ended up conceding on November 22 (Barone and McCutcheon 2011, 1602).

Farenthold did not mention moral issues as a candidate, and, like Black, the Tea Party support he received was surely related to his economic conservatism. However, in addition to introducing legislation during his first year in office that required federal agencies to display their receipts and expenditures every two weeks on their websites, Farenthold actively supported efforts to ban funding for Planned Parenthood. Furthermore, his Family Research Council rating was 90 percent in 2011 and 100 percent in 2012 (Barone and McCutcheon 2013, 1645–47). Farenthold, along with all but six of his GOP colleagues, voted for the twenty-week abortion ban championed by Diane Black (Cohen and Barnes 2015, 1798). Despite a few personal scandals, Farenthold had made the seat his own, winning 71 percent in the 2012 GOP primary and 57 percent against the Democrat (Cohen and Barnes 2015, 1798). However, in December 2017, Farenthold could not overcome very public and very ugly staff complaints about the office he ran. He was portrayed as a tantrum-throwing, sexually harassing boss. As a result, Farenthold announced he would retire rather than seek reelection in 2018. Regardless, Farenthold was yet another example of a Tea Party–backed candidate taking a Democratic seat in 2010 and becoming a strong vote for moral traditionalism once in Washington. Both Farenthold and Black are morally conservative members of Congress, and both are from the South. In those respects, they are apt examples of a new Republican majority that was forged in the early 1990s and reinforced in 2010.

A Southern-Fried Majority

At the presidential level, the South has been solidly Republican since 2000, and if you exclude the elections when Southerners Jimmy Carter and Bill Clinton headed the Democratic ticket, Republicans have fared very well south of the Mason-Dixon Line all the way back to 1972. But as shown in Figure 1.3, white Southerners were slower to warm to congressional candidates from the Republican Party. During the Reagan-Bush years, when those two presidential candidates did very well in the South, their House counterparts never won more than 40 percent of Southern seats and averaged 36 percent over the span of those seven congressional elections. Republicans could not win a majority elsewhere but did slightly better, winning an average of 42 percent during the same period. It was not until

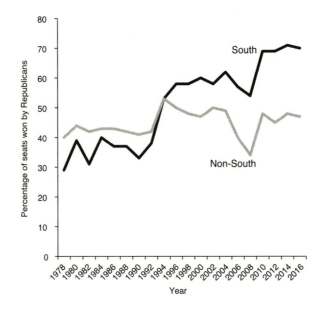

Figure 9.1. U.S. House seats won by Republicans in the South versus the non-South

1994 that Southern Republicans began winning at the same clip as non-Southern Republicans, and since that watershed election, the gap between Southern success and non-Southern success has steadily grown. Figure 9.1 displays these trends graphically. In 2016, Republicans won 70 percent of Southern House contests and only 47 percent elsewhere. In fact, John Barrow's defeat in Georgia's Twelfth District two years earlier meant that there are now a grand total of zero white Southern Democrats in the House of Representatives. Thus it is now the Republicans who can lay claim to the term "solid South" as far as the U.S. House is concerned. In Figure 9.2, the reader can see that as of 2016, the Republican House delegation is almost half Southern. That is noteworthy considering that based on the 2010 apportionment, Southern states possess only 37 percent of the nation's House seats.

A Morally Traditional Majority

Along with being much more Southern based, the new Republican House majority is also much more conservative on moral issues than it has ever

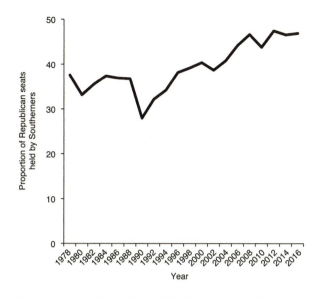

Figure 9.2. Proportion of Republican U.S. House seats held by Southerners

been. This has largely been the result of new Republican members of Congress coming to Washington with culturally conservative views on issues of moral traditionalism. Before 1990, the percentage of new Republican House members who espoused culturally conservative messages in their most recent campaign never exceeded 14 percent, and the average percentage from 1978 to 1988 was 8.3 percent. Starting in 1990 and moving forward to 2012, the percentage in any one cycle never fell below 28 percent, and the average over that period was 45.7 percent. Figure 9.3 shows the relevant trend over time. Turnover of this type and magnitude has produced the type of House delegation that has sought to curtail women's reproductive rights time and time again. In 2017, H.R. 7, a bill to make the Hyde Amendment permanent, and renewed efforts to slash Planned Parenthood's federal funding are the most recent high-profile legislative pushes made by morally conservative members of Congress.

Issues, Activists, and Candidates

Many of the so-called moral issues that have been the focus of this book have been with us for roughly half a century. When the Supreme Court

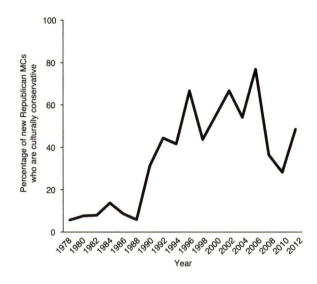

Figure 9.3. Percentage of new Republican members of Congress who were morally conservative

ruled on January 22, 1973, in *Roe v. Wade* that abortion would be legal nationwide for any reason during the first trimester, it took what had previously been mostly a medical issue and made it political. A vibrant pro-life movement, led primarily at the outset by Catholics, organized and mobilized against what they saw as nothing less than a tragic decision by the High Court (Risen and Thomas 1999). Pro-choice activists then countermobilized to protect the gains that had been granted by the judicial branch. When *Roe* came down, religious conservatives were already furious with the Supreme Court for banning school prayer in *Engel v. Vitale* eleven years earlier. Impeach Earl Warren signs popped up throughout the nation as the chief justice was vilified for that ruling. The gay rights movement that burst onto the scene in the late 1960s and into the 1970s led to a backlash amplified by Anita Bryant's efforts to repeal local ordinances designed to protect gay men and lesbians from discrimination in housing and employment. And the main event during this period for many on both sides of the cultural divide was the battle over the Equal Rights Amendment. Phyllis Schlafly and her minions successfully kept the ERA from ratification by blocking it three states shy of the thirty-eight needed for it to become a constitutional amendment (Mansbridge 1986, Crichtlow 2008).

Starting around 1980, the two major parties in this country began to take opposite stands on abortion, school prayer, gay rights, and the ERA. The birth of the Christian right around the same time was both cause and effect, fanning the flames and sparking a liberal response. Chapter 1 presents the context surrounding these macro-level changes in national politics.

But as my congressional candidate coding shows, very few candidates for the House of Representatives were mentioning these issues at the time. It was not until the mid-1980s that a nontrivial number of candidates began taking public stands and espousing moral campaign messages. And not until the 1990s did a significant number start injecting moral traditionalism into House races across the country. Figure 2.1 tracks the change over the period of study. Once the Republicans took more conservative stands on moral issues, Democrats were forced to follow suit, creating the polarization on these issues that dominates American politics to this day. Chapter 2 highlights this polarization and contains a preliminary test that shows the potential importance of these issues to a voter's choice for the House of Representatives.

Chapter 3 surveys prominent theories about how party coalitions change; conversion versus replacement, bottom-up versus top-down, and candidate centered versus party centered. I argue that these moral issues began to play a role in congressional elections mostly as a result of local activists pushing them into the public discourse. In many districts across the country, these culturally conservative activists originally found themselves on the outside looking in when it came to the Republican Party hierarchy. Either the party apparatus was moderate on moral issues or it did not put a lot of emphasis on such subjects as abortion, gay rights, and school prayer. Diverging with other theories regarding the increased importance of these issues at the grassroots, I do not believe the national Republican Party made a conscious effort to recruit morally conservative challengers around the country. Even after they succeeded with these issues at the presidential level, my research suggests it simply was not a strategic play emanating from the upper echelons of Republican power. The first year where internecine battles within the GOP became a major influence on congressional elections in America was 1986. The results were not pretty for Republicans. Democrats repeatedly defeated Republican nominees who were weakened by divisive primary campaigns. The Republican Party had a difficult time marrying their two main factions: the so-called country-club Republicans and Christian Republicans.

In Chapters 4, 5, and 6, I detail three examples of this political and social phenomenon. Many people—such as Mark Gietzen and David Gittrich in Kansas's Fourth; Bob Jones University faculty, staff, and students, and Pat Robertson's legion of supporters in South Carolina's Fourth; and Doug Daugherty and Jim Golden in Tennessee's Third—fought their way into prominence, first within the local Republican party structure and then within the larger political landscape. These morally traditional activists excited the local population in a variety of ways, forcing them to consider issues such as abortion when thinking about politics and who might represent them in Congress. Then these activists helped nominate candidates who espoused conservative messages on these issues. Finally, there was a full-bore effort to get them elected over more liberal Democratic opponents.

In the early 1990s, this story played out around the country, producing a series of wins for the Republican Party that gave them control of the House of Representatives in 1994 for the first time in four decades. In Chapter 7, I present a congressional voting model that can account for the impact that issues can have on U.S. House elections. It is a two-stage, communications-based interaction model that finds great potential for moral, economic, and racial issues to affect the electoral choice of voters. *Potential* is the key word, however. Without polarization on the issues in question, there cannot be an effect on the vote. Chapter 8 goes further, examining and quantifying the overall effect of these three issue dimensions, taking into consideration not just the potential effect on the vote coming from the model explicated in Chapter 7 but also the polarization data first presented in Chapter 2, and presenting new data regarding how close the parties are to the voters on the three issue dimensions in question. Considering the raw effect on the vote, levels of polarization, and party proximity, I conclude that the Republican Party largely realized the positive potential of being conservative on moral issues and leveraged that new position to achieve many "moral victories" that led to the GOP's control of the House for all but four of the previous twenty-four years.

Where We're at and Where We Might Be Headed

In the era of Donald Trump, it would be foolish to try to predict exactly where we are headed in American politics at the national level. I have argued throughout this book that moral issues and morally traditional candidates have given the Republican Party an edge in U.S. House elections, and that edge has enabled the GOP to control the lower chamber of Congress throughout most of the past two-and-a-half decades. Going into the 2018 election cycle, the scandal-plagued Trump administration figured to be a significant drag on Republican House candidates. A president's party almost always loses seats in the first midterm election, and even the most diehard Republican was conceding this outcome on election eve. The only question was whether the Democrats would be able to pick up enough seats to regain control of the chamber. In the end they did just that, winning more than the twenty-three they needed to once again take back the speakership. The Republican Party suffered major losses in districts that Hillary Clinton won in 2016, as well as some defeats in suburban areas Trump carried two years earlier. Where they did not lose and who they did not lose is instructive and relevant as a coda to this book. The Bible belt continues to almost exclusively send Republicans to Washington, and self-described evangelical Christians voted 75 percent to 22 percent for Republican House candidates in 2018. The core of the Republican House delegation remains as it was before the most recent midterm election cycle. For this and other reasons, I believe much of our current political landscape has been shaped by the events I highlight in this book. The polarization, the bitter cultural divide that has emerged, the tremendous salience of such issues as abortion, contraception, gay rights, and the broader role of religion in public life are not going away anytime soon. I believe this current environment was nurtured, if not born, during the late 1980s and early 1990s. This was a time when the culture wars heated up and seeped into all levels of American politics. The battle lines hardened, the parties moved farther apart, and the issues became woven into the fabric of our discourse. I would argue that a new era of American politics dawned when the Republicans took over the Congress in 1994. And that takeover was made possible by a new breed of Republican congressional candidates. A type of candidate that stressed moral traditionalism in the many districts where voters were amenable to that ideology. These candidates often had to fight their fellow Republicans just to be able to compete directly with Democrats. But once they broke through and started winning primaries, consolidating competing party factions, and harnessing the energy of their religiously conservative supporters, marrying sophistication with intensity, they were able to achieve a host of wins throughout the country. These "moral victories" that I have described in the preceding pages made it possible for the Republicans to achieve a majority in the House of Representatives and influence American politics for more than a generation.

Notes

Chapter 1

1. This notable congressional race is the centerpiece of Chapter 4 and will be discussed at much greater length there.

2. This book went to print just after the 2018 midterm election, when the Republican Party lost its House majority primarily because of President Donald Trump's low approval ratings and a relatively large number of GOP retirements.

3. Many scholars divide Christian right activism into two waves. The first wave began in the late 1970s with the formation of the Moral Majority and other national groups, and lasted until Pat Robertson's unsuccessful bid for the Republican presidential nomination in 1988. The second wave arose out of the ashes of Robertson's failed attempt and was catalyzed by the creation of the Christian Coalition. There were real substantive and stylistic differences between the two waves of organizing and activism. This framework will be evident not just in this section but throughout the entire book.

4. Gerrymandering, in particular the creation of majority-minority districts after the 1990 census, has been linked to improved Republican fortunes in the South in 1992 and 1994 (Hill 1995, 384–401). Of the nine districts taken by Republicans in 1992 in the eight states where majority-minority districts were created, Hill concludes that four were the result of racial redistricting. Incidentally, South Carolina's Fourth District, which is the second case study presented in this book, was one of the five that flipped for reasons other than racial redistricting. My take on why it flipped is addressed thoroughly in Chapter 5. Susan Banducci and Jeffrey Karp (1994) also posit a role for gerrymandering in the success of Republican House candidates in the South. However, John Petrocik and Scott Desposato (1998) argue that the first-order effect of a reduced black constituency was less important than the second-order effect of losing familiar voters. Regardless of this debate, redistricting effects would only show up in the number of seats won, and Figures 1.2 to 1.4 deal with trends in the overall congressional vote that would be independent of how the lines have been drawn.

5. For the former interpretation, see John Aldrich (1995). For the latter, see Marty Cohen et al. (2008) and Kathleen Bawn et al. (2012).

Chapter 2

1. I ended up coding 7,412 Democratic candidates and 7,193 Republican candidates. Of course, many candidates show up in multiple years, but each time they were coded anew to account for positions changing, new issues arising, or old issues fading. The raw candidate data are available on request from the author.

2. With these economic calamities, we might expect economic issues to become more relevant to candidates and voters. Indeed, the percentage of Republican candidates espousing conservative economic messages spikes in 2010 and 2012 (see Figure 2.5).

3. Other works have displayed growing polarization over the same period using Nominate scores, including Schier and Eberly (2016, 92) and Marty Cohen, Hans Noel, and John Zaller (2004, 10).

Chapter 3

1. These two races figure prominently in the case studies presented later in the book.

2. And there are also Geoffrey Layman (2001) and Jonathan Knuckey (2005) who argue forcefully for the primacy of moral issues when it comes to voters' partisanship and voting behavior.

3. Dick Armey, one of Gingrich's closest allies, wanted school prayer to be in the contract, but Newt disagreed, saying it was too controversial and would distract from the other more popular issues. So it was excluded, and many religious conservative leaders chided Reed for his backing of a program that failed to include such important moral issues as abortion and school prayer. Days after the election, however, Gingrich signaled that he wanted school prayer brought up on the floor of the House by July 1995. See Nigel Ashford (1998) for a discussion of the compromises between Reed and the Christian right on one side and Gingrich and the Republican congressional leaders on the other.

4. South Carolina's Fourth District is the subject of Chapter 5 of this book, where the Christian Coalition's role in the 1992 congressional elections will be discussed in greater detail.

5. There is a natural tendency for local activists to inflate their own importance by downplaying the role of national forces. I recognize this bias and attempt to address it by speaking to as many objective observers as possible (i.e., reporters and academics) to corroborate the activists' stories. I speak to this and other general concerns I had with the validity of my interview data at the end of this chapter.

6. Many prominent scholars have written on these subjects, including but not limited to David Mayhew (1974), Morris Fiorina (1977), Richard Fenno (1978), John Aldrich (1995), Alan Ehrenhalt (1991), Nelson Polsby (1983), and Gary Jacobson (2001).

7. See also Paul Herrnson (2004) and Linda Fowler and Robert McClure (1989).

8. Data come from various editions of *The Almanac of American Politics*, and the percentiles were calculated by the author.

Chapter 4

1. The Kansas state legislature works only part time, so Tiahrt retained his middle management position at Boeing after getting elected.

2. The exception that proved the rule in Kansas was Jim Jeffries. Jeffries was one of the first New Right candidates to be elected. He defeated the Democratic incumbent in the Second District (northeastern Kansas) in 1978. However, Jeffries was seen as one of the lousiest legislators and had no real base of support other than what national direct mail could provide. He was strongly challenged in the Republican primary in 1980 and was held under 50 percent, proving that many Republicans wanted someone else. He was targeted for defeat in 1982 and decided to retire.

3. Glickman's religion was something else he had to overcome in the rural areas. While there certainly was not any virulent, overt anti-Semitism in the region, Norman believes that in such towns as St. John's and St. Joseph's, it was something to overcome nonetheless. Of course, this was only true to the extent people out in the country actually realized Glickman was Jewish. Early in the young Democrat's career, an adviser was not at all displeased to read a misrepresentation of Glickman's place of worship in a small-town newspaper. The article said Glickman attended Temple Immanuel Church.

4. Several of these rebel lawmakers would go on to prominent roles within the Republican Party, and two even went on to run for governor. Of course, this is a testament to the changing political dynamic within the GOP and Kansas politics in general. I will have more to say on that evolution later in this chapter.

5. I believe the Sedgwick County old guard is more aptly described as Chamber of Commerce, or business, Republicans rather than moderate Republicans as others have depicted them. As two political reporters, including Bud Norman, pointed out to me, these well-entrenched activists were not all that moderate in their beliefs. While not able to comment on the politicians, Norman believed that the rank-and-file "moderates" he knew who were involved in the GOP infighting were all staunch economic and foreign policy conservatives and would even be considered cultural conservatives in many circles. He went on to say that the "moderates" were by and large white-collar small-business owners and corporate workers who were more likely to have a college education than their more "conservative" counterparts. (I have added the quotation marks to highlight the weakness of those terms.) Class differences often exacerbated what were sometimes fairly insignificant policy disagreements. This is addressed to some extent throughout Thomas Frank (2004). Although Frank grew up in Johnson County in the Third District and focuses on that area in his book, he does have a chapter that concentrates on Sedgwick County.

6. The importance of precinct positions was highlighted in Tom McCann (1998).

7. One of the precipitating events that led to the 1992 takeover of the Sedgwick County Republican Party was the feeling of pro-life members that the party was unfairly favoring the pro-choice candidate in the congressional primary. There will be more on this later.

8. The Sedgwick County Republican Party under Mark Gietzen gained a large amount of media exposure and national notoriety. Rush Limbaugh referred to the takeover and subsequent increase in party activity on his radio show, and Gietzen was interviewed by ABC News, Canadian Radio, and the BBC. Much of the publicity was in fact negative and, according to Gietzen, betrayed a lack of public knowledge as to how party politics can work. "It seemed so odd to me that later on when it was talked about on Rush Limbaugh and so on, it was something we had done in secret. Or that we had come in with guns and taken over the Republican Party—like we had done something unspeakable." Gietzen argues that they did not "steal" the party and that it was not done in secret. They were successful because they were organized, and it was all done legally and out in the open (Gietzen, interview with author).

9. It is worth noting that a drastic shift in party identification had already occurred in Sedgwick County during the 1980s. Observers credit Ronald Reagan's enormous popularity and a shifting local workforce for sizable Republican gains. See Al Polczinski (1990).

10. On the 1990 race, see "Anti-Tax Activist" 1990, 1D. See also Jean Hays (1990, 10A).

11. Incidentally, Peggy Jarmin was also Dr. George Tiller's spokeswoman during the Summer of Mercy.

12. Adding to the inequity was Yost's need to spend large sums of money in the Republican primary while Glickman could save all of his funds for the general election.

13. My recounting of the 1992 general election campaign comes mainly from Anne Fitzgerald (1992, 1D) and Jim Cross (1992e, 1C; 1992f, 3D; 1992g, 1D; 1992h, 1B; 1992i, 1A).

14. Tiahrt's triumph must have been all the more satisfying considering he lost a state house race in 1990 by only eight votes.

15. In Fowler and McClure (1989), the authors argue that there are many promising candidates who decide not to run for Congress. They explore what drives some to make the race and others not to, and discuss the consequences of those decisions for our democracy.

16. Here is how the candidates were described in an April 1994 *Wichita Eagle* article: "Tiahrt, 42, has served two years of a four-year state senate term representing western and southern Sedgwick County. He is a proposal manager at Boeing and part of a group of fiscally and socially conservative legislators who oppose abortion and gun control and support school vouchers and abstinence-based sex education." "Ojile, an attorney in private practice, was known for his opposition to abortion while on the City Council." These descriptions are from Julie Wright (1994, 1D).

17. The dialogue presented here is most certainly not verbatim. It was Dave Hanna's ten-year-old memory of Tiahrt's version of what was said. The gist is surely correct. Hanna also recalls with humor Tiahrt and his advisers thinking shortly after the Ojile decision was made, "How are *we* going to raise $3,500 a day?" (interview with author)}

18. The brain trust behind Todd Tiahrt consisted of Dave Hanna (a veteran political consultant from the area), Matt Schlapp (another politico who ended up rising in the Republican Party and eventually landing a job in the White House), David Gittrich (the political director of Kansans for Life), and Vicki Tiahrt (the candidate's wife). Mark Gietzen, as the powerful chair of the Sedgwick County Republican Party, certainly played a large role, but he did so under the guise of the county party and not within the formal campaign organization.

19. Early on, Gittrich admitted that Kansans for Life was not politically savvy. At first, they just sent out questionnaires and simply chose to endorse the candidate with the best position on abortion, regardless of how good or bad the candidate was otherwise. They did not even bother to check in many cases. This led to some embarrassments for the organization. They often endorsed sure losers who were clobbered in November. They even endorsed someone with a criminal record for child abuse.

20. David Gittrich also takes credit for developing the advertising symbol that dominated the visual campaign. Gittrich convinced Tiahrt to agree to the placement of a picture of a heart with a "T" traced inside it on the first set of yard signs. There was nothing else on those original signs. People wondered what they were when they saw them around the neighborhoods. This uncertainty created a buzz, and later on the symbol found its way onto the Tiahrt for Congress signs. People had already been primed and, because of the T-heart symbol, knew how to pronounce a name that might otherwise have been awkward to say.

21. The Contract with America itself deliberately omitted abortion, school prayer, and other moral issues that were exceedingly controversial and might alienate swing voters. Ralph Reed and the Christian Coalition got on board despite this exclusion with the idea that a Republican Congress would be much friendlier to their viewpoints in the future. For an interesting look at the Contract with America, including its role in the 1994 congressional elections, see James Gimpel (1996).

22. To a lesser extent, the Second Amendment groups in the Fourth District did the same thing for Tiahrt on guns. In the state senate, Tiahrt had sponsored a concealed-carry law that was seen as out of the mainstream by many local observers. Naturally, Tiahrt did not want to be portrayed as a "gun nut," so he largely steered clear of gun issues in public statements during the campaign. Gun rights groups were not as influential in local politics as the pro-life groups were, and guns did not have quite the salience that abortion had. However, the Second Amendment people were important members of Tiahrt's electoral coalition.

23. In the early 1990s, many liberals were downright apoplectic about the notion of stealth candidates and stealth campaigns. Opponents of the Christian right claimed that some socially conservative candidates, especially in such low-information contests as city council and school board races, purposely hid their views on controversial issues while making sure *their* supporters knew where they stood. Ralph Reed heightened the paranoia in an oft-quoted comment he made about how as a campaign strategist he sneaks in under the cover of darkness and before his opponents know it, they are in body bags. Reed later disavowed that statement as part of an effort to defend the Christian Coalition and himself against charges of extremism.

24. George H. W. Bush won Kansas's Fourth District in 1992 with 40 percent of the vote. Clinton came in second with 33 percent, which was only six points better than Ross Perot's showing.

25. The 86 percent ad is a good example of national forces playing a role in this congressional campaign. However, the money used to produce the ad was strictly local and collected through a tireless grassroots effort.

26. Dave Hanna related to me the story of how while flying cross-country, Dole called Haley Barbour, the chairman of the RNC, and told him that he "smelled a winner in KS04." Dole went on to demand the maximum donation from the RNC, and if it was not forthcoming, the Senate majority leader said he would "get off the plane, go to Wichita, and raise it myself." Needless to say, the money was sent. Dole's active involvement is a nice illustration of the broadening of the Republican tent and the growing rapprochement between the two factions.

27. Most of the following discussion of the debate comes out of my interview with Dave Hanna.

28. Another example of how the candidates were perceived differently came out of a pit stop at a southeastern Kansas convenience store. Tiahrt bought a packet of chewing tobacco, and the girl behind the counter remarked, "Mr. Glickman never bought any Red Man." This story was told to me by Dave Hanna.

29. The exact count was 111,653 to 99,366. These vote totals are from Michael Barone and Grant Ujifusa (1995, 538).

30. One might go back further and compare 1994 with pre-1992 campaigns against Glickman. Of course, the differences will be greater, but the races are less directly comparable. Many things had changed between, say, 1986 and 1994. Considerably fewer changes marked the period between 1992 and 1994, but those would seem to be most relevant.

31. Dan Glickman's conversation with his pollster was related to me by Dave Hanna who spoke extensively with Glickman after the election was over.

32. The only unknown about the General Aviation Revitalization Act was where Cessna would open their new plant. With this new plant would come thousands of new jobs and a

general boost to the local economy. It was not clear during the campaign whether the new plant would be placed in the Fourth District. Even if it was not, the aviation act was still guaranteed to benefit the entire district's economy. The new plant would just be an added bonus and another feather in the cap for Dan Glickman. In December, Cessna announced that a small town in southeastern Kansas named Independence would be the site of their new plant. Independence was indeed in the Fourth District—Dan Glickman's district—but alas, only for a few more days.

33. Glickman certainly landed on his feet, though. He was appointed secretary of agriculture by Bill Clinton and subsequently became the president of the Motion Picture Association of America.

Chapter 5

1. The impact of Bob Jones University on local life cannot be overestimated. Bob Jones College was founded in 1927 by evangelist Bob Jones in Florida. It moved to Tennessee and finally settled in Greenville, South Carolina, in 1947. With just short of four thousand students (85 percent of whom are from out of state), BJU is South Carolina's largest private school. Bob Jones theology is extremely conservative and separationist. The university, through the strong signals it sends to its graduates around the world, has become a pacesetter for fundamentalist politics. See Oran Smith (1997, 102).

2. Greenville and Spartanburg are the names of the county seats as well, and these cities are the major population centers in each county.

3. Ron Romine, a professor at the University of South Carolina–Upstate, believed Atwater was behind the Jew baiting.

4. Charismatic Christians, also known as Pentecostals, are born-again believers and followed the same separatist path as fundamentalists. However, their worship style is more emotive, open, and nontraditional. Charismatics place special emphasis on healing, miracles, and speaking in tongues. These differences have led to strife between the two groups, manifesting itself politically, not only in Greenville County but on a national level. Pat Robertson has been the best-known charismatic Christian leader in America, and his 1988 presidential campaign failed in part because he was not supported by Jerry Falwell and other fundamentalists.

5. Rigdon, for his part, endorsed Workman.

6. The background on Bill Workman comes from my interview with him as well as from Baker (1986b, 1C).

7. Adams describes "constitutional government" as a system of government in which one group of people cannot use the power of government to benefit themselves at the cost of the citizens.

8. With all this discussion about a city-county rivalry, an attentive reader might wonder why Workman did not do better in the city compared with his showing in the county. When one considers the relatively large African American population within the Greenville city limits, the parity makes more sense. Setting aside the African American vote, Workman did indeed do much better in the city of Greenville than he did in the county.

9. After a bit of prodding, the saga of the mini-bottles was related to me by my anonymous source at the *Greenville News*. When I first mentioned my personal experience the night before with the mini-bottles and my confusion as to why they had them, he simply responded,

"Those goddamned mini-bottles." After that visceral response, he recounted their history (interview with author).

10. The differences range from the doctrinal to the socioeconomic and were detailed in note 4.

11. It is a testament to his power and influence that almost every person I interviewed in South Carolina made mention of Carroll Campbell. In addition to the quotes in the text, comments made by Lee Bandy, Bob Taylor, and Ron Romine also helped me piece together these two paragraphs on Campbell.

12. Bob Taylor, who was one of the most politically influential members of the Bob Jones University administration, supported Knox White. Taylor did not support Workman in 1986.

13. Knox White happened to be the mayor of Greenville at the time I interviewed him. He still holds that office.

14. Incidentally, Patterson's high-wire act did not come without cost. She was known to agonize over every vote, wondering how it might play at home. A fellow member said she would call her husband in Spartanburg moments before a roll call asking him how she should vote. Mayor White tells a story of how Patterson kept a box of Rolaids in her desk drawer in Washington because of all the flipping and flopping she had to do to hold onto a district that was not only more conservative than she was but way more conservative than the national Democratic party.

15. This anecdote was offered to me by Knox White. White also mentioned that Inez Tenenbaum, the Democratic candidate for the U.S. Senate in 2004, completely skipped John Kerry's nominating convention for fear of being linked to the liberalism of the national party.

16. Incidentally, a well-connected political reporter blamed White's loss in 1988 on the old city-county rivalry.

17. According to a reporter who covered the campaign, Patterson's position on abortion was somewhat misrepresented. The incumbent was furious when she found out about the voter guides and saw how they portrayed the two candidates. Democrats have routinely charged that these voter guides are far from nonpartisan, and therefore such groups as the Christian Coalition are violating their tax-exempt status when engaging in this type of political activity. Ron Romine alerted me to the disparity in the photography presented in the guides and vehemently argued against the notion that the Christian Coalition literature could reasonably be considered dispassionate and nonpartisan. My anonymous source at the *Greenville News* generally agreed with Romine's characterization. "I think it was good versus evil. . . . It [the religious right] set things up that there is a Republican running for Truth, Justice, and the American Way against the evil Democrat who would undo all this" (interview with author).

18. Lee Bandy, Ron Romine, and Knox White all emphasized Patterson's complacency as an important factor in her defeat. Naturally, Mayor White seemed very disappointed that Patterson did not show similar laxity four years earlier.

19. Dan Glickman also took his Republican challenger lightly owing to Todd Tiahrt's grassroots, stealth campaign.

20. Ralph Reed bemoans the labeling of religious conservatives as "stealth candidates" in his first book, *Politically Incorrect* (1994). Reed writes in a "who me?" tone on this subject and accuses liberals of trying to marginalize and denigrate pro-family candidates by saying that they can only be successful by running stealth campaigns. However, in one of his earlier, brasher comments, Reed bragged openly about this strategy with his infamous "body bag" quote that I refer to in note 23 in Chapter 4.

Chapter 6

1. Wamp also benefited in his battle with Meyer because he had run a close race against the Democratic incumbent two years earlier. In fact, it was widely assumed he would avoid a primary challenge because of that impressive effort. Undoubtedly, his previous run increased his credibility with the Republican primary electorate and made him a more attractive candidate. However, I would argue, as would Gary Jacobson based on his coding scheme, that Meyer was still the higher-quality challenger. That said, party activists were even more responsible for Wamp's nomination in 1992 when he had no experience as a candidate. In that contest, he ousted another formidable challenger with the help of local political and economic elites. The story of the 1992 Republican congressional primary is extremely important and a terrific example of how an informal party organization, such as described by Seth Masket in *No Middle Ground* (2009), can control congressional nominations. It will be discussed in great detail later on in this chapter.

2. This brief political history of East Tennessee was culled from personal interviews with two professors from the political science department at the University of Tennessee, Chattanooga, including Bob Swansbrough, as well as from several *Chattanooga Times-Free Press* political reporters, including Tom Griscom.

3. A longtime Republican political operative in Chattanooga laid out the routes various individuals took into the Republican Party.

4. There will be much more on Pat Brock and his political activism later in this chapter. As for Bill Brock, after his defeat at the hands of Jim Sasser in 1976, he tailored his organizational expertise to national politics, becoming RNC chair in the late 1970s. After a stint as a special U.S. trade representative, Brock moved to Maryland and eventually challenged incumbent senator Paul Sarbanes in 1994, where he was defeated by eighteen points.

5. Dave Flessner, a local political reporter, related to me the details regarding Marilyn's acceptance of the offer to run in place of her deceased husband.

6. I spoke with two of those constituents, and they agreed that Lloyd's legacy was the Brainerd Levee. Pamela and Robin Rudd were not big fans of the congresswoman, but they conceded she was good on constituency service and knew how to listen.

7. Admittedly, Lloyd's conservative positions made it difficult for Davis to attack the incumbent on issues of moral traditionalism, such as abortion and the Equal Rights Amendment, even if he was so inclined. However, it was possible, and there was room on the right of Lloyd on these types of issues. The 1986 Republican nominee would prove that.

8. In a show of the increasing strength of the pro-life movement, those protests eventually resulted in the closing of the clinic. The owners were then bought out of their lease by anti-abortion activists and the one-time abortion clinic was transformed into the National Memorial for the Unborn.

9. Dave Flessner believes the media at the time missed much of the intensive religious appeal of the Golden campaign. This kind of campaign is reminiscent of Bob Inglis's and Todd Tiahrt's, albeit several years earlier.

10. As with Lloyd's achievements for the district in the 1970s, her constituents continue to give her credit for the Trade Center and the Riverport. More than one interviewee mentioned these projects in connection with Congresswoman Lloyd.

11. Siljander quickly realized his mistake, telling the *Washington Times* that if "evangelical candidates go out thumping Bibles on street corners, then they are going to lose no

question." This quote from Siljander and the one in the text are from Andy Sher (1986, A1). Incidentally, Siljander did send a letter of endorsement to Golden during the Tennessean's nominating contest. Referring back to Chapter 2, Siljander and Golden would be considered very conservative and receive scores of 2 in my candidate coding scheme.

12. Here, Daugherty neatly encapsulates the classic dilemma a candidate faces when running for office. He or she has to win not one election but two, each with vastly different electorates.

13. Apparently, my interview spurred Pamela Rudd to get in touch with Jim Golden regarding his run for Congress; however, I did not suggest the overture nor did I know about it until she related to me his views on this subject.

14. Incidentally, Todd Gardenhire was the only person I asked who pointed in a different direction when attributing responsibility for the anti-Golden letters. Gardenhire always believed that the Lloyd people sent those letters out, although he has no evidence for his hunch.

15. My election night source was Dave Flessner, who covered the party as a reporter for the *Chattanooga Times*.

16. Liz Patterson also made a concerted effort to put some distance between her and the Democratic ticket in 1988. However, she was not as successful as Marilyn Lloyd, considering she did spend one day at the national convention in Atlanta.

17. This strategic calculation is quite interesting and touches on many larger issues in political science. For that reason, I will discuss and analyze this further at the end of the chapter.

18. Gardenhire related this story, and what follows in the next two paragraphs, to me during our interview.

19. Once again, local and state Republicans did not want to stir up the Democratic vote in the Third District with what figured to be a close presidential race on the ballot.

20. See Judy Frank (1992, A1) for an in-depth treatment of Wamp's personal problems. Against the advice of his political advisers, Wamp opened up about his past drug use in an effort to empty his closet of skeletons.

21. Indeed, a local abortion rights organization noticed Marilyn Lloyd's recent evolution. Tennesseans Keeping Abortion Legal and Safe changed Lloyd from an "anti" to a "mixed" rating based on that vote. See Sher (1992, A1).

22. The following quote from Zach Wamp was reported in Jeff Powell (1992, A1). "I think government should be based on moral principles. All our laws have a moral principle to them—right and wrong, our laws are based on fundamental values." Further, Powell relates the following in the same article. "Mr. Wamp says he believes the biblical Ten Commandments are a firm foundation on which to build. Other religions may call them something else, but Mr. Wamp says he has found 'very few sources of the differences between right and wrong that would deny the fundamental principles found in the Ten Commandments.' He says he wants to be a 'congressman who sets those values into laws. I think we've veered away from that in the last twenty years,' he says. 'Those are the things family values are all about. The country has been sinking since we said we can give our kids a value-free education in the public schools,' he insists. 'We don't have the basic values we had before.'" And Jon Meacham commented, "Where they do differ is access to abortions, with Rep. Lloyd favoring access while Wamp has taken a strong anti-abortion-rights stand" (1992c, A1). Elsewhere in the article, Wamp hammers Lloyd's vote on allowing military personnel access to abortions.

23. They also concurred on extending unemployment benefits and developing a space station. Interestingly, they both came out against family leave, which was an issue championed by many women and liberals during the early 1990s. Liz Patterson voted against family leave, and it damaged her credibility with the liberal Democratic base in South Carolina's Fourth District.

24. The issue positions presented in this paragraph come from Meacham (1992c, A1).

25. Interestingly enough, Lloyd may have been saved by redistricting. In the four new counties brought into the district after the 1990 census, Lloyd won by 1,900 votes. In addition, some of Bradley County—where Wamp won 61 percent to 39 percent—was taken out of the district. This development was ironic considering many Republicans in the early 1990s were aided by the creation of several majority-minority districts after the 1990 reapportionment. In this case, redistricting did not revolve around race, and it did not help the Republican candidate. In fact, it may have cost him the race. Election returns were drawn from Meacham (1992g, A1).

26. In our discussions, Todd Gardenhire repeatedly mentioned the signaling power of Pat Brock.

27. Zach Wamp also got a big lift from an establishment figure from outside the district who will be familiar to readers from Chapter 5. Outgoing South Carolina governor and potential 1996 presidential candidate Carroll Campbell traveled to Chattanooga in March to campaign with Wamp. Campbell was the main draw at a fund-raising event that was expected to bring in $50,000. The story of Carroll Campbell's endorsement comes from Mary Gabel (1994b, B1).

28. This may have had more to do with Wamp's strengths with this community than Meyer's weaknesses considering Meyer was helped by anti-abortion activists in his 1992 state legislative race. See Sher (1994, A1).

29. Despite his religious background and morally conservative pronouncements, Wilson could not claim the backing of the entire movement as he only polled 50,000 total votes (11 percent) in the Senate primary won by future Senate majority leader Bill Frist. Fowler, on the other hand, defeated Albright and served twelve years in the Tennessee state senate. According to Bob Swansbrough, Fowler was one of the early successes of the social conservative movement that was gaining power in the early 1990s. He seemed to be a more refined, politically savvy version of Jim Golden. Like Golden, Fowler was also a lawyer, and he had never held any public office when he defeated a twenty-six-year incumbent in the 1994 Republican primary. Fowler went on to become an instructor at Bryan College in Dayton, Tennessee, where he also directed the Center for Law and Government. Bryan College is named after William Jennings Bryan and is located in the small town where the Scopes Monkey Trial took place. From its website, Bryan is an "independent, non-denominational Christian liberal arts school which opened in 1930 . . . educating students to become servants of Christ to make a difference in today's world and to think critically and Biblically." Fowler ran in 1994 on term limits, low taxes, personal responsibility, fighting crime, educational choice, and traditional values. All of the material in this note on David Fowler is from my interview with him.

30. Wamp also managed to get to the right of Meyer on taxes. While Meyer could not rule out the possibility of voting to raise taxes if necessary, Wamp told the voters that under no circumstances would he vote to increase taxes. See Gabel (1994e, A1).

31. For his part, Meyer endorsed Wamp, albeit in a very impersonal way. See Silence (1994c, A7).

32. The information on the Chattanooga Resource Foundation's political activities and their role in the 1994 congressional election comes from my interviews with Doug Daugherty and State Senator David Fowler.

33. These updates were called Salt and Light because Jesus admonished his followers to be salt and light in the world. This is found in Matthew and is part of what is known as the Sermon on the Mount.

34. This is Linville's opinion, but it is corroborated closely by David Rosenbaum (1994, A1).

35. Victor Miller (1994, B1) characterizes Button as running against Wamp but Wamp running against Bill Clinton. Wamp tried to paint Button as a liberal Democrat. Gabel (1994g, A1) notes that Wamp had been running ads morphing Button's face into Clinton's and vice versa. These attempts to link an ostensibly moderate Democrat to the seemingly more liberal policies of Bill Clinton echoes what Todd Tiahrt's campaign succeeded in doing to Dan Glickman in Kansas's Fourth District in the same year. On the salience of abortion, Miller writes, "The candidates continued to spar over when abortion should be allowed, with Mr. Button saying he personally opposes abortion but that it is a 'moral decision. It's not a legislative decision.' Mr. Wamp opposes abortion except to save the life of the mother."

Chapter 7

1. This is the preliminary model presented at the end of Chapter 2. The model in Chapter 2 also did not account for the other two issue dimensions (economics and race) that the more complex model presented in this chapter includes.

2. An alternate specification would be to run one regression on the entire data set and include a triple interaction between voter ideology, district issue polarization, and voter knowledge. The difficulty in interpreting triple interaction terms and displaying their effects led me to the simpler formulation described and implemented in the text. Reassuringly, the triple interaction model did produce similar substantive effects to what is reported in these pages.

3. The equation is as follows: Congressional vote $= 1/(1 + \mathrm{EXP}(b0-b1^*\mathrm{party\ identification}-b2^*\mathrm{incumbency}-b3^*\mathrm{education}-b4^*\mathrm{south}-b5^*\mathrm{male}-b6^*\mathrm{white}-b7^*\mathrm{age}-b8^*\mathrm{moral\ traditionalism}-b9^*\mathrm{guaranteed\ job}-b10^*\mathrm{aid\ to\ blacks}-b11^*\mathrm{moral\ issue\ polarization}-b12^*\mathrm{economic\ issue\ polarization}-b13^*\mathrm{racial\ issue\ polarization}-b14^*\mathrm{moral\ traditionalism}^*\mathrm{moral\ issue\ polarization}-b15^*\mathrm{guaranteed\ job}^*\mathrm{economic\ issue\ polarization}-b16^*\mathrm{aid\ to\ blacks}^*\mathrm{racial\ issue\ polarization}-i1^*1988-i2^*1990-i3^*1992-i4^*1994-i5^*1996-i6^*1998-i7^*2000-i8^*2004-i9^*2008-i10^*2012))$.

4. The quoted responses come from the cumulative ANES data file (VCF0838).

5. This is VCF0809 from the ANES cumulative file: "Some people feel that the government in Washington should see to it that every person has a job and a good standard of living. Suppose these people are at one end of a scale, at point 1. Others think the government should just let each person get ahead on his/their own. Suppose these people are at the other end, at point 7. And, of course, some people have opinions somewhere in between, at points 2, 3, 4, 5, or 6. Where would you place yourself on this scale, or haven't you thought much about this?"

6. This is VCF0830 from the ANES cumulative file: "Some people feel that the government in Washington should make every possible effort to improve the social and economic position of blacks. Suppose these people are at one end of a scale, at point 1. Others feel that the government should not make any special effort to help blacks because they should help

themselves. Suppose these people are at the other end, at point 7. And, of course, some other people have opinions somewhere in between, at points 2, 3, 4, 5, or 6. Where would you place yourself on this scale, or haven't you thought much about it?"

7. The equation is as follows: Willingness to rate Republican candidate $= 1/(1 + EXP(-b0-b1*$political information$-b2*$Republican spending$-b3*$incumbency status$-b4*$media coverage$))$.

8. The equation is as follows: Willingness to rate Democratic candidate $= 1/(1 + EXP(-b0-b1*$political information$-b2*$Democratic spending$-b3*$incumbency status$-b4*$media coverage$))$.

Chapter 8

1. Partisan gerrymandering, especially after the 2010 census, has been well documented, creating many "safe" districts for both parties and making my hypothetical districts not so hypothetical after all.

2. Of course, some contests featured candidates who differed on more than one issue dimension.

Chapter 9

1. Harper did benefit from the endorsement of former Senate Republican leader Trent Lott who appeared at a fund-raiser with the candidate.

Interviews

Kansas Fourth Congressional District

Marvin Barkis, former speaker of the Kansas state house—May 13, 2005, Louisburg, Kansas

Mark Gietzen, pro-life activist and former chair of the Sedgwick County Republican Party—May 18, 2005, Wichita, Kansas

David Gittrich, former head of Kansans for Life—May 16, 2005, Wichita, Kansas

Dave Hanna, campaign manager for U.S. Representative Todd Tiahrt, 1994 and 1996—May 17, 2005, Wichita, Kansas

Mike Hayden, former governor of Kansas—May 12, 2005, Topeka, Kansas

Bud Norman, former political reporter for the *Wichita Eagle*—May 18, 2005, Wichita, Kansas

Tom Schaefer, former religion reporter for the *Wichita Eagle*—May 17, 2005, Wichita, Kansas

South Carolina Fourth Congressional District

Ted Adams, congressional candidate, 1986 and 1988—January 26, 2005, Greenville, South Carolina

Lee Bandy, former political reporter for the *Columbia State*—January 31, 2005, Columbia, South Carolina

Liz Patterson, former U.S. Representative—May 10, 2005, via email

Ron Romine, former professor of political science at the University of South Carolina Upstate and campaign manager for former U.S. Representative Liz Patterson, 1986—January 28, 2005, Spartanburg, South Carolina

Oran Smith, head of Palmetto Family Council—January 31, 2005, Columbia, South Carolina

Bob Taylor, Republican activist and former faculty member of Bob Jones University—January 27, 2005, Greenville, South Carolina

Knox White, mayor of Greenville and congressional candidate, 1988—January 27, 2005, Greenville, South Carolina

Bill Workman, congressional candidate, 1986—January 27, 2005, Greenville, South Carolina

Tennessee Third Congressional District

Doug Daugherty, former head of Chattanooga Resource Foundation and campaign manager for Republican congressional candidate Jim Golden, 1986—September 22, 2005, Chattanooga, Tennessee

David Flessner, former political reporter for the *Chattanooga Times-Free Press*—September 20, 2005, Chattanooga, Tennessee

David Fowler, former Tennessee state senator—October 31, 2005, via email

Todd Gardenhire, Republican activist and congressional candidate, 1992—October 26, 2005, by telephone

Tom Griscom, former editorial page editor for the *Chattanooga Times-Free Press*—September 22, 2005, Chattanooga, Tennessee

Billy Linville, campaign manager for Democratic congressional candidate Randy Button, 1994—September 21, 2005, Atlanta, Georgia

Ken Meyer, former Tennessee state representative and congressional candidate, 1994—September 2, 2005, Pentagon City, Virginia

Pamela and Robin Rudd, pro-life activists—September 23, 2005, East Brainerd, Tennessee

Robert Swansbrough, former professor of political science at University of Tennessee, Chattanooga—September 23, 2005, Chattanooga, Tennessee

Bibliography

Abramowitz, Alan. 1995. "The End of the Democratic Era? 1994 and the Future of Congressional Research." *Political Research Quarterly* 48: 873–89.

———. 2012. "Grand Old Tea Party: Partisan Polarization and the Rise of the Tea Party Movement." In *Steep: The Precipitous Rise of the Tea Party*, edited by Lawrence Rosenthal and Christine Trost, 195–211. Berkeley: University of California Press.

———. 2013. *The Polarized Public: Why American Government Is So Dysfunctional*. Boston: Pearson.

Abramowitz, Alan, and Kyle L. Saunders. 2008. "Is Polarization a Myth?" *Journal of Politics* 70: 542–55.

Aldrich, John H. 1995. *Why Parties? The Origin and Transformation of Political Parties in America*. Chicago: University of Chicago Press.

American Rhetoric. "Patrick J. Buchanan: Address to the Republican National Convention," delivered August 17, 1992. Accessed March 9, 2017. http://www.americanrhetoric.com/speeches/patrickbuchanan1992rnc.htm.

"Anti-Tax Activist to Challenge Glickman, Grund Accuses Democrat of Helping Boost Spending." 1990. *Wichita Eagle*, January 27.

Ashford, Nigel. 1998. "The Republican Policy Agenda and the Conservative Movement." In *The Republican Takeover of Congress*, edited by Dean McSweeney and John E. Owens, 96–116. New York: St. Martin's.

Baker, Bill. 1986a. "Deficit, Role of Religion Dominate GOP Debate." *Greenville News*, May 5.

———. 1986b. "Greenville's Workman Follows Family Tradition in His Political Career." *Greenville News*, May 26.

———. 1986c. "Adams Takes Pride in Neophyte Status." *Greenville News*, May 29.

Baker, Bill, and Linda Perry. 1986a. "Congressional Race Heats Up in Final Weeks." *Greenville News*, June 3.

———. 1986b. "Majority of Republican Leaders Throw Support to Workman." *Greenville News*, June 19.

Banducci, Susan, and Jeffrey A. Karp. 1994. "Electoral Consequences of Scandal and Redistricting in the 1992 House Election." *American Politics Quarterly* 22: 3–26.

Bandy, Lee. 1988a. "S.C. Congressmen Get Ready to Run." *Columbia State*, February 1.

———. 1988b. "Upstate GOP Rivals Save Harsh Words for Democrat." *Columbia State*, June 10.

———. 1988c. "Strategists Believe Patterson Could Be Vulnerable." *Columbia State*, September 4.

———. 1988d. "Outcome of Close Fourth District Race Is Linked to Bush." *Columbia State*, October 30.

———. 1988e. "South Carolina Voters Continue Their Ticket-Splitting Ways." *Columbia State*, December 4.

———. 1988f. "Patterson, Spence Hold 'Safe' Seats." *Columbia State*, November 10.

———. 1990a. "Thomas Lacked Support in Race." *Columbia State*, April 8.

———. 1990b. "Haskins Was Never in Race." *Columbia State*, November 11.

———. 1992. "Faithful, in Churches and in GOP, Beat Patterson." *Columbia State*, November 5.

Barone, Michael, Richard E. Cohen, and Grant Ujifusa. 2007. *The Almanac of American Politics, 2008*. Washington, DC: National Journal.

Barone, Michael, and Chuck McCutcheon. 2011. *The Almanac of American Politics, 2012*. Chicago: University of Chicago Press.

———. 2013. *The Almanac of American Politics, 2014*. Chicago: University of Chicago Press.

Barone, Michael, and Grant Ujifusa. 1973. *The Almanac of American Politics, 1974*. Washington, DC: National Journal.

———. 1975. *The Almanac of American Politics, 1976*. Washington, DC: National Journal.

———. 1977. *The Almanac of American Politics, 1978*. Washington, DC: National Journal.

———. 1979. *The Almanac of American Politics, 1980*. Washington, DC: National Journal.

———. 1985. *The Almanac of American Politics, 1986*. Washington, DC: National Journal.

———. 1995. *The Almanac of American Politics, 1996*. Washington, DC: National Journal.

Bartels, Larry. 2006. "What's the Matter with What's the Matter with Kansas." *Quarterly Journal of Political Science* 1: 201–26.

Bawn, Kathleen, Marty Cohen, David Karol, Seth Masket, Hans Noel, and John Zaller. 2012. "A Theory of Political Parties: Groups, Policy Demands and Nominations in American Politics." *Perspectives on Politics* 10, no. 3: 571–97.

Brewer, Mark D., and Jeffrey M. Stonecash. 2007. *Split: Class and Cultural Divides in American Politics*. Washington, DC: CQ Press.

Bumiller, Elisabeth. 2008. "Talk of McCain's No. 2 Concerns Conservatives." *New York Times*, August 20.

Casteel, Bill. 1983. "Political Upstart Davis Hopes to Return 3rd District Seat to GOP." *Chattanooga Times*, December 3.

———. 1984. "Davis Running for Rep. Lloyd's Post Cites Her Lack of 'Clout' in House." *Chattanooga Times*, February 8.

———. 1986. "First Golden-Davis Face-Off Brings Up Few Differences." *Chattanooga Times*, May 20.

Center for Reproductive Rights. 2013. *Under Attack: Reproductive Rights in the 112th Congress*. New York: Center for Reproductive Rights.

Cigler, Allan J., Mark Joslyn, and Burdett A. Loomis. 2003. "The Kansas Christian Right and the Evolution of Republican Politics." In *The Christian Right in American Politics*, edited by John C. Green, Mark J. Rozell, and Clyde Wilcox, 145–66. Washington, DC: Georgetown University Press.

Cohen, Marty. 2012. "The Future of the Tea Party: Scoring an Invitation to the Republican Party." In *Steep: The Precipitous Rise of the Tea Party*, edited by Lawrence Rosenthal and Christine Trost, 212–41. Berkeley: University of California Press.

Cohen, Marty, David Karol, Hans Noel, and John Zaller. 2008. *The Party Decides: Presidential Nominations Before and After Reform.* Chicago: University of Chicago Press.

Cohen, Marty, Hans Noel, and John Zaller. 2004. "Local News and Political Accountability in U.S. Legislative Elections." Paper presented at the annual meeting of the American Political Science Association, Chicago, September.

Cohen, Richard E., and James Barnes. 2015. *Almanac of American Politics, 2016.* Bethesda, MD: Columbia Books and Information Services.

Cooper, Kenneth. 1994. "Democrats on Defensive in Georgia Where GOP Has High Expectations." *Washington Post,* October 28.

Cooper, Michael, and Mitchell L. Blumenthal. 2008. "McCain Picks Governor of Alaska; Obama Vows to Fix 'Broken Politics'; Surprise Choice as Running Mate, 44, Is an Appeal to Women Voters." *New York Times,* August 30.

CQ Press. 1986. *CQ Guide to Current American Government: Fall 1986.* Washington, DC: CQ Press.

Crichtlow, Donald. 2008. *Phyllis Schlafly and Grassroots Conservatism.* Princeton, NJ: Princeton University Press.

Cross, Jim. 1992a. "Candidates Using Abortion as a Money-Raising Lever." *Wichita Eagle,* July 1.

———. 1992b. "Abortion Views, and the 4th District Four Reluctantly Give Their Opinions." *Wichita Eagle,* July 5.

———. 1992c. "LaMunyon Trailing in Race for Campaign Funds." *Wichita Eagle,* July 16.

———. 1992d. "Yost Gets the Fight He Wanted, Now He Confronts Glickman. *Wichita Eagle,* August 5.

———. 1992e. "Glickman Rejects Slant on 'Values.' " *Wichita Eagle,* September 21.

———. 1992f. "Support for Yost Stops Short of Baptists' Pulpit." *Wichita Eagle,* September 30.

———. 1992g. "Money Flows to Glickman: Yost's Fund-Raising Trails Badly Despite Dole's Help." *Wichita Eagle,* October 17.

———. 1992h. "Yost Welcomes Help in Battle with Glickman." *Wichita Eagle,* October 25.

———. 1992i. "Glickman Has the Last Laugh, Beating Yost by Wide Margin." *Wichita Eagle,* November 4.

Diamond, Sara. 1995. *Roads to Dominion: Right-Wing Movements and Political Power in the United States.* New York: Guilford.

———. 1998. *Spiritual Warfare: The Politics of the Christian Right.* Boston: South End.

Dochuk, Darren. 2011. *From Bible Belt to Sunbelt: Plain-Folk Religion, Grassroots Politics, and the Rise of Evangelical Conservatism.* New York: W. W. Norton.

Dowd, Maureen. 1994. "The GOP Leader; GOP's Rising Star Pledges to Right Wrongs of the Left." *New York Times,* November 10.

Ehrenhalt, Alan. 1991. *The United States of Ambition: Politicians, Power, and the Pursuit of Office.* New York: Times Books.

Evans, Rowland, and Robert Novak. 1980. "The Trouble with Bush." *Washington Post,* July 16.

Fenno, Richard F. 1978. *Home Style: House Members in Their Districts.* Boston: Little, Brown.

Fiorina, Morris P. 1977. *Congress, Keystone of the Washington Establishment.* New Haven, CT: Yale University Press.

Fiorina, Morris P., Samuel J. Abrams, and Jeremy C. Pope. 2006. *Culture War? The Myth of a Polarized America.* Boston: Longman.

Fitzgerald, Anne. 1992. "Glickman, Yost Make Their Pitches." *Wichita Eagle*, September 2.

Flessner, Dave. 1986. "3rd District Republicans Regrouping to Challenge Rep. Lloyd in 1988 Race." *Chattanooga Times*, November 6.

———. 1988a. "Lloyd Leading by 20 Percent in 3rd District." *Chattanooga Times*, October 27.

———. 1988b. "Lloyd and Sasser Easy Victors." *Chattanooga Times*, November 9.

———. 1990a. "Lloyd Likely to Win Easily, but GOP Focusing on '92." *Chattanooga Times*, October 13.

———. 1990b. "NOW Endorses Melcher in Race for Lloyd's Seat." *Chattanooga Times*, November 1.

Flessner, Dave, and Dick Kopper. 1986. "Golden: Lloyd an 'Indecisive Leader'; Lloyd: Region 'A Real Success Story.'" *Chattanooga Times*, October 13.

Flessner, Dave, and Andy Sher. 1988. "With Rep. Lloyd in Picture, Democrats Like Their Chances." *Chattanooga Times*, February 4.

Fowler, Linda L.. and Robert D. McClure. 1989. *Political Ambition: Who Decides to Run for Congress?* New Haven, CT: Yale University Press.

Francia, Peter L., and Nathan S. Bigelow. 2010. "What's the Matter with the White Working Class? The Effects of Union Membership in the 2004 Presidential Election." *Presidential Studies Quarterly* 40: 140–58.

Frank, Judy. 1984. "Davis: High Jobless Rate Partly Fault of Rep. Lloyd." *Chattanooga Times*, April 24.

———. 1992. "Wamp Opens Up on Drugs." *Chattanooga Times*, July 27.

Frank, Thomas. 2004. *What's the Matter with Kansas? How Conservatives Won the Heart of America.* New York: Metropolitan.

Frankel, Glenn. 1980. "Reagan Triumph Parallels YAF's Resurgence." *Washington Post*, July 21.

Fretwell, Sammy. 1992a. "Patterson's Opponents a Diverse Trio." *Columbia State*, August 23.

———. 1992b. "Inglis, Horne Will Run for U.S. House Seats." *Columbia State*, August 26.

———. 1992c. "Upstate Roots May Aid Patterson Again." *Columbia State*, October 9.

Gabel, Mary. 1994a. "Button's Congressional Campaign Opens Today." *Chattanooga Times*, January 8.

———. 1994b. "Wamp Gains Endorsement." *Chattanooga Times*, March 29.

———. 1994c. "Meyer Playing Catch-Up in GOP Bid for Congress." *Chattanooga Times*, May 16.

———. 1994d. "Meyer Still Determined to Fight Vested Interests." *Chattanooga Times*, May 21.

———. 1994e. "Candidates Differ Mainly in Style." *Chattanooga Times*, July 13.

———. 1994f. "Wamp, Button: A Lot Alike." *Chattanooga Times*, September 14.

———. 1994g. "Randy Button." *Chattanooga Times*, October 26.

———. 1994h. "GOP Sweeps State." *Chattanooga Times*, November 9.

Gaines, Gay Hart. 1994. "GOPAC Trains Leaders in Conservative Ideals." *New York Times*, September 7.

Gimpel, James G. 1996. *Legislating the Revolution.* Boston: Allyn and Bacon.

Green, John C., James L. Guth, Corwin E. Smidt, and Lyman Kellstedt. 1996. *Religion and the Culture Wars: Dispatches from the Front.* Lanham, MD: Rowman and Littlefield.

Green, John C., and Mark J. Rozell. 2000. *Prayers in the Precincts: The Christian Right in the 1998 Elections*. Washington, DC: Georgetown University Press.

Green, John C., Mark J. Rozell, and Clyde Wilcox. 2003. *The Christian Right in American Politics*. Washington, DC: Georgetown University Press.

———. 2006. *The Values Campaign: The Christian Right and the 2004 Elections*. Washington, DC: Georgetown University Press.

Harper, Gregg. "Biography." Accessed June 14, 2017. https://harper.house.gov/about-gregg/biography.

Hanshaw, Mark. 1985. "They're Off." *Chattanooga Times*, December 16.

Hasson, Judi. 1994. "The Bullish Newt: Gingrich Has No Plans to Back Down." *USA Today*, November 11.

Hays, Jean. 1990. "Glickman Appears Headed to Victory." *Wichita Eagle*, November 7.

Herberg, Will. 1960. *Protestant, Catholic, Jew: An Essay in American Religious Sociology*. Chicago: University of Chicago Press.

Herrnson, Paul. 2004. *Congressional Elections: Campaigning at Home and in Washington*. Washington, DC: CQ Press.

Hicks, Brian. 1990. "Rhoden Calls Himself 'Kamikaze' Candidate in 3rd District Race." *Chattanooga Times*, June 29.

Higdon, Dave. 1993. "Beech to Lay Off 480 More: Declining Sales Forcing Job Cuts, Company Says." *Wichita Eagle*, June 5.

Hill, Kevin A. 1995. "Does the Creation of Majority Black Districts Aid Republicans? An Analysis of Congressional Elections in Eight Southern States." *Journal of Politics* 57, no. 2: 384–401.

Hillygus, Sunshine D., and Todd G. Shields. 2005. "Moral Issues and Voter Decision Making in the 2004 Presidential Election." *PS: Political Science and Politics* 38: 201–9.

Hoover, Dan. 1988a. "Candidates See Patterson, Liberals as Main Foes." *Greenville News*, May 27.

———. 1988b. "White Rolls to Victory." *Greenville News*, June 15.

Hunter, James Davison. 1991. *Culture Wars: The Struggle to Control the Family, Art, Education, Law, and Politics in America*. New York: Basic.

Jacobson, Gary. 1990. *The Electoral Origins of Divided Government*. Boulder, CO: Westview.

———. 2001. *The Politics of Congressional Elections*. New York: Longman.

Karol, David. 2009. *Party Position Change in American Politics: Coalition Management*. Cambridge: Cambridge University Press.

Kellstedt, Lyman A., John C. Green, James L. Guth, and Corwin E. Smidt. 1996. "Grasping the Essentials: The Social Embodiment of Religion and Political Behavior." In *Religion and the Culture Wars: Dispatches from the Front*, edited by John C. Green, James L. Guth, Lyman A. Kellstedt, and Corwin E. Smidt, 174–92. Lanham, MD: Rowman and Littlefield.

Knuckey, Jonathan. 2005. "A New Front in the Culture War? Moral Traditionalism and Voting Behavior in U.S. House Elections." *American Politics Research* 33: 645–71.

Kopper, Dick. 1990. "Lloyd Re-elected, but House Race Surprisingly Close." *Chattanooga Times*, November 7.

———. 1992. "Lloyd, Wamp Begin Battle." *Chattanooga Times*, August 7.

Krimmel, Katherine. Forthcoming. "The Efficiencies and Pathologies of Special Interest Partisanship." *Studies in American Political Development*.

Layman, Geoffrey. 2001. *The Great Divide: Religious and Cultural Conflict in American Party Politics*. New York: Columbia University Press.

Lipton, Eric. 1994. "GOP's Davis Bolstered by Party's Momentum." *Washington Post*, October 23.

Manegold, Catherine. 1994. "The GOP Leader; Gingrich, Now a Giant, Claims Victor's Spoils." *New York Times*, November 12.

Mansbridge, Jane. 1986. *Why We Lost the ERA*. Chicago: University of Chicago Press.

Masket, Seth. 2009. *No Middle Ground: How Informal Party Organizations Control Nominations and Polarize Legislatures*. Ann Arbor: University of Michigan Press.

Mayhew, David. 1974. *Congress: The Electoral Connection*. New Haven, CT: Yale University Press.

McCann, Tom. 1998. "GOP Battle Close in Sedgwick County: Moderates Make Gains in Precinct Posts Held by Social Conservatives, but the Conservatives Still May Have Slight Majority." *Wichita Eagle*, August 7.

Meacham, Jon. 1988. "Candidates' Positions on National Tickets Offer Some Insights into Lloyd-Coker Race." *Chattanooga Times*, August 12.

———. 1992a. "Wamp Kicks Off 3rd District Race." *Chattanooga Times*, January 22.

———. 1992b. "Gardenhire Enters Race for Lloyd's Seat." *Chattanooga Times*, February 28.

———. 1992c. "Crime, Defense, Abortion." *Chattanooga Times*, July 28.

———. 1992d. "Lloyd, Wamp Duel." *Chattanooga Times*, October 15.

———. 1992e. "Melcher Backs Lloyd Effort Against Wamp." *Chattanooga Times*, October 23.

———. 1992f. "3rd District Awash in Negative Wave." *Chattanooga Times*, November 3.

———. 1992g. "Lloyd Wins in a Squeaker; Margin Less Than 3 Percent." *Chattanooga Times*, November 4.

———. 1992h. "Area's Close Races: A Chill and a Rerun." *Chattanooga Times*, November 5.

———. 2015. *Destiny and Power: The American Odyssey of George Herbert Walker Bush*. New York: Random House.

Miller, Victor. 1994. "Wamp, Button Differ on Political Aims in Debate." *Chattanooga News-Free Press*, October 25.

Montgomery, Peter. 2012. "The Tea Party and the Religious Right Movements: Frenemies with Benefits." In *Steep: The Precipitous Rise of the Tea Party*, edited by Lawrence Rosenthal and Christine Trost, 242–74. Berkeley: University of California Press.

Moreland, Laurence W., Robert P. Steed, and Tod A. Baker. 1986. "South Carolina." In *The 1984 Presidential Election in the South*, edited by Robert P. Steed, Laurence W. Moreland, and Tod A. Baker, 123–56. New York: Praeger.

Norman, Bud. 1994a. "Race for 4th District Seat Winding Down Partisan Path." *Wichita Eagle*, October 3.

———. 1994b. "Candidates Face Off on TV in Close 4th District." *Wichita Eagle*, November 8.

———. 1994c. "Tiahrt Credits Volunteers for Beating Glickman." *Wichita Eagle*, November 9.

Nyhan, David. 1994. "The GOP's Newtron Bomb Is All Set to Detonate." *Boston Globe*, November 13.

Parish, Norm, and Paul Brinkley-Rogers. 1994. "Shadegg Breezes to Win over District 4 GOP Rivals." *Arizona Republic*, September 14.

Paslay, Bob. 1986. "Marchant Running on Confidence." *Greenville News*, May 27.

Perry, Dale. 1986. "GOP Expects Larger Turnout for Congressional Primary." *Greenville News*, June 8.

Perry, Linda. 1986. "Rigdon Running Low-Key Campaign." *Greenville News*, May 28.

Petrocik, John R. 1996. "Issue Ownership in Presidential Elections, with a 1980 Case Study." *American Journal of Political Science* 40: 825–50.

Petrocik, John R., and Scott W. Desposato. 1998. "Partisan Consequences of Majority-Minority Redistricting in the South, 1992 and 1994." *Journal of Politics* 60, no. 3: 613–33.

Polczinski, Al. 1986. "GOP Wants Docking to Pay $57.40 Tab." *Wichita Eagle*, October 11.

———. 1990. "Democrats Lose Sedgwick County Edge, Presidential Coattails Blamed for Voter Shift." *Wichita Eagle*, March 10.

Polsby, Nelson. 1983. *Consequences of Party Reform*. Oxford: Oxford University Press.

Powell, Jeff. 1992. "Lloyd's Rivals Riding Anti-Incumbent Mood." *Chattanooga News-Free Press*, July 26.

Rawlins, Wade, and Dave Flessner. 1988. "Campaign Themes Recur in Debate by Coker, Lloyd." *Chattanooga Times*, October 24.

Reed, Ralph. 1994. *Politically Incorrect*. Dallas: Word Publishing.

Risen, James, and Judy Lundstrom Thomas. 1998. *Wrath of Angels*. New York: Basic.

Rosenbaum, David. 1994. "Party, Clinton Denied Credit." *Chattanooga Times*, October 18.

Rozell, Mark, and Clyde Wilcox. 1997. *God at the Grass Roots: The Christian Right in the 1996 Elections*. Lanham, MD: Rowman and Littlefield.

Schattschneider, E. E. 1942. *Party Government*. Westport, CT: Greenwood.

Schier, Steven E., and Todd E. Eberly. 2016. *Polarized: The Rise of Ideology in American Politics*. Lanham, MD: Rowman and Littlefield.

Schlozman, Daniel. 2015. *When Movements Anchor Parties: Electoral Alignments in American History*. Princeton, NJ: Princeton University Press.

Schram, Martin. 1980. "Reagan Would Rather Go It Alone, but Choose He Must." *Washington Post*, July 10.

Sedgwick County. 2017. "About." Accessed May 10, 2017. http://sedgwickcounty.org/about/history.asp.

Shafer, Byron. 1998. "The Mid-Term Election of 1994: An Upheaval in Search of a Framework." In *The Republican Takeover of Congress*, edited by Dean McSweeney and John E. Owens, 7–32. New York: St. Martin's.

Sher, Andy. 1986. "A Shadow Behind the Issues: Religion Plays a Role in the 3rd District Race." *Chattanooga Times*, October 28.

———. 1988. "GOP Talks of Uniting Behind 1 Candidate." *Chattanooga Times*, February 18.

———. 1992. "Abortion-Rights Group Endorses 37; None in the City." *Chattanooga Times*, July 2.

———. 1993a. "3rd District Battle Brewing for GOP." *Chattanooga Times*, May 24.

———. 1993b. "Brocks on List of Wamp Campaign Donors." *Chattanooga Times*, July 19.

———. 1994. "GOP Enlists in Values War." *Chattanooga Times*, July 5.

Sher, Andy, and Dave Flessner. 1986. "Incumbent Wins 54 Percent of the Ballots, Loses Bradley." *Chattanooga Times*, November 5.

Shribman, David. 1994. "A Son of Newt Battles in Tennessee." *Boston Globe*, November 4.

Silence, Michael. 1994a. "Four Win a Dinner." *Knoxville News Sentinel*, May 6.

———. 1994b. "Contenders for Third District Seat Face Off at Mall." *Knoxville News Sentinel*, July 4.

———. 1994c. "Wamp's Ex-Foe Urges GOP Election Unity." *Knoxville News Sentinel*, August 18.

Smith, Oran. 1997. *The Rise of Baptist Republicanism*. New York: New York University Press.

Smith, Rhoten A., and Clarence J. Heil. 1958. *Republican Primary Fight: A Study in Factionalism*. New York: Holt.

Soper, Christopher J. 1996. "The Politics of Pragmatism: The Christian Right and the 1994 Elections." In *Midterm: The 1994 Elections in Context*, edited by Philip A. Klinkner, 115–24. Boulder, CO: Westview.

Thomas, Judy Lundstrom. 1992a. "GOP Leader Quits After Contentious Vote." *Wichita Eagle*, August 14.

———. 1992b. "County GOP Is a House Divided After Leaders Squabble, Is Unity Possible?" *Wichita Eagle*, August 15.

———. 1992c. "The New GOP Religious Right Making Huge Inroads with Political Networking at Local Level." *Wichita Eagle*, September 20.

"Tiahrt Plans Run for 4th District Seat." 1994. *Wichita Eagle*, May 29.

U.S. Congress. 2017. "H.R. 2956: Parental Notification and Intervention Act of 2017." 114th Cong. Accessed August 17, 2017. https://www.congress.gov/bill/115th-congress/house -bill/2956/text.

Wamp, Zach. 1992. "Wamp Thanks Supporters." *Knoxville News Sentinel*, November 20.

Wann, Libby. 1986. "Lloyd Issues Challenge to Debate." *Chattanooga Times*, August 8.

Warthen, Brad. 1990. "Avowed Thugs and Anti-Thugs Have Some Fun." *Columbia State*, April 1.

Webb, Tom. 1993. "Cessna Will Make Piston-Engine Planes as Soon as Reform Passes." *Wichita Eagle*, September 15.

———. 1994. "Light Plane Industry Hopes Soar: Clinton Ready to Sign Bill." *Wichita Eagle*, August 4.

Williams, Daniel K. 2010. *God's Own Party: The Making of the Christian Right*. New York: Oxford University Press.

Wright, Julie. 1994. "Ojile, Tiahrt to Decide Which of Them Will Run." *Wichita Eagle*, April 13.

Index

Adams, Ted, 111, 115, 124–25, 228n5; as primary candidate in 1986, 107–114; as primary candidate in 1988, 120, 122–24, 129; refusal to endorse Bill Workman, 114, 117–19

Affordable Care Act, 17, 29. *See also* Obamacare

Albright, Ray, 156–57, 170, 232n29

American Civil Liberties Union, 31–32

Armey, Dick, 55, 91, 224n3

"at-risk" districts, 49, 55, 59, 103, 136, 139–40, 158, 175–76

Baker, Howard, 142, 145–46, 161

Baker, LaMar, 141; as challenger in 1970, 141–42; as challenger in 1976, 144; as incumbent in 1972, 143; as incumbent in 1974, 143–44

Barkis, Marvin, 72–73, 78

Black, Diane, 213–14

Bob Jones University, 103, 108–9, 112, 114, 116, 123, 126, 134–35, 136, 220, 228n1

Brock, Bill, 140, 146, 161, 165–66, 168; as challenger in 1962, 141; as U.S. Senate candidate in 1970, 141, 160; as U.S. Senate candidate in 1994, 230n4

Brock, Pat, 141, 155, 157–58, 161, 164, 168, 175, 230n4, 232n26; building the GOP in Tennessee, 141–42

Buchanan, Pat, 19–20

Bush, George H. W., 3, 7, 50, 61, 161, 215; as friend of Carroll Campbell, 121; as incumbent in 1992, 81, 84, 98, 131, 135, 166, 227n24; as presidential candidate in 1988, 158; as Reagan's vice-presidential choice, 5–6

Bush, George W., 3, 8, 17, 213

Button, Randy, 15, 60; as challenger in 1994, 171; why he lost in 1994, 174–75, 233n35

Campbell, Carroll, 107, 125; as candidate for governor in 1986, 107; as challenger in 1978, 107; assisting Bill Workman in 1986, 113–14; assisting Zach Wamp in 1994, 232n27; leading South Carolina's GOP, 121–22, 229n11

Carter, Jimmy, 6, 58, 103, 106, 144, 216

Chattanooga Resource Foundation, 171–72, 178, 233n32

Christian Coalition, 3, 22, 43, 118, 169, 223n3; and stealth campaigns, 227n23; assisting Bob Inglis in 1992, 59, 130–33, 224n4, 229n17; role in 1994 midterm elections, 54–55, 98, 101, 170, 172, 175, 226n21. *See also* Reed, Ralph; Robertson, Pat

Clinton, Bill, 8, 29, 66, 81, 215, 227n24, 228n33; as a factor in Liz Patterson's 1992 defeat, 135; as a factor in the 1994 midterm elections, 52–55, 91, 93–94, 174, 233n35

Clinton, Hillary, 3, 11, 52, 102, 137, 174, 221

Club for Growth, 31–32, 212

Coker, Harold, 157, 169; as challenger in 1988, 158–59; as primary candidate in 1988, 157–58

Conlan, John, 104
Contract with America, 51, 53–55, 92, 226n21
crime bill, 52, 91, 93, 164, 171

Daugherty, Doug, 148, 220; as Jim Golden's campaign manager, 149–51, 154–55; as leader of Chattanooga Resource Foundation, 171–73, 178–79
Davis, John, 145, 166; as challenger in 1984, 146–47, 230n7; as primary candidate in 1986, 147–52, 155
DeMint, Jim, 128, 136
district issue polarization, 15, 26, 28, 32 (fig.), 180, 181 (fig.), 182, 193, 195–96, 233n2
Dole, Bob, 66, 69–70, 84, 94–95, 98, 227n26

electoral blind spot, 44–45

Faith and Freedom Coalition, 43. *See also* Reed, Ralph
Falwell, Jerry, 3, 54, 228n4
Family Research Council, 18, 31–32, 102, 137, 176, 213, 215
Farenthold, Blake, 214–15
Fleischmann, Chuck, 176
Ford, Gerald, 5, 70, 106, 146, 161
Fowler, David, 156, 170, 173, 232n29
Franks, Trent, 211–12
Freedom Caucus, 10

Gardenhire, Todd, 160, 168; as primary candidate in 1992, 161–63; as Republican activist, 160–61
Gietzen, Mark, 42, 220; as pro-life activist, 73–74; as Republican organizer, 42, 76–80, 83, 99, 211, 255n8; assisting Todd Tiahrt in 1994, 85, 88, 90–91, 93, 100–101, 226n18
Gingrich, Newt, 8, 53–55, 91, 167, 224n3
Gittrich, David, 73, 172, 220; as leader of Kansans for Life, 73–76, 88, 226n19; assisting Todd Tiahrt in 1994, 85, 88–93, 99–100, 226n18, 226n20

Glickman, Dan, 2, 14, 43, 55, 68, 102, 152; after defeat, 228n33; and the airplane liability law, 1, 65–67, 228n32; as challenger in 1976, 70–71; as incumbent in 1986, 72; as incumbent in 1988, 81; as incumbent in 1990, 81; as incumbent in 1992, 83–84, 226n12; as incumbent in 1994, 85–87, 89, 91–97, 227n28, 227n30, 227n31; his position on abortion, 82–83, 89; his religion, 225n3; why he lost in 1994, 98–101, 229n19
Golden, Jim, 147, 166, 168, 171, 220, 231n13, 232n29; as challenger in 1986, 151–56, 231n14; as primary candidate in 1986, 148–51, 230n9, 231n11; supporting Zach Wamp in 1992, 162–63
Gore, Al Jr., 135, 147, 165
Gore, Al Sr., 141, 160
Gowdy, Trey, 137, 176
Graham, Lindsey, 4
Grund, Roger, 81

Hanna, Dave, 85–87, 89, 91–96, 226n18
Harper, Gregg, 212–13, 234n1
Haskins, Terry, 126; as challenger in 1990, 126–27
Hayden, Mike, 71–74
Humphrey, Hubert, 6
Hunt, Gene, 157; as primary candidate in 1988, 157–58

Inglis, Bob, 14, 54, 59, 174, 230n9; as challenger in 1992, 128–131; as challenger in 2004, 136; as incumbent in 2010, 137; why he won in 1992, 131–36
intense policy demanders, 13, 43–44, 46

Jarmin, Peggy, 82, 225n11
Jeffries, Jim, 224n2
Jones, Bob, 228n1
Jones, Bob Jr., 108, 110
Jones, Bob III, 108, 110

Kansans for Life, 73, 172–73; as an educational organization, 73–74; helping Eric Yost in 1992, 84; helping Todd Tiahrt in

1994, 88–95; protesting outside abortion clinics, 75. *See also* Gittrich, David
Kassebaum, Nancy, 66, 79
Knight, Bob, 72, 81

LaMunyon, Richard, 82
Lieberman, Joe, 4–5
Limbaugh, Rush, 4, 225n8
Lloyd, Marilyn, 15, 60, 178; as challenger in 1974, 143; as incumbent in 1976, 144; as incumbent in 1978, 144; as incumbent in 1980, 145; as incumbent in 1982, 145; as incumbent in 1984, 145–47, 230n7, as incumbent in 1986, 148, 151–52, 154–56, 157, 231n14; as incumbent in 1988, 157–59, 231n16; as incumbent in 1990, 159–60; as incumbent in 1992, 160–61, 163–66, 168, 231n21, 231n22, 232n25; as U.S. Representative, 143–44, 145, 163, 167, 230n6, 230n10
Lookout Mountain Power Structure, 155, 160–62, 166, 168

Marchant, Thomas, 107; as primary candidate in 1986, 107–11
McAteer, Ed, 147, 170
McCain, John, 3–5, 146, 212
Melcher, Pete, 159–60, 163, 165
Meyer, Ken, 55, 139, 142, 167–71, 230n1, 232n28, 232n30, 232n31
Moral Majority, 3, 223n1. *See also* Falwell, Jerry

NAFTA, 52, 91, 93
Nichols, Bill, 82–83
Nixon, Richard, 3, 143; employing Southern strategy, 6

Obama, Barack, 8–10, 17, 29, 60, 137, 212–14
Obamacare, 10, 17, 214. *See also* Affordable Care Act
Ojile, Frank, 85–86, 88, 226n16, 226n17
Operation Rescue, 41, 74–75, 77, 88, 99. *See also* Summer of Mercy

Palin, Sarah, 3–4, 214
Patterson, Liz, 14, 152; as challenger in 1986, 108, 114–17, 119; as incumbent in 1988, 122, 124–26, 229n14, 231n16; as incumbent in 1990, 126–28; as incumbent in 1992, 129–31, 229n17, 229n18, 232n23; why she lost in 1992, 131–36
Planned Parenthood, 18, 102, 137, 176, 213–15, 217
Pompeo, Mike, 102, 137, 176

Reagan, Ronald, 3, 7, 42, 47, 61; elected president in 1980 and 1984, 6, 50, 54, 215; impact on Republican Party in Kansas, 69–71, 73, 98, 225n9; impact on Republican Party in South Carolina, 106–7, 115, 125; impact on Republican Party on Tennessee, 144–47, 161; selecting George H.W. Bush as running mate, 5–6
Reed, Ralph, 3, 9, 224n3; and stealth campaigns, 44, 132, 227n23, 229n20; as leader of Christian Coalition, 43, 54, 130–31, 226n21. *See also* Christian Coalition; Faith and Freedom Coalition
Rhoden, Grady, 159, 161
Rigdon, Richard, 228n5; as primary candidate in 1986, 107–11
Robertson, Pat, 3; as leader of Christian Coalition, 131; as presidential candidate in 1988, 14, 21, 223n3, 228n4; endorsing James Butcher, 45; endorsing Jim Golden, 148; inspiring organization in South Carolina, 120, 220. *See also* Christian Coalition
Rosell, Paul, 76

Schlafly, Phyllis, 211, 218
Schlapp, Matt, 226n18
Shriver, Garner, 70; as incumbent in 1974, 70; as incumbent in 1976, 71
Sloan, Jerry, 79, 120, 151
stealth campaigns, 44, 227n23, 229n20; strategy of Bob Inglis, 132; strategy of Todd Tiahrt, 87, 93, 229n19
Summer of Mercy, 14, 41–42, 59, 74–78, 81, 88–90, 97, 99, 225n11. *See also* Operation Rescue

Taylor, Bob, 104, 136, 229n12

Tea Party, 8–10, 17, 25, 102, 137, 213–15

Thomas, David, 126–27

Tiahrt, Todd, 1–2, 14, 43, 55, 59, 68, 129, 174, 230n9, 233n35; as challenger in 1994, 67, 85–97, 226n16, 226n17, 226n18, 226n20, 227n22, 227n28, 229n19; as challenger in 2014, 102; as state senator, 67, 84, 224n1, 226n14; as U.S. Senate candidate in 2010, 102; supported by religious conservatives, 69; why he won in 1994, 97–102

Tiahrt, Vicky, 226n18

Tiller, George, 41, 74–76, 89, 225n11

Trump, Donald, 10–11, 102, 137, 210, 220–21, 223n2

voter ideology, 15, 179–80, 182, 188, 189 (fig.), 193, 195–96, 201–2, 203 (fig.), 204 (fig.), 206, 233n2

voter knowledge, 15, 179, 182, 189, 195, 196, 206

Wallace, George, 6

Wamp, Zach, 15, 55, 60; as candidate for governor in 2010, 176; as challenger in 1992, 162–66, 231n20, 231n22, 232n25; as challenger in 1994, 139, 167–71, 230n1, 232n27, 232n28, 232n30, 232n31; considering a run for U.S. Senate, 175–76; why he won in 1994, 174–75, 233n35

Watergate, 6, 142–44

White, Knox, 133, 146, 229n13, 229n14; as challenger in 1988, 122–27, 129, 135, 229n12, 229n16

white Southern Protestants, 3, 6, 11; Republican House vote of, 7, 7 (fig.), 12 (fig.), 49

Wilson, Steve, 170; as candidate for U.S. Senate in 1994, 170, 232n29

Workman, Bill, 106, 122–25, 127, 146; as challenger in 1986, 114–19, 129, 134–35, 228n8, 229n12; as primary candidate in 1986, 107–14, 129, 228n5

Yost, Eric, 81–85, 87, 89, 92, 98–101, 226n12

Young Americans for Freedom, 5, 161